D0039212

ALASKA-YUKON
HANDBOOK

this book is available from: AUSTRALIA—Bookwise (Australia) Pty. Ltd., 101 Argus St., Cheltenham, Victoria 3192 (Box 204, Cheltenham, 3192), tel. (03) 584 4109/3507; NEW ZEALAND—Bookwise (New Zealand), Pty. Ltd., 28 Fitzherbert St., Tetone, Wellington; SINGAPORE—MPH Distributors (S) Pte. Ltd., 116-D JTC Factory Building, Lorong 3 Geylang Square, Singapore 1438, tel. 4461088; THAILAND—Chalermnit Bookshop, Erawan Arcade 1-2, Bangkok; HONG KONG—The Book Society, 16-18 Conduit Road, Flat 2 (G.P.O. Box 7804), tel. 5-241901; JAPAN—Charles E. Tuttle Co. Inc., 2-6 Suido, 1-Chome, Bunkyo-ku, Tokyo 112, tel. 811-7106/9; NETHERLANDS—Nilsson & Lamm BV, Postbus 195, Pampuslaan 212, 1382 JS Weesp, tel. 02940-15044; WEST GERMANY—Nelles Verlag GmbH, Schleissheimer Str. 37lb, 8000 Munchen 45, tel. (089) 351 5786; UNITED KINGDOM—Roger Lascelles, 3 Holland Park Mansions, 16 Holland Park Gardens, London W14 8DY, tel. 01 603 8489; CANADA—Firefly Books, 3520 Pharmacy Ave., Unit 1-C, Scarborough, Ontario M1W 2T8, tel. (416) 499 8412; USA—Publishers Group West, 5855 Beaudry Street, Emeryville CA 94608, tel. (415) 658 3453; Bookpeople, 2940 Seventh Street, Berkeley CA 94704, tel. (415) 549 3030; Pacific Pipeline, Box 3711, Seattle WA 98124, tel. (206) 872 5523; Bradt Enterprises, 95 Harvey St., Cambridge MA 02140, tel. (617) 492 8776; or directly from Moon Publications, Box 1696, Chico CA 95927, tel. (916) 345 5473.

ALASKA-YUKON HANDBOOK

DAVID STANLEY

PUBLICATIONS

ALASKA-YUKON HANDBOOK

Published by
  Moon Publications
  P.O. Box 1696
  Chico, CA 95927, USA
  tel. 916-345-5473

Printed by
  Colorcraft Ltd., Hong Kong

© David Stanley 1983

Library of Congress Cataloging in Publication Data

    Stanley, David.
      Alaska-Yukon Handbook.

      Bibliography: p.
      Includes index.
      1. Alaska--Description and travel--1981-   --
    Guide-books. 2. Yukon Territory--Description and
    travel--Guide-books. 3. Washington (State)--
    Description and travel--1981-   --Guide-books.
    4. British Columbia--Description and travel--
    Guide-books. I. Title.
    F902.3.S7 1983   917.95'0443   83-1031
    ISBN 0-9603322-5-1

photo credits: Cover photograph: National Park Service (Joe Standart). Black and white photographs: National Park Service—pages 10 (M. Woodbridge Williams), 18 (Charles J. Gebler), 19, 52, 53, 54, 127; Provincial Archives of British Columbia—pages 20 (74461), 22 (42639), 69 (9160), 79 (7408), 94 (33784), 136 (51512); Alaska Marine Highway—pages 26, 28; David Stanley—pages 30, 43, 46, 50, 57, 61, 63, 70, 74, 80, 82, 86, 98, 101, 103, 108, 111, 114, 123, 132, 145, 146, 155, 168, 174, 178, 181, 185, 186, 191, 194, 198, 201, 204, 206; Tourism British Columbia—pages 35, 60, 68, 77, 91; Seattle-King County Convention and Visitors Bureau—page 42; B.C. Steamship Company—page 49; B.C. Parks and Outdoor Recreation Division—page 64; Greater Vancouver Convention and Visitors Bureau—page 67 (Brian Stablyk); Federal Archives, Seattle—pages 90, 106; U.S. Forest Service—pages 118, 120; Alaska Discovery—pages 125, 214; White Pass and Yukon Corporation—page 134 (Rand E. Snure); Yukon Archives—pages 144, 152, 153; Fairbanks Convention and Visitors Bureau—pages 164 (Randolph W. Brand), 166 (Roxanne Kent), 219 (Sr. Margaret Larsen, O.P.); Division of Tourism, State of Alaska—page 184; Alyeska Pipeline Service Company—page 202; Naval Historical Center, Washington, D.C.—pages 210, 215 (Howard W. Curtis), 216 (William G. James). Illustrations: Gordon Ohliger—pages 9, 13, 23, 29, 32, 34, 41, 55, 58, 59, 66, 73, 87, 88, 93, 96, 97, 100, 105, 106, 111, 112, 113, 121, 124, 130, 135, 139, 141, 150, 156, 157, 158, 161, 165, 176, 177, 188, 205, 208, 209, 218, 219, 220; Foster A. Carr—pages 14, 15, 16, 17, 31, 36, 117, 128, 137, 160, 169, 172, 190, 192, 195, 201; Grey Rabbit—page 24; David Hurst—pages 33, 109, 138; U.S. Forest Service—page 116.

CONTENTS

PREFACE 7

INTRODUCTION 9

THE INSIDE PASSAGE 41

ALASKA–YUKON 139

BOOKLIST 221
GLOSSARY 225
INDEX 227

LIST OF MAPS

PREFACE

Most travel guidebooks to North America cater to the American dream of open freeways blinking with Exxon stations and Holiday Inns. Jet setters are told how to rent a car and where to locate gourmet restaurants and resorts, while overloaded motorists are directed to the great outdoors, complete with plug-ins, dump stations, and laundromats. Hotel chains and tour companies feed the condo mentality, because that's where the money is. Tourist information offices often hand out brochures so slanted they're practically useless to anyone without a car. The gas-powered travel habits of middle-class North Americans thwart the growth of the kind of rail, bus, and other public transportation systems Europeans and Japanese depend on at home. And in the shuffle, energy-conscious bus travelers and hitchhikers are left to fend for themselves. This pattern changes, however, once you move N of Seattle and Vancouver. The Inside Passage route through British Columbia to Alaska is a world apart, with rugged mountains and islands, where passenger ferries replace bridges and road building is impossible. This region is the one great exception to the North American public transport wasteland, the only place where the automobile addict is plagued by delays and heavy charges, while the foot passenger goes cheap and easy. Mother Earth, smiling down on those who comport themselves most kindly towards her, has made the Northwest coast the scenic highlight of the continent, the meeting point of cultures, the haven of wildlife, the final frontier. All this offers the budget traveler an opportunity unequalled elsewhere N of the Mexican border. This book explores that opportunity.

current trends: As Reaganomics works its wonders across the U.S. and the slump spills over into Canada, more people are seeking a way to holiday that won't bankrupt or put them deep in debt. This book gives it to them. Herein an adventurous American or Canadian will learn how to do the loop up the coast by ferry and return down the Alaska Highway, meals and lodging included, and take a summer to do it, for less than it costs for just air passage to Europe. A similarly enterprising European can fly over the Pole to Anchorage and do the same trip in reverse for only his/her airfare more. Age and lifestyles are not barriers. Virtually everyone can share the thrill of making their own travel arrangements as they go. A variety of ferry routes are available and regular scheduled bus services cover most of the highways. The railroads are peak travel experiences. Youth hostels welcome everyone (except small children) and campgrounds are accessible to all. This book explains how to eat, travel, and sleep through this exciting area on your own, for the very least amount of money. If you have a little more to spend, it insures you get top value for every dollar. You readers who have never traveled this way before are in for the time of your lives.

an endangered environment: Most of the North is still wilderness, that last corner of our continent where wildlife survives in numbers and the land is less torn by the greed of developers. Yet the further reaches of this wilderness are threatened by business interests who measure progress only in terms of mileposts, megawatts, and money, and road builders who press asphalt into hard lines that divide animal trails and bring the outposts closer to the grasp of the modern spoiler. In this fragile environment, the scars remain long after the men who make them. It is a land that must be protected. This book will help you find that land, help you leave behind the motorized madness of today and come closer to things as they once were everywhere. But in your travels, please walk lightly. Respect your fellow creatures, no matter how insignificant they may seem, and look for beauty in the tiniest of things. Those who resist nature with gadgetry and machines will be deprived; those who seek it in the canoe-slap of the waves, the tent-fly patter of the rain, and the wild howl of the wolf, will find something they have long sought.

ACKNOWLEDGMENTS

Many thanks to all the wildlife, park, and tourism officials who provided valuable information and materials used in the preparation of this book. Many of the area maps are based on originals published by the U.S. Geological Survey. The extract from "The Spell of the Yukon" on page 18 is reprinted from *The Collected Poems of Robert Service* by permission of Dodd, Mead and Company, Inc., New York, and McGraw-Hill Ryerson Ltd., Canada. Special thanks should go to Royce and Garth Wilson of Seattle, who agreed to share 35 years of dining experience in the city, to Phil Esmonde of Victoria, and to the staff of WestCan Treks Adventure Travel in Vancouver. The author would also like to recognize the assistance of all the kind people who stopped to give him a ride as he researched this book. Here's hoping I can do the same for you some day! There are several people to whom I am deeply indebted and whose assistance enriched the book in many ways. Most obvious were my illustrators, Gordon Ohliger and Foster A. Carr, who gave my vague images graphic form. Gordy drew most of the illustrations contained herein in his isolated cabin in the Sierra Nevada foothills, while Foster released all the pent-up enthusiasm gleaned on several backpacking trips to Yukon and Alaska. Less visible, but equally essential,

were my editors, Deke Castleman and Diana Hume. Deke is better known as the master of Alaskan Krosswords, but he was equally adept at unraveling my obscure rantings and moulding them into useful shape. Deke also typeset the entire book on a mad hatter schedule. Diana brought grammatical order to this otherwise disorderly work and was a constant source of encouragement and optimism. All of the maps were drawn, labeled, and photographed by David Hurst. Dave was forced to contend with a demanding, impatient author who mailed him obscure, smudged base maps sketched on picnic tables by the light of the midnight sun. His success is illustrated 70 times in this book. Typographical errors were eliminated by our globetrotting proofreader, Clara Pryor, who managed to squeeze her reading in between junkets to Tunisia and Antarctica. Trickiest mistakes were nabbed by Gordon Smith, greengrocer extraordinaire. Also I am much obliged to the production staff, Cathy Shilts, Kerry Hardy, and Tom Jacobson, for working so hard on the book. Thanks too to Ed Edwards B.A. of Chico for arranging office space for the staff. Finally, there's Bill Dalton, my publisher. Bill was the inspiration of this book, the patient teacher of an unruly student, and the mastermind behind getting it out in record time.

IS THIS BOOK OUT OF DATE?

Conditions in the North change quickly and what is true one week could be completely different the next. A hostel opens or closes; a good restaurant or bar changes hands; a bus company goes out of business. Although we make herculean efforts to check our facts, the task is an enormous one and sometimes gets away from us. You can help us keep up. If something we mention no longer exists, if certain suggestions are misleading, or if you've uncovered anything new, please write in. Women travelers sometimes run up against situations which warrant special attention and if you share them with us, we'll share them with others. Letters from Alaskans and Western Canadians are particularly appreciated. If you take a photograph during your trip which you feel we might like to use in the book, you are welcome to send it. Good photographs by individuals always get preference over stock photos from agencies. Be aware, however, that the publisher is not responsible for unsolicited manuscripts, artwork, or photographs and, in most cases, cannot undertake to return them. Send only good quality duplicate Kodak slides-or glossy black and white

prints. Moon Publications will own the publication rights on all photographic material submitted. If we use your photos, you will be mentioned in the photo credits and receive a free copy of the book. Although we try to make our maps as accurate as possible, we are always grateful when readers point out any omissions or inaccuracies. If you feel we've overlooked a certain map, please let us know and we'll try to include it in the next edition. When writing, always be as specific and accurate as possible. Notes made on the spot are better than later recollections. Write your comments into your copy of *Alaska-Yukon Handbook* as you go along, then send us a summary when you get home. This book is a spokesperson for you, the budget traveler, so please help keep us up to date. Address your letters to:

David Stanley
c/o Moon Publications
P.O. Box 1696
Chico, CA 95927, USA

INTRODUCTION

THE LAND

The broad physical features of North America continue unbroken into that great head of land that is Alaska. The Coastal Mountains, which begin in California, continue up the edge of the continent to become the Alaska Range and the Aleutian Islands. Between these chains and the Rockies is a high plateau which runs from British Columbia through the interiors of Yukon and Alaska to the delta of the Yukon River, where it dips into the Bering Sea. The Rocky Mountains form an inland spine from Mexico to the Brooks Range, while the Great Plains of the midwest U.S. extend to become the Mackenzie Lowlands and North Slope.

the Coastal Mountains: Nowhere else on the continent is so much raw beauty and grandeur jammed into one area as it is in the Coastal Mountains of the U.S. and Canada. Most of the places described in this book are within or near this mighty barrier, which contains the highest peaks, largest glaciers, and only

remaining active volcanoes in North America. Two parallel chains and an intervening depression can be traced all the way from Mexico to Alaska: the Sierra Nevada of California becomes the Cascades of Washington, the Coast Mountains of B.C., the St. Elias and Wrangell mountains, the Alaska Range, and finally the Aleutian Range, which then sinks into the Pacific just short of Asia. Closer to the ocean, the Coast Range of California becomes the Olympic Mountains of Washington. Further N a string of islands from Vancouver Island to the Queen Charlottes and the Alexander Archipelago runs into the St. Elias Mountains, where the 2 chains unite in a jagged icecapped knot. In Alaska they divide again, with the Chugach and Kenai mountains swinging SW toward Kodiak Island. Between these parallel chains is a depression starting with the Central Valley of California, then Puget Sound, the Inside Passage, the Susitna Basin in Southcentral Alaska, Cook Inlet, and Shelikof Strait in Southwest Alaska. There are only 4 low-level breaks in the Coastal Mountains: the valleys of the Columbia, Fraser, Skeena, and Stikine rivers.

GLACIATION

Glaciers once covered most of the areas included in this book. Glaciers form from the accumulation of snow on a mountain or plateau. High precipitation and altitude are required, as the snow must pile up to great depths, compacting the bottom layers. The great weight above this ice causes it to become fluid and flow down the mountainside in a great frozen river. When the rate of advance is balanced by melt-off, the face of the glacier remains more or less stationary. If the glacier flows more quickly than it melts, it advances; if it melts faster than it flows, it recedes. All air bubbles are squeezed out of glacial ice by this tremendous pressure. This makes glacial ice extremely dense, so compacted that the higher spectrums of light cannot escape or penetrate it, which explains the dark blue tinge. It also melts at fantastically slow rates; a small chunk or two will keep a beer cooler cold for a week.

signs of the glaciers: As you travel up the coast or hike in the national parks of the interior, it's a satisfying accomplishment to be able to identify glacial landforms and to be able to read the signs. As a glacier moves down a valley it bulldozes rubble ahead of it or carries it on top. The typical V-shaped river valley becomes a U-shaped glacial trough. Valleys and ridges branching from the main valley are sliced off to create hanging valleys and truncated spurs. A side valley which once carried a tributary glacier may be left a hanging trough. Waterfalls often tumble from hanging valleys and troughs. Alpine glaciers cut back into the headwalls of their accumulation basins to form cirques. Bare, jagged ridges between cirques are known as aretes. The debris carried and dumped by a glacier becomes a moraine. Lateral moraines are at the sides of glaciers, while a terminal moraine is what is left at the point of furthest advance

Cirques, aretes, and medial moraines are easily identified in this spectacular photograph of Nabesna Glacier in the Wrangell Mountains.

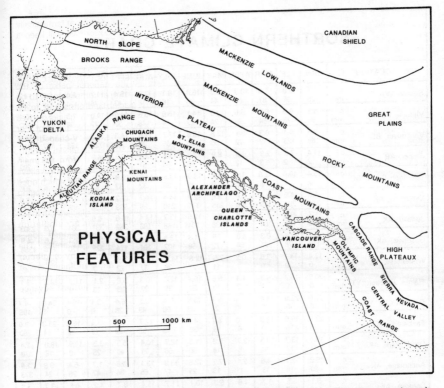

PHYSICAL
FEATURES

0   500   1000 km

of the face. A medial moraine is formed when a pair of glaciers unite. These ribbon-like strips of rubble can be followed back to the point where the lateral moraines come together. When looking at a glaciated landscape, watch for gouges and scrape marks on the bedrock which indicate the direction of glacial flow. Notice erratics, huge boulders carried long distances by the glacier, which often differ from the surrounding rock. Glacial runoff is heavy with powdered stone or "flour," which gives it a distinctive milky-white color. The abundance of silt carried by glacial streams creates a twisting, braided course. With a little practice, you'll soon learn to recognize glacial features at a glance.

climate: Contrary to popular misconception, the North is not a frozen wasteland; there is a wide variety of climates. Temperatures in Alaska, for example, range from -61 degrees C

to 38 degrees C and above. In some places it always seems to be raining, while just over the mountains may be a desert. It is possible, however, to generalize and distinguish 3 climatic zones: coastal maritime, interior continental, and arctic. The main factor affecting the coasts is the warm so-called "Japanese Current" (North Pacific Drift) which flows toward Vancouver Island. There it is deflected N along the coast of SE Alaska and finally W around the Gulf of Alaska as far as Kodiak Island. These currents keep the sea from freezing in winter and cause temperatures to be much milder than the norm at that latitude. They also bring continuous year-round rain as the humid Pacific air is forced up over the Coastal Mountains. However, these mountains shield the interior plateaus from the maritime air streams, so precipitation there is low. The mountains also protect the coastal areas from cold interior air masses. The interior gets more rain during

NORTHERN CLIMATE CHART

LOCATION		JAN.	FEB.	MAR.	APRIL	MAY	JUNE	JULY	AUG.	SEPT.	OCT.	NOV.	DEC.	ALL YEAR
Seattle, WA	c	4.7	5.9	7.6	10.3	13.3	15.8	18.1	17.9	15.4	11.7	8.0	5.9	11.2
	mm	126	98	81	56	44	35	16	18	43	76	124	139	856
Victoria, BC	c	4.1	5.2	6.8	9.6	12.3	14.1	15.6	15.6	14.2	11.0	7.3	5.6	10.1
	mm	99	76	54	30	24	27	14	18	32	72	98	123	667
Vancouver, BC	c	2.9	4.1	6.3	9.1	12.8	15.8	17.7	17.6	14.3	10.2	6.2	4.3	10.2
	mm	168	123	119	72	55	56	35	35	70	137	158	197	1225
Jasper, AB	c	-11.4	-7.6	-2.9	3.5	8.9	12.3	15.2	13.8	10.2	4.8	-3.6	-8.1	2.9
	mm	2	2	3	12	31	55	50	51	36	26	9	5	282
Telegraph Creek, BC	c	-15.4	-10.4	-2.8	3.5	9.8	13.9	15.8	14.8	10.9	4.4	-5.3	-11.4	2.3
	mm	2	1	5	8	9	18	30	32	37	47	13	4	206
Ketchikan, AK	c	1.0	1.9	3.4	6.0	9.6	12.7	14.4	14.7	12.2	8.3	4.7	2.1	7.6
	mm	351	294	319	300	215	171	210	289	339	556	485	412	3941
Juneau, AK	c	-1.7	-0.9	1.3	4.8	8.9	12.6	13.7	13.4	10.6	6.6	2.5	-0.6	5.9
	mm	190	155	164	152	136	104	148	188	262	331	264	209	2303
Gustavus, AK	c	-3.1	-2.1	0.3	4.0	7.9	11.3	13.0	12.4	9.8	5.6	1.3	-1.6	4.9
	mm	118	76	74	64	72	58	102	104	174	228	170	126	1366
Whitehorse, YT	c	-17.4	-14.1	-7.6	-0.2	7.5	12.6	14.2	12.4	7.9	0.7	-8.2	-15.1	-0.7
	mm	0	0	0	1	11	27	35	37	22	7	2	0	142
Haines Junction, YT	c	-20.9	-16.7	-8.9	-1.4	5.6	10.4	12.1	10.3	5.8	-2.1	-11.7	-19.2	-3.1
	mm	0	0	1	2	10	27	35	27	25	13	9	8	157
Dawson City, YT	c	-27.6	-23.9	-14.6	-1.4	8.1	13.8	15.4	12.5	6.4	-3.1	-16.4	-24.9	-4.7
	mm	0	0	0	2	24	33	50	49	28	8	0	1	195
Fairbanks, AK	c	-23.8	-19.6	-12.8	-2.0	8.7	14.7	15.8	12.7	6.6	-3.4	-16.0	-23.3	-3.6
	mm	18	15	10	6	18	36	48	52	32	19	12	14	280
Denali Park, AK	c	-16.1	-13.7	-10.8	-2.7	5.3	11.3	12.7	10.4	5.3	-3.2	-11.9	-16.0	-2.4
	mm	21	17	10	15	19	50	66	71	40	25	18	18	370
Anchorage, AK	c	-10.9	-7.7	-4.8	2.1	7.7	12.5	13.9	13.1	8.8	1.7	-5.4	-9.8	1.8
	mm	20	18	13	11	13	25	47	65	64	47	26	24	373
Cordova, AK	c	-5.1	-3.6	-1.7	1.9	6.3	10.1	11.7	11.4	8.7	4.2	-0.6	-3.7	3.3
	mm	170	126	105	108	146	93	184	228	358	321	229	194	2262
Homer, AK	c	-5.3	-3.5	-2.3	2.0	5.9	9.5	11.6	11.4	8.3	3.4	-1.8	-5.2	2.8
	mm	55	35	36	34	25	25	44	76	68	90	68	67	623
Kodiak, AK	c	-0.9	-0.2	-0.1	2.6	6.1	9.8	12.1	12.9	9.8	5.2	1.7	-1.2	4.8
	mm	131	128	96	100	141	100	97	95	151	169	152	118	1478
Cold Bay, AK	c	-2.1	-1.8	2.2	0.2	4.1	7.2	9.7	10.7	8.2	4.5	1.2	-1.7	3.2
	mm	60	68	49	41	71	55	56	124	92	118	109	56	899
Adak, AK	c	0.7	0.6	1.3	2.8	4.5	6.8	9.2	10.8	8.9	5.7	2.7	1.0	4.6
	mm	171	138	156	110	123	85	76	109	140	178	186	195	1667
Nome, AK	c	-16.0	-15.8	-13.6	-7.3	2.3	7.7	10.0	9.5	5.4	-1.7	-8.4	-15.4	-3.6
	mm	27	17	20	17	19	30	64	117	67	38	27	21	464
Barrow, AK	c	-26.4	-28.0	-26.2	-17.7	-7.4	0.9	4.2	3.5	-0.8	-8.5	-17.8	-23.9	-12.3
	mm	5	4	3	3	9	9	23	23	15	14	7	5	114

NOTES ON THE CLIMATE CHART: The top figure indicates the average monthly temperature in degrees and tenths Centigrade, while the monthly rainfall average in millimeters (mm) is given below. The last column gives the annual average temperature, and the total precipitation during the year. These figures have been averaged over a minimum of 14 years, and in most cases, much longer. Altitude may be a factor at Jasper (1,058 m), Telegraph Creek (335 m), Whitehorse (703 m), Haines Junction (619 m), Dawson City (320 m), Fairbanks (133 m), and Denali Park (638 m); all of the others are near sea level. While extreme temperature variations are limited to the interior and far N, the coastal areas experience heavy rainfall year-round. Throughout the region May to Sept. are the best months with temperatures in Yukon and Alaska nearly as warm as those experienced thousands of km south.

summer, the coast during winter. The interior experiences great temperature extremes, from biting cold in winter, to summer heat waves. Permafrost covers most of the northern third of Alaska, and scattered areas in the center and to the west. The long hours of darkness in winter cause even colder temperatures, yet on 21 June a point at 60 degrees N latitude receives as much warmth from the sun as does a spot on the equator. Fairbanks has 22 hours of daylight that day. The climate makes budget travel possible in the interior May to Sept. only. Most trails are closed to hikers in winter, although cross-country skiing is an attractive alternative. Winter travel in Southeast and Southcentral Alaska would be feasible, but even here you must be prepared for near freezing rain and day-long twilight. Sea water never gets much warmer than 10 degrees C anywhere N of Puget Sound: you have to be crazy or a polar bear to swim in it.

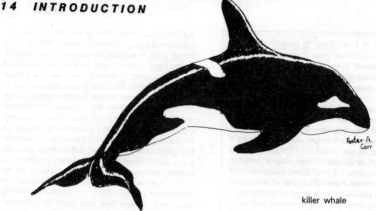

Foster A. Carr

killer whale

FLORA AND FAUNA

vegetation: You can categorize the vegetation of the North Pacific Coast and the Yukon/Alaskan interior by dividing it into rainforest, taiga, and tundra. The lush coastal rainforests of British Columbia feature giant conifers: Douglas fir, hemlock, and cedar. Spruce is common in the Queen Charlotte Islands. Cedar continues into Southeast Alaska, but spruce and hemlock predominate. Sparser forests of hemlock and spruce stretch across Southcentral Alaska, with the latter continuing through northern Kodiak Island and onto the adjacent mainland. Dense thickets of alder are found in the higher, sub-alpine areas near the coast. The boreal forest of the interior lowlands consists primarily of scattered, open stands of white spruce and paper birch. Taiga, the interface between boreal forest and tundra, is characterized by stunted black spruce, dwarf shrubbery, and swampy areas known as muskegs. Alpine fir, lodgepole pine, and balsam poplar (cottonwood) grow throughout the interior, with alder on the sub-alpine heights. There are 2 treelines in Alaska: one is determined by elevation, the other by latitude. Generally, the treeline descends as you move further north. Although alder and poplar also exist in isolated stands near the Brooks Range, the Arctic region on the North Slope is mostly treeless tundra. Dwarf willow, alder, grasses, and moss give tundra the appearance of a shag carpet. This tundra belt continues along the shores of the Bering Sea to the Alaska Peninsula and Aleutian Islands. Southward, the Arctic plant vegetation is gradually replaced by Pacific coastal. *fireweed:* Fireweed is a wildflower that you will come to know intimately during your travels. It enjoys sunlight and grows profusely in open areas along roads and rivers. Given proper conditions, fireweed can grow to be 2 m tall. Its long stalk of pink flowers blossoms from bottom to top; sourdoughs claim they can predict the earliness and severity of winter by the speed with which fireweed finishes blooming.

fauna: Most of the animals of North America migrated from Asia across the Bering Land Bridge; they are very different from South American creatures. Along the North Pacific coast are found Sitka deer, bear, wolves, and mountain goats. This is the home of the bald eagle; Alaska is the only American state where it is not endangered. There are as many eagles in Alaska as in the rest of the U.S. combined. Across the interior range bear, wolves, foxes, lynx, moose, caribou, Dall sheep, beaver, and snowshoe hare. Unlike the moose and caribou, which shed their antlers annually, the Dall sheep grows permanent horns: a dark ring is added yearly. The larger the horns of a Dall ram, the older he is and the more prominent position he holds in the herd. Dall ewes grow small, spiked horns. The fauna of the Arctic region consists of timber wolves, red foxes, caribou, and polar bear, while the Aleutians are inhabited by great numbers of shore birds, sea lions, and sea otters. *marine mammals:* The largest summer visitors to Alaska are the whales. Each spring grey whales are seen migrating N from Baja California; in the fall they swim south. Also in the spring humpback whales move N from Hawaii and are easily distinguished by their hump-like dorsal fin, 5-m-long flippers, and large tail which shows as they dive. These 15-m creatures often breach (jump) or beat the water with their tail, as if trying to send a message. Smaller 9-m minke whales are also common. The killer whale (orca), which is not actually a whale but the largest of the dolphins (up to 7½ m long), hunts fish and other mammals in schools. Their high (2 m), triangular-shaped dorsal fin easily identifies them. Also watch for the Dall porpoise (white patches on a black body), harbor porpoise, sea lion, and harbor seal. Sea otters are once again common in Prince William Sound.

man and beast: For centuries, primitive man, with his crude weapons and limited needs, had little impact on the wildlife population. This all changed in the mid-1700s with the coming of the white man. The sea otters, fur seals, and grey whales were hunted to the verge of extinction. By the 1850s, the Alaskan musk ox, largest member of the sheep family, had become extinct. It has only recently been reintroduced from Greenland. A domesticated herd at Unalakleet near Nome produces a rare type of wool (*qiviut*) from which exquisite garments are woven. The caribou have been

Dall ram

reduced to a tenth of their former numbers, and because, as nomadic grazers, they depend on trails, road building poses a continuing threat to the surviving herds. Because wolves hunt the same prey as man, they have been ruthlessly exterminated. Yet wolves rarely attack humans, and, among themselves, they show highly social traits of loyalty, courage, and affection. _conduct:_ Visitors to the North should be aware that wildlife may be encountered almost anywhere outdoors. Many animals are well prepared to defend their territories against intruders (you) and even the smallest animals can bite. Never attempt to feed an animal. It is seldom good for it, you, or those who follow. Do not surprise or corner one—stay alert and keep your distance. Wolves and foxes which appear unafraid or "tame" may be rabid, so keep away from them. If you have a pet with you, watch it carefully; dogs harassing Alaskan wildlife or domestic animals may be shot. If you appreciate wildlife, do not buy souvenirs made from their body parts. For example, avoid walrus-tusk ivory carvings, candles made from whale or seal oil, or clothing lined with wild fur. Any mosquitos or other insects reading this are urged not to bite visitors. One thing you don't have to worry about are snakes; there are none in Alaska.

the brown bear: These splendid animals, which once ranged over all of northwestern America, are now an endangered species limited to the mountains and forests of Alaska and Northern Canada, and a few protected areas in the Rocky Mountains. Brown bears and grizzlies are now considered the same species (*Ursus arctos*), but there are differences. The brown bear is primarily coastal, with a much higher percentage of protein (fish) in its diet, while the grizzly, found in the interior, consumes a large proportion of roots and berries. Standing 2 m tall, brown bears can weigh up to 550 kg. The king of the brown bears, the Kodiak bear, is the largest meat-eating animal in the world. Since their claws are adapted for digging rather than climbing, big adult brown bears can't climb trees, an advantage for you if you've climbed one to escape (but remember their 3-m reach). Their color varies from blackish-gray to blonde, often with white-tipped fur which gives them a grizzled look. The best way to differentiate a brownie from the smaller, less-dangerous black bear is to look for the massive head, concave or dish-shaped face,

COEXISTING WITH THE BEARS

at the campsite: When choosing a campsite, avoid places like salmon streams, ground squirrel mounds, or berry patches, were there are most likely to be bears. Watch for fresh signs of bears (droppings, tracks, diggings). Make sure you're not on a bear trail, which are likely to be in these same areas or in saddles on ridge tops. In mid-summer bears tend to move up to the cooler alpine areas, while in fall they will be anywhere the salmon are spawning or berries are ripening. If possible, camp near a climbable tree. *food and garbage:* Your best security is a clean campsite. Avoid smelly foods such as fish, fresh meat, cheese, sausage, or bacon; freeze-dried food is light and relatively odorless. Keep food in airtight containers or several layers of plastic bags. Your cooking, eating, and food storage area should be at least 50 m away from your tent. Wash up after eating. Burying garbage is useless as animals soon dig it up; burn what garbage you can and wash and flatten tin cans. Store unburnable garbage and the clothes you were wearing while cooking in the same place. Put your food in a plastic bag inside a sleeping bag stuff sack and suspend it from a branch or between 2 trees, at least 3 m off the ground. Tie 2 cups or pots to it so you will hear if it's moved. In the absence of trees, store food well downwind of your tent. Many campgrounds provide bear-proof metal food caches, which are handy. Perfumes, deodorants, and sexual smells are all thought to attract bears. Women should be especially cautious during their periods. Used tampons should be stored in air-tight containers and packed out with all other garbage.

bear encounters: If you take all of the above precautions, your chances of a serious bear encounter are greatly reduced. Most bears are shy or fearful and go the other way when they sense humans (though a startled bear, a sow with cubs, or a wounded bear is always dangerous and unpredictable). Bears have poor eyesight, but excellent senses of smell and hearing. Avoid unexpected encounters with bears by letting them know you are there. If you walk with a breeze hitting your back, any bears ahead of you will know you are coming. If you are unable to see everything around you for at least 50 m, warn any possible animals by talking, singing,

BEAR PAWS

black bear (*Ursus americanus*)   brown bear (*Ursus arctos*)

clapping your hands, tapping a cup, rattling a can of pebbles, or wearing a bell. Whistling is not recommended as you might inadvertently imitate a bird. Don't get mauled because a bear mistakes you for a long-tailed jaeger! Be especially wary when traveling through thick brush or high grass, into the wind, along streams, or at twilight. Safety is in numbers: the more of you there are, the more likely a bear is to notice you and stay away. If you unexpectedly come upon a bear while hiking, make a wide detour around it or back off and give it time to go away. To a bear, man is unpredictable. It may feel its territory is being invaded at 200 m, threatened at 50 m. If you happen to find yourself closer than this, don't panic. The worst thing you can do is to run; this could trigger the chase instinct, and there is no human capable of outrunning a bear. Too, any sudden moves might startle the animal. Speak *quietly* and wave your hands slowly above your head to let the bear know what you are. If the bear is very close, slowly back off while continuing to face it. If the bear stands on its hind legs and waves its head from side to side it may only be trying to identify you. When it does, it will usually run away. If a bear follows as you back off, drop a hat or piece of clothing for it to smell. Move cautiously towards a climbable tree, if one is nearby. If a bear woofs and postures, don't imitate, as this is a challenge. Retreat. Most bear charges are also a bluff; the bear will often stop short and amble off. If it charges, however, don't move. When contact is imminent, drop down and play dead. Put your hands behind your neck, pull your legs up to your chest, and think of Jesus. Keep your pack on for protection. It takes a lot of courage to do this, but often the bear will only sniff you and leave after a nip or two. The injury you might sustain would be far less than if you had tried to resist.

other precautions: Photography is one of the main causes of bear incidents. Never, under any circumstances, approach a bear, even if it appears to be asleep. Move off quickly if you see bear cubs, especially if one comes towards you; the mother is always close by and will invariably attack to protect her young. Dogs create dangerous situations by barking and exciting bears—leave yours at home. In most places it is illegal to feed or

black bear (*Ursus americanus*)

harass bears, or deliberately leave food or garbage in such a way as to attract them. Fed bears lose their natural feeding instincts and fear of man. They become garbage bears, and wildlife officials are eventually forced to destroy them. Report anyone you see doing this, as quickly as possible, for they are not only endangering their own lives but also yours. Bear incidents of any kind should be reported to park and wildlife authorities so they can act to minimize the problem. Remember, bears are dangerous, wild animals which may be encountered anywhere in the North. This is *their* country, not a zoo. By going in you accept the risk of meeting a bear.

entering bear country: Enter bear country with respect but not fear. Know that bears rarely attack man; you're 50 times more likely to be injured in a highway accident than by a bear. Actually, more people are hurt each year by moose than by bears. Observe all the precautions and you have little to worry about. It's a sad commentary on the human condition that many people's reaction to bears is a desire to kill them. If you feel the need to carry a rifle for protection, it's better that you stay out of the wilderness. You have plenty of alternative places to go, the bears do not. Every Northerner has a bear story. Listen to them, but take them with a grain of salt. If you see a bear yourself it will probably be the most memorable event of your trip, and the one you will talk about most to the folks back home. Let us hope that the great bears always remain an intriguing part of the northern wilderness.

big hump over the front legs, sloping back, and long, curved claws.

the black bear: The black bear (_Ursus americanus_) may be found in almost any forested area, except on certain islands which are exclusively brown bear territory. A blackie can weigh up to 136 kg and stand up to 1.5 m tall. They are expert tree climbers. Color is a poor way to distinguish black bear from brown as the "black" bear can be brown or even cinammon-color, though he is usually black. Most have a patch of white hair on the front of their chest. Black bears have a straight facial profile with a tapered nose, a straight shoulder and back line, and a raised hump.

The winter! the brightness that blinds you,
    The white land locked tight as a drum,
The cold fear that follows and finds you,
    The silence that bludgeons you dumb.
The snows that are older than history,
    The woods where the weird shadows slant;
The stillness, the moonlight, the mystery,
    I've bade 'em good-by—but I can't.

Robert Service, "The Spell of the Yukon"

HISTORY

prehistory: The Athapaskan Indians of Canada have a legend which tells how one of their ancestors helped a giant in Siberia slay a rival. The defeated giant fell into the sea forming a bridge to America. The ancestors then crossed this bridge, bringing the caribou with them. Eventually the giant's body decomposed, but parts of his skeleton were left sticking above the ocean to form the Aleutian Islands. Low ocean levels during the pleistocene (some 30,000-40,000 years ago) offered to the nomadic peoples of Asia a land bridge 1,500 km wide over the Bering Sea. The interior lowlands of Alaska and the Yukon Valley were never glaciated and would have provided an ice-free migration route. As the climate warmed and the great ice sheets receded towards the Rocky Mountains and Canadian Shield, a corridor opened down the middle of the Great Plains, allowing movement further south. One of the earliest records of man in the Americas is a caribou bone with a serrated edge found at Old Crow in northern Yukon. Almost certainly used by man as a tool, carbon dating of the bone has placed it at 27,000 years old.

the Indians: The last Indian group to cross the Bering Land Bridge was the Déné or Athapaskans, whose language is spoken today from Interior Alaska to the American Southwest (Navajos and Apaches). These Indians of the interior followed the great caribou herds which supplied them with most of their necessities of life. Agriculture was unknown to them, but they did fashion crude implements from the copper of their region. Eventually, certain tribes found their way down the great rivers of British Columbia to the coast. The Tlingits, who are related to the Athapaskans, migrated down the Nass River near Prince Rupert and spread N through Southeast Alaska. The rich environment provided these coastal Indians with abundant fish and shellfish, as well as with the great cedar logs from which they fashioned community houses, totem poles, and long dugout canoes.

the Eskimos: The last group of all to arrive from Asia were the mongoloid Eskimos, probably some 10,000 years ago, near the end of the last Ice Age. Today they are found in Siberia and across Alaska and Arctic Canada to Greenland. Their language, which in Alaska is divided into the Inupiak dialect in the N and the Yupik dialect in the S, is unrelated to any other in North America except that of the Aleuts. They lived near the coast, along the migratory routes of the marine mammals they hunted in kayaks and *umiaks.* They also relied upon caribou, birds, and fish. Their homes were partly underground and constructed of driftwood, antlers, whale bones, and sod. The

The dignity of the Coast Salish is evident in this photo of an Indian woman taken by Edward S. Curtis in 1899.

Chirikof, in command of Bering's second ship, reached the site of Sitka. Bering died of scurvy on the return journey but survivors reached Siberia with a load of sea otter pelts. This provoked a rush of Russian hunters and traders toward Alaska. Reports of Russian advances alarmed the Spaniards in Mexico who considered the entire coast theirs. Juan Perez and Bruno Hecata were ordered N in 1774 and 1775. The Spanish explorer Juan Francisco Quadra sailed as far N as Sitka in 1775. However, Spain failed to back up its claim with any permanent settlement N of San Francisco. It was the Englishmen, James Cook (1776-1780) and George Vancouver (1791-1795), who were the first to carefully explore and chart this coast. In 1778 Cook landed on Vancouver Island, then sailed N into Cook Inlet in Southcentral Alaska, in search of a Northwest Passage to the Atlantic. He continued to the Aleutians and entered the Bering Sea and Arctic Ocean. A decade and a half later, Vancouver, on board his ship the HMS *Discovery,* charted the entire W coast of North America from California to Southeast Alaska. His was the first extensive exploration of Puget Sound and circumnavigation of Vancouver Island. He also claimed the region for England.

well-known snow and ice igloo was exclusive to Canadian Eskimos. In the summer skin tents were used at fish camps. The Eskimos did not utilize the dog sled until the coming of the white man. _the Aleuts:_ Marine mammals and fish provided the Eskimo-related Aleuts with food, clothing, and household materials. They were famous for their tightly woven baskets. Prior to the arrival of the Russians, 20,000 Aleuts inhabited almost all of the Aleutian Islands; by the end of the 18th C. there were about 2,000 survivors. These intermarried with the conquerors and today scattered groups of their descendents are found in the eastern Aleutians and the Pribilofs to the north.

EUROPEAN EXPLORATION

exploration by sea: The first Europeans to see the North Pacific coast were Russians. In 1728 Vitus Bering sailed through the Bering Strait to the Arctic Ocean, but did not discover Alaska on this trip. His second voyage in 1741 took him much further E, to within sight of the St. Elias Mountains. The expedition naturalist, George Steller, explored Kayak Island. Alexis

Captain Cook from Payne's *System of Geography* (London, 1791).

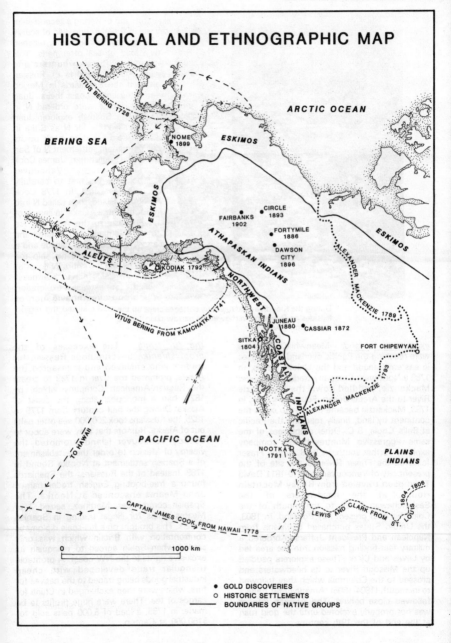

During the Klondike gold rush tiny cottages crept up the hillsides as Dawson overflowed its narrow plain beside the Yukon River.

exploration by land: Meanwhile, explorers were reaching the Pacific overland from bases in eastern Canada and the United States. In 1789 a Northwest Company trader, Alexander Mackenzie, paddled down the Mackenzie River to the Arctic Ocean. Four years later, in 1793, Mackenzie became the first to cross the continent by land, finally reaching the Pacific at Bella Coola, B.C. Other employees of the same aggressive Montreal-based company explored further south. In 1808, Simon Fraser followed the Fraser River to the site of the present city of Vancouver; in 1810-1811 David Thompson traveled from Rocky Mountain House, at the headwaters of the Saskatchewan River, to the mouth of the Columbia near present-day Portland. In 1803, the United States purchased Louisiana from Napolean and President Jefferson ordered a military fact-finding mission into the area led by Lewis and Clark. These explorers paddled up the Missouri River to its headwaters and crossed to the Columbia which they followed to its mouth (1804-1806). American fur traders followed close behind. The Alaskan interior was not properly explored until the gold rush at the end of the 19th century.

the fur trade: The excesses of the *promyshleniki,* unscrupulous Russian fur traders who enslaved and massacred the Aleuts, prompted the Czar in 1799 to create the Russian-American Company which, by 1821, had a monopoly along the coast of Alaska. During the half century from 1775 to 1825, the Russians took 200,000 sea otter pelts out of Alaska. Rumors that they were about to occupy Vancouver Island prompted the viceroy of Mexico to order the establishment of a Spanish settlement at Nootka Sound in 1789. Instead of the Russians, the Spaniards found a free-booting English trader named John Meares ensconced at Nootka. The Spanish commander, Martinez, seized 2 of Meares' ships for illegal trading in Spanish waters. This brought on a full-scale diplomatic confrontation with Britain which was only settled when Spain agreed to relinquish its exclusive rights to the NW coast. A profitable triangular trade developed with cheap industrial goods being traded to the natives for furs, which were then exchanged in China for cargos of tea. There were huge profits to be made; in 1785, a load of 5,000 pelts sold for $160,000 at Canton.

THE MODERN ERA

political units form: In 1824 and 1825, Russia signed agreements with the U.S. and Britain which fixed the southern limit of Russian America at 54 degrees 40' N latitude, near present-day Ketchikan. The vast territory S of this line was up for grabs. The American claim to the Oregon Country around the Columbia River was based on its discovery by Robert Gray in 1792, and the first overland exploration by Lewis and Clark. Britain based its claim on its effective occupation of the land by the Northwest Company, which in 1821 merged with the Hudson Bay Company. As American settlers began to inhabit the area, feelings ran high—President Polk was elected in 1846 on the slogan, "Fifty-four Forty or Fight." War between Britain and the U.S. was averted when both agreed to draw the boundary line to the Pacific along the 49th parallel, the current Canadian/American border. All of Vancouver Island went to Britain. Largely because of bad relations between Britain and Russia in the aftermath of the Crimean War (1853-1856), the Russian government sold its unprofitable Alaskan possessions to the United States in 1867 rather than face their inevitable loss to the English. The new Canadian nation purchased all the territorial holdings of the Hudson Bay Company (Rupert's Land) in 1870. In 1871, British Columbia joined Canadian Confederation on the promise of a railroad to extend there from the east.

the search for gold: It was goldmining which really opened up Interior Alaska and Yukon. After the California gold rush of 1848, the search moved north. In 1858 there was a rush up the Fraser River to the Cariboo goldfields. In 1872, gold was found in the Cassiar region of B.C. Strikes in Alaska and Yukon followed one another in quick succession: Juneau (1880), Fortymile (1886), Circle (1893), Dawson City (1896), Nome (1899), Fairbanks (1902), and Iditarod (1908). For centuries, placer deposits had accumulated in the unglaciated interior valleys. Gold could be extracted there by individuals using simple means. A very mobile group of men and women followed these discoveries on riverboats, dog sleds, and foot, creating many of the legends which continue to draw tourists. Gold also caused the Canadian and American governments to take a serious look at their possessions for the first time; the administrative histories of both Yukon and Alaska date from those times. *note:* For a history of the North during WW II see under "Southwest Alaska"; recent events in the area are discussed in the "introduction" to "Alaska and the Interior."

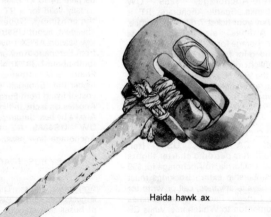

Haida hawk ax

GETTING THERE

BY AIR

from the Lower 48: The main U.S. carriers to Alaska are Alaska Airlines, Northwest Orient, Western Airlines, and Wien Air Alaska. All 4 have toll-free numbers (call toll-free information at tel. 800-555-1212), which you can use to check the latest fares. When you call these airlines, tell them you want the cheapest possible fare. You'll find early morning and evening rates are lower; there are other discounts if you buy your ticket 7 days in advance. The current night coach fare is $203 OW Seattle-Anchorage, $259 OW Seattle-Fairbanks. Seattle-Anchorage RT is $348 if you buy your ticket 7 days in advance. Western Airlines also has flights Honolulu-Anchorage for $306 OW and Seattle is often included for free. Be aware, however, that the highlight of a trip to Alaska is what you see on the way N, not Anchorage. A RT by air is not recommended, but a flight back may be advisable to avoid having to retrace your steps.

charters: O.C. Tours, 800 S. Airport Blvd., Burlingame, CA 94010, USA (tel. 415-348-6300), has periodic charter flights from Oakland, California, to Anchorage for $99 OW ($15 membership extra). Bookings must be made 21 days in advance; call or write for details. *from Canada:* Pacific Western airlines flies from Edmonton to Whitehorse, while CP Air flies Vancouver-Whitehorse. Both charge CDN$220 OW. Western Airlines offers Calgary-Anchorage for CDN$300 OW, CDN$362 RT (APEX).

the Polar Route: Fares from Europe to Alaska vary according to the season, with the lowest rates available for travel before 14 May. Mid-summer prices are about 25 percent higher. Since Western Airlines dropped their London-Anchorage service, fares on the Polar Route have soared. A regular OW ticket from London to Anchorage on British Airways, for example, is now US$942. You can reduce this to only US$342 OW by going standby (low season). British Airways also has an APEX (advance purchase excursion) fare of US$800 RT (low season). If you want a RT always ask about APEX fares which are cheaper, but must be paid 14 to 21 days in advance. These are usually valid for a RT within one year. From the continent, Sabena Belgian Airlines is cheapest, about US$536 OW, US$838 RT for low-season APEX travel. Other airlines flying from Europe to Anchorage are KLM and SAS (both about US$100 higher than Sabena), Air France and Lufthansa (both about US$200 higher than Sabena). You might compare the cost of flying from Europe to New York or Los Angeles on a cheap flight, then proceeding to Alaska by bus. Japan Airlines charges US$595 OW, US$685 RT (APEX) for Tokyo-Anchorage (low season).

BY BUS, TRAIN, AND TOUR

Greyhound Lines: This giant company, the largest of its kind in the world, has thousands of buses and stations all over the U.S. and Canada. You buy a ticket and you're on your way. Bus travel is very flexible because you never need a reservation. If one bus fills up, they just roll out another. Greyhound's maximum OW fare from anywhere in the Lower 48 to Port Angeles, Seattle, or Vancouver, varies between US$100-135. In Canada you can buy a bus ticket to Vancouver, Prince Rupert, or Beaver Creek, Yukon, for only CDN$100, so long as you begin no further E than Montreal. A OW ticket is valid in the U.S. for 15 days, in Canada for 60 days, and unlimited stopovers are allowed. Greyhound buses run round the clock so you save a lot on hotels. Instead of going straight through, however, stop off once in awhile for a night or two in some of the exciting cities along the way. Remember, you're on holidays! There's almost always a YMCA, YWCA, or YH where you can arrange inexpensive accommodations. Greyhound also has an unlimited travel Ameripass which is valid throughout the U.S. and Canada (but not Alaska). The Ameripass is sold for periods of 7 days (US$187), 15 days (US$240), and 30 days (US$347). Use your Ameripass to visit Banff and Jasper in the Canadian Rockies, travel to Yellowknife, N.W.T., then follow the Alaska Highway to Beaver Creek, Yukon. Otherwise, terminate in Prince Rupert, B.C., and board the ferries north. Enjoy the freedom that public transport travel offers: do yourself a favor and leave your car at home.

magic buses: Green Tortoise travel is more than just a bus ride—it's an inexpensive vacation. This alternative bus line uses recycled Greyhounds with the seats ripped out and foam-rubber mattresses laid in their place on elevated platforms. Up front there's a lounge area with seats and tables, which converts to another sleeping area at night—just roll out your sleeping bag and forget everything. Food is not included in the fare, but passengers can pool their grocery money for tasty vegetarian meals prepared by the wayside. Unlike Greyhound, you're allowed to drink beer and wine on board (in moderation), but tobacco smoking is prohibited. One of the best things about these trips is the people—alternative travel attracts good company. The removal of the seats eliminates barriers and leads to new friendships. Passengers are encouraged to bring along musical instruments or cassettes for all to enjoy. Stops are made at out-of-the-way hot springs for relaxing. On the San Francisco-Seattle run, for example, you can soak for a couple of hours at Wilbur Hot Springs. The cross-country buses spend whole days touring national parks such as

Yellowstone or Big Bend. If you've never done anything like this before, give it a try.

services: Green Tortoise has a shuttle bus between San Francisco and Seattle ($49) twice a week. From June-Oct. there's a weekly trip all the way from San Francisco to New York and Boston. You can board this bus in Seattle; the journey takes 10 days. In winter (Oct.-Jan.) there's a faster run E from San Francisco through Texas to Boston ($159). Tours from the West Coast to places like Baja California (Nov.-May, $249 RT) and Mardi Gras in New Orleans (Feb., $249 RT) are offered. Ask about their 4-week tour of Alaska in June and July which costs a low $499 RT from San Francisco or Seattle. Despite the casual approach, Green Tortoise buses are reliable and have a good safety record. For more information write: Green Tortoise Alternative Travel, Box 24459, San Francisco, CA 94124, USA. Telephone numbers are: 415-386-1798 in California; 206-324-RIDE in Seattle; 212-431-3348 in New York; 617-265-8533 in Boston. *others:* The Grey Rabbit, 2000 Center St. #1092, Berkeley, CA 94704, USA, offers a similar service. For information call 206-223-0287 in Seattle or 415-621-1550 in San Francisco.

by train: A Canrailpass is available in Canada for unlimited travel on VIA trains. The service to Churchill on Hudson Bay is included, but not the Ontario Northland train to Moosonee nor Viarail buses in Newfoundland. During the low season (1 Oct. to 31 May, Christmas excluded) the pass costs CDN$240 for 22 days, CDN$280 for 30 days, whereas high-season

Almost anything can happen in the solarium of the Alaska state ferries.

travel is CDN$345 for 22 days, CDN$395 for 30 days. This is for travel right across Canada; if you don't go beyond Winnipeg, the fare is less. Reservations are required. With trains running from both Prince Rupert and Vancouver, the Canrailpass is a creative way to begin or end your trip. In the U.S., unfortunately, Amtrack has dedicated itself to providing luxury service for the affluent instead of basic transportation. Bus travel is much cheaper.

driveaways: Driveaway cars are another way of getting around North America. You pick up a car from an agency in one city, pay a deposit, then drive the car to the destination, where your deposit is refunded. If you have a rider or two to share the gas and driving, it's cheap transportation. Europeans and Australians are welcome but should have an International Drivers License. Canadians are not allowed to drive American cars into the U.S., nor Americans drive Canadian cars into Canada. Aaacon is one of the largest driveaway agencies in the U.S.; look for others in the classified ad section of the daily newspapers or yellow pages of the telephone book.

tours: For an illustrated free brochure listing dozens of excellent outdoor-oriented tour programs in Western Canada write: Adventure Canada, No. 101 Recreation Square, 1414 Kensington Road N.W., Calgary, Alberta T2N 3P9, Canada. On-the-spot information about these tours can be obtained from any office of WestCan Treks Adventure Travel (in Toronto tel. 922-7584; in Calgary tel. 283-6115; in

Edmonton tel. 439-0024; in Vancouver tel. 734-1066) or Goway Travel (in Toronto tel. 863-0799; in Vancouver tel. 687-4004). In the U.S. contact the Adventure Center, 5540 College Ave., Oakland, CA 94618 (tel. 415-654-1879). Besides offering worthwhile package tours around Canada and the U.S., the above companies know of many exciting travel opportunities abroad. Another travel-oriented company, Ecosummer Canada Expeditions Ltd., 1666 Duranleau St., Vancouver, B.C. V6H 3S4 (tel. 604-669-7741), offers outstanding kayaking and hiking tours to some of the most remote corners of the Queen Charlotte Islands and Yukon. Prices begin at CDN$1,000 pp for 10 days, but are excellent value if you have the money. Also, Alaska Discovery, Box 26, Gustavus, AK 99826, USA, offers excellent canoe and kayak expeditions on the waterways of Southeast Alaska (see under "Juneau" for details).

TRAVEL WITHIN THE REGION

by ship: The Inside Passage route from Seattle to Skagway cuts between mountains far higher and wilder than the famous Norwegian fjords. It even surpasses a trip down the coast of Chile to Punta Arenas. One difference is that the North American journey is cheaper and more easily arranged than its South American or Scandinavian counterparts. Another difference is the variety of services, routes, and destinations on this route. The Washington State Ferries offer regular service throughout Puget Sound and

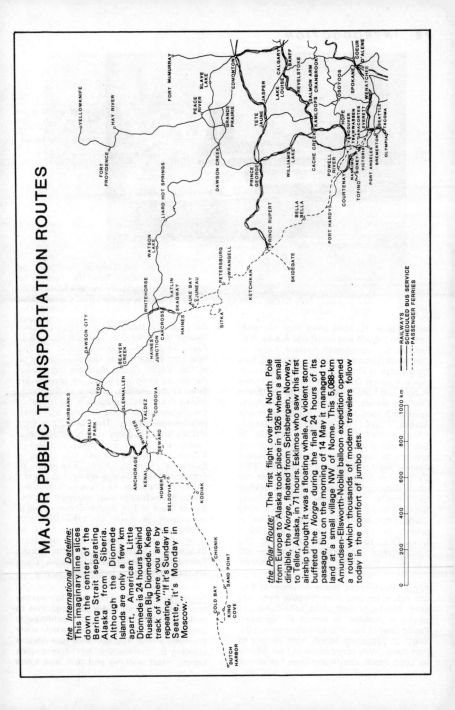

MAJOR PUBLIC TRANSPORTATION ROUTES

the International Dateline: This imaginary line slices down the center of the Bering Strait separating Alaska from Siberia. Although the Diomede Islands are only a few km apart, American Little Diomede is 24 hours behind Russian Big Diomede. Keep track of where you are by repeating, "If it's Sunday in Seattle, it's Monday in Moscow."

the Polar Route: The first flight over the North Pole from Europe to Alaska took place in 1926 when a small dirigible, the *Norge*, floated from Spitsbergen, Norway, to Teller, Alaska, in 71 hours. Eskimos who saw this first airship thought it was a floating whale. A violent storm buffeted the *Norge* during the final 24 hours of its passage, but on the morning of 14 May it managed to land at a small village NW of Nome. This 5,088-km Amundsen-Ellsworth-Nobile balloon expedition opened a route which thousands of modern travelers follow today in the comfort of jumbo jets.

RAILWAYS
SCHEDULED BUS SERVICE
PASSENGER FERRIES

0   200   400   600   800   1000 km

The *Columbia,* flagship of the Alaska Marine Highway, sails from Seattle north to Alaska once a week in the summer.

to Vancouver I., while other lines run from Seattle to Victoria and Southeast Alaska. B.C. Ferries has commuter service between Vancouver Island and the B.C. mainland, plus long distance ships through the Canadian Inside Passage from Port Hardy to Prince Rupert, and from Prince Rupert to the Queen Charlotte Islands. The Alaska Marine Highway operates 2 ferry networks: one in Southeast Alaska (see "Southeast Alaska— Introduction" for details), another in Southcentral Alaska. The 2 far-reaching systems do not interconnect, but the Alaska Airlines' flight from Juneau to Cordova ($108 OW) makes it possible to travel almost the whole distance from Seattle to Dutch Harbor by regular passenger ferry (ferry Seattle-Juneau, plane Juneau-Cordova, ferry Cordova-Kodiak-Dutch Harbor). The ferries operate year-round and fares are 25½ lower from Oct. to April. A glance at the transportation routes map in this section will give you an idea of the tantalizing possibilities.

by bus: Bus services, highly developed in B.C. and Yukon, become more primitive when you enter Alaska. Nonetheless, scheduled bus service is available on almost all highways. Pacific Coach Lines offers excellent service the length of Vancouver Island, from Victoria to Port Hardy, with connections in Port Alberni for Long Beach. Greyhound Lines has almost

daily service from Edmonton and Prince George to Whitehorse, with connections to Fairbanks 3 times a week. Norline Coaches runs from Whitehorse to Dawson City and on to Tok. Within Alaska there are many small companies using minibuses; all services are listed in the relevant sections of this book. Alaska-Yukon Motorcoaches is the largest of the Alaskan carriers and the only one which requires reservations. Their buses run from Haines and Skagway to Anchorage, and Fairbanks to Valdez. Be aware that buses in Yukon and Alaska do not run at night. Everyone arriving from Skagway or Edmonton/Prince George will have to spend a night in Whitehorse. All passengers transiting Yukon to Anchorage must overnight in either Beaver Creek or Tok. Accommodations are at your own expense, so take this into consideration when calculating your costs. *by train:* A narrow-gauge railway runs from Skagway to Whitehorse, and the Alaska Railroad links Anchorage to Fairbanks. There are daily services on both in the summer.

hitchhiking: One of the best ways to meet the local people and get where you're going is to stick out your thumb and hitch. Hitchhiking is possible throughout the North; mostly what you need is time. Tourists rarely give rides. If standing by the roadside for hours sounds boring, start walking and turn and hitch whenever a car comes along. Most of the North is uninhabited, so you'll have no trouble finding a place to pitch your tent when night falls. One or 2 women get rides easiest, then couples, then solo males, then 2 guys, and last, a guy and a dog. Having small children or a guitar with you often helps. If you're from somewhere other than Canada or the U.S., a flag on your backpack might assist you in getting a lift. Often the people who stop are former hitchhikers themselves, so offer to contribute for gas. At stops, try to be the one who pays for cigarettes or soft drinks. Buying the driver lunch will make you both feel good, and is a lot cheaper than a bus ticket. Ask people you meet on ferries and at campgrounds if they can give you a lift. A good number of the motorists leaving the ferry at Haines head for Fairbanks or Anchorage. Tape a notice outside the ship's cafeteria offering to share the gas and driving in exchange for a ride. If you have your own car, save money by looking for riders to share expenses. The notice board outside the tourist office in Dawson City is a great clearinghouse for people offering/looking for rides. In Anchorage, check the classifieds in the daily papers.

by bicycle: Taking along a bicycle is an excellent idea, and most of the ferries will let you bring it at no extra charge. In Southeast Alaska, bicycle campers have a definite advantage — campgrounds can be far from the towns and terminals. Almost all of the bus companies and railways will carry your bike as accompanied baggage for a nominal amount, although a few ask you to crate it. If you're planning to cycle all the way to Anchorage, be aware that the Haines Highway is a lot shorter and easier than the Klondike Highway out of Skagway. Most airlines also accept bicycles as luggage, usually at no extra charge. Take off the pedals and panniers, and clean off the dirt before checking in. There are 4 airlines flying between Anchorage and Seattle; before you buy a ticket, compare prices, then ask each about taking a bicycle. *maintenance and supplies:* Know how to fix your own bike. Take along a good repair kit as bicycle shops are few and far between. You should have a spare tube, a patch kit, a tire pump, extra cables, a spare chain, a chain tool, and perhaps extra wheels with you. Carry your gear in saddlebag panniers lined with plastic bags. Fenders would be nice to shield you from the rain. Warm, waterproof clothing is essential, particularly rain pants, poncho, rain hat, wool shirt, wool socks, and waterproof shoes. Bicycling gloves, shorts, and clear goggles are also necessary. Everything you need may be purchased in Seattle or Vancouver.

ACCOMMODATIONS AND FOOD

hotels and hostels: Within these pages you'll find reasonably-priced hotel accommodations listed wherever they exist. The hotel rates given are for the cheapest category of room (shared bath). Also check the classifieds in the daily papers or the yellow pages of the phone book. Naturally you won't find a phone in every room. The TV is in the lounge and you'll share a bathroom. In other words, it's just like being at home. Reservations are usually not accepted in the cheapest hotels. The older hotels in the big cities look a lot worse than they actually are, but ask to see the room. If you have any doubts about staying in one, try the YHs, YMCAs, and YWCAs, which are invariably pleasant and acceptable. A sleeping sheet is sometimes required at YHs, although you can usually rent them. Cooking facilities are often available and the hostels are good meeting places. Hostelers are expected to help with hostel housekeeping work and the YHs close during the day. Note that YHs do not accept small children and charge more to non-members. Joining the YH Association before you leave home is recommended. Write: American Youth Hostels, Inc., National Campus, Delaplane, Virginia 22025, USA, or Canadian Hosteling Assn., 333 River Rd., Vanier City, Ontario K1L 8B9, Canada.

camping: The only consistent way to sleep cheap in the North is to camp. Camping is easy from May to Sept. but be prepared for occasional cold and rain (see "what to take" below). Most of the land is owned by the government; so long as you stay out of sight of the road, don't chop down any trees, and are careful with fire, no one is likely to bother you. Avoid places with NO TRESPASSING signs, if possible. In Canada you may camp anywhere on Crown Land without a permit; in Alaska camping is allowed on state land and within the national forests. The national parks of both countries ask that you first obtain a free backcountry use permit. Camping on public property within city limits, however, is usually prohibited. The lengths to which officials will go to enforce this prohibition varies, but the worst that might happen is you'll be asked to leave. Avoid problems and insure your privacy by keeping your tent well hidden. Don't invite trouble by building a campfire. See under "coexisting with the bears" above and "wilderness etiquette" below for general backcountry camping tips.

campgrounds: Generally, 2 distinct types of campgrounds are available: state, provincial,

The youth hostel at Denali National Park in Alaska is 3 old railway cars parked near the station.

ALASKAN WILD BERRIES

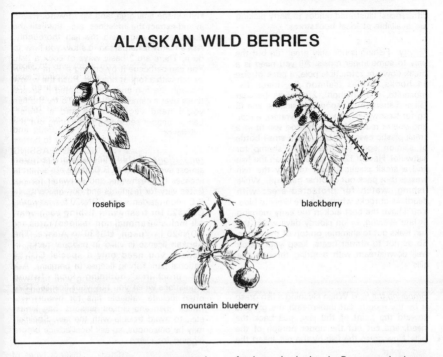

rosehips

blackberry

mountain blueberry

and federal government-operated campgrounds which offer a basic outdoor experience with a minimum of facilities; and municipal and private campgrounds which usually offer hot showers, laundromats, stores, dump stations, plug-ins, etc. The latter cater primarily to RV drivers, and some don't even accept tenters! They still call themselves campgrounds, though. Often you have no choice which type to stay at and must take what you can get. The government campgrounds are usually cheaper than the commercial variety. Whenever you are quoted a fee at a campground always assume, unless told otherwise, that it is for your whole group rather than per person.

FOOD

The cheapest, healthiest, and most enjoyable way to eat is to buy groceries and prepare your own meals. A lot can just be eaten cold. Sandwiches, anyone? Freeze-dried food is recommended for hikers and campers. Canned food can also be handy. Buy canned salmon: the goodness of the northern oceans is locked in every tin. Avoid canned tuna: every year thousands of dolphins drown in tuna nets, victims of the tuna industry's drive for higher profits. Some hostels have kitchens, or cook on your camp stove. At restaurants, breakfast is usually your best-value meal. Food is generally more expensive in Canada than in the U.S., and more expensive in Alaska than either. Nineteen is the drinking age throughout the area (except Washington, where it is 21).

berry collecting: Blueberries, cranberries, blackberries, elderberries, and raspberries can often be found along northern trails. They provide a refreshing treat, but it's best to know what you're eating as certain varieties are poisonous. Blueberries, for example, grow on a low shrub and have small, tough, light green leaves which are glossy all over. The poisonous false blueberry is a near look-alike; it grows on a vine and has succulent leaves which are glossy on top but fuzzy underneath. You must look carefully to note the differences! Illustrated guides to berry picking are available at local bookstores.

fishing: Fishing is not only great fun but the way to some super meals. All you need is a break-down or retractible pole, a pack of size 14 hooks, 5 flies (salmon fly, black fly, mosquito, gnat, nymph), 2 spinners (rooster tail and shannon), 2 spoons, 4 sinkers, line (5 kg for freshwater, 14 kg for saltwater), a reel, and you're ready. All but the rod will fit in a small plastic case. For bait, get a small bottle of salmon eggs for freshwater, shrimp for saltwater. Have a 12-cm knife to clean the fish and a small plastic trowel to bury the fish wastes (but pack out all other garbage). While fishing, watch for protected areas with deadfalls or rocks where fish are likely to hide. You'll have the best luck in the early morning or late evening, or on cloudy days when the sun leaks out to shimmer on top of the water. So as not to attract bears, keep your catch well downstream with a string through the gills.

preparing the fish: When cleaning a fish grasp it by the mouth, cut underneath the gill slits toward the point of the jaw, pull back the head, and cut out the upper portion of the gills. Now grasp the fish by the tail, insert the knife in the anal area, and slit forward. Reach in and extract the intestines, etc., then slit the dorsal artery and wash the fish thoroughly. Ask a fellow fisherperson to show you how to do it. There are 2 basic ways to cook a fish. You can barbecue it by cutting a ½ m willow switch with a fork at one end. Push the willow through the fish and roast, turning it several times over a campfire till done. To fry the fish you'll need vegetable oil and a skillet. Lemon-pepper seasoning helps bring out the full flavor.

regulations: Fishing licenses are required almost everywhere. In B.C. there are separate licenses for freshwater and saltwater fishing. Rates vary for residents and non-residents. In B.C., non-residents pay CDN$20 for saltwater, CDN$23 for freshwater fishing each year. All-inclusive annual non-resident rates are CDN$20 in Yukon, US$30 in Alaska. The Alaskan license is valid in national parks; in Canada you need only a special CDN$4 national park fishing license (a bargain). Ask for brochures outlining local fishing regulations when you buy your license. They often include valuable tips for newcomers. Check open and closed seasons, bag limits, etc., to avoid trouble with the law. Shellfish may be poisonous, so ask local advice before digging for clams.

MONEY, MEASUREMENTS, VISAS

Unless otherwise stated, all prices in this handbook are in the local currency: Canadian dollars in Canada, U.S. dollars in the United States. Assume that all hotel and restaurant prices are pp (per person) per day or per meal. Campground charges are usually per site. The prices and hours of all attractions and services throughout the book refer to the peak season in midsummer. The travel suggestions in this book are meant to be used from May to Sept. only. Some prices are lower in the off season and many businesses close. By the time you get there, all of the prices given in this book will have changed. Nevertheless, you should find them a useful basis for comparison as what was once the cheapest is still likely to be reasonable. Always ask the price of a room, meal, or service before accepting it. Tipping, like in the Lower 48, is expected at most sit-down eating places above the level of a snack bar or takeaway counter, usually 15 percent of the bill. Employees of the large hotel chains often receive such poor wages that tips are their only real income. All transportation fares and traveling times are OW (one way), unless otherwise noted. Be aware that tickets or exact change are required on all forms of public transport in North America; drivers rarely carry change. Hiking times are also OW and are those of a strong, fast walker, so figure accordingly. Almost all of the maps in this book have been drawn with north at the top. Exceptions are the large regional maps where an indication of north is difficult due to the curvature of the earth's surface. Be careful to read the instructions before using public telephones in the North. Often you do not pay until your party answers; if you put the coin in before that, it will be lost. The basic trick to economy travel is to live on the road as you do at home, or cheaper. With a little creative planning and flexibility, you can have a whale of a time on a minnow's worth of money. Try it.

measurements: All measurements are according to the metric system:

    1 inch   = 25.4 millimeters (mm)
    1 foot   = .3048 meters (m)
    1 mile   = 1.609 kilometers (km)
    1 sq mile = 2.59 sq km
    1 acre   = .4047 hectares (ha)
    1 pound   = .454 kilograms (kg)

To compute centigrade temperatures, subtract 32 from fahrenheit and divide by 1.8. To avoid confusion, all clock times in this handbook are expressed according to the 24-hour military or European train timetable system, i.e. 0100 is 1:00 a.m., 1300 is 1:00 p.m., 2330 is 11:30 p.m. From noon to midnight, merely add 12 on to regular time to derive military time. For a list of abbreviations used, consult the glossary near the end of this book.

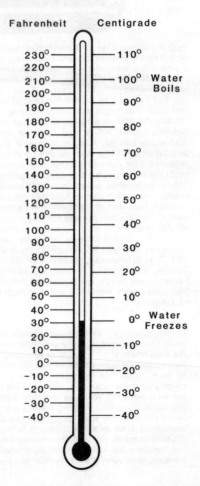

mail: If you would like to receive mail en route, have it sent to yourself c/o General Delivery to a post office along the way. American post offices hold General Delivery mail 10 days, while Canadian post offices keep it 15 days. If you had mail sent to a Canadian post office and think you might not arrive in time, a "Holding of Mail" card may be obtained at any Canadian post office and sent to the appropriate address. Postage stamps in the amount of CDN$1.50 must be affixed to the notice card for each month that you request mail to be held, up to a maximum of 3 months. This is an excellent service, but don't bother phoning; verbal requests to hold mail are not honored. Note that all mail posted in Canada must carry Canadian postage stamps, just as all U.S. mail must have American stamps. Convenient General Delivery addresses are: Vancouver, B.C. V6B 3P7; Prince Rupert, B.C. V8J 3P3; Whitehorse, Yukon Y1A 2BO; Seattle, WA 98101; Juneau AK 99801; Fairbanks, AK 99701; Anchorage, AK 99510. Mail takes several weeks to travel from Alaska to Yukon.

border crossings: Immigration officials are trained to be suspicious, so try to look as much like a legitimate short-term visitor as you can. Never admit (or even infer) that you are going to work, study, do business, or live in a country other than your own. They may ask to see your money. If you have less than $250, you stand the chance of being refused entry. Some unscrupulous souls get around this by borrowing $500 or more, using it to buy travelers cheques, claiming the cheques were lost, repaying the loan with the replacement cheques, then using the "dummies" to crash

borders with. We do not recommend that you do this as it is illegal and unfair to kindly immigration officers. If you were ever to cash the "lost" cheques, even by mistake, you would go straight to jail. The best approach is just to be as polite and submissive as you can. Never argue or get angry with an official—it never helps. They have unlimited institutionalized force on their side and know it.

entry into Canada: No visa is required of visitors from Western Europe, most Commonwealth countries, or the United States. Americans can enter Canada by showing a birth certificate or voters registration card; a driver's license may not be sufficient. Everyone other than Americans must have a passport. Travelers under 18 must have written permission from a parent or guardian to enter Canada. Handguns, rifles less than 66 cm overall length, and automatic weapons are not allowed into Canada. (James Bond take note!) *entry into the U.S.:* Everyone other than Canadians requires a passport and visa to enter the United States. Canadians must show a birth certificate or other identification. U.S. residents returning from Canada may bring back US$300 worth of duty-free merchandise once every 30 days.

WORKING HOLIDAYS

boomers: Reports of astronomical wages paid during the building of the Trans-Alaska Oil Pipeline (1973-1974) created the impression in the rest of the U.S. that Alaska was the place to achieve instant wealth. Now, almost a decade later, those construction jobs no longer exist, and Alaska is plagued with high inflation and unemployment. Alaska's summer unemployment is 10 percent, but in winter it's twice that. Couple this with a cost of living almost double that of the Lower 48 and you have all the makings of hard times. Brochures from the Alaska Job Service do everything they can to discourage people from coming to Alaska to seek work. Yet you occasionally meet someone who tells you how they made thousands of dollars in a couple of weeks. What's the truth?

summer jobs: Although easy money is nowhere to be found, it's possible to pay for your trip by picking up odd jobs along the way. Forget the oil industry—they only take highly trained specialists. Canneries are an obvious place to apply; you'll often learn through the grapevine when they're hiring. Summer resorts, hotels, and tourist restaurants often need dishwashers, janitors, and odd-jobbers during the summer. Jobs with tour companies as guides, drivers, hostesses, etc., are almost always filled at the company's head office in Seattle or elsewhere, long before the season begins. Westours, for example, hires mostly "Christians" who are less likely to cause trouble. Jobs with the Forest Service are generally paid minimum wage ($3.85 an hour) and disappear towards the end of the summer. It doesn't hurt to ask. If you can get on a profitable fishing boat where you're paid a percentage of the catch you're lucky, but be aware that jobs like this are highly sought after and usually filled by word-of-mouth among people known in the area. While on a summer vacation you could choose a place you'd like to work, then return with a job the following

year. If you're really serious about working in Alaska, start looking and applying in January. Otherwise, to avoid disappointment and even real hardship, looking for a summer job in Alaska should be thought of only as a working holiday. Take enough money to get by even if you find nothing, but if you actively seek work everywhere you go, chances are you'll pay your way.

others: If you're thinking of heading N to look for work in the canneries or on a fishing boat, get hold of *A Season in Alaska* by Beau Westover (available from Moon Publications, Box 1696, Chico, CA 95927, USA). Westover outlines the job situation clearly and realistically and explains how to arrange jobs in canneries in advance, so the company pays your way north. Every bit as good is *The North Pacific Deckhand's and Alaska Cannery Worker's Handbook* by John Higgins (Albacore Press, Box 355, Eastsound, WA 98245, USA). The many intriguing photographs, the informative essays, and the first-person narratives by a fishing boat captain make the *Deckhand's Handbook* worthwhile for both general reader and serious job seeker. If the U.S. and Canadian governments ever give final approval to the Alaska Highway Gas Pipeline, destined to bring natural gas SE from Prudhoe Bay to the Lower 48, a whole range of new construction jobs could materialize. Most will be union jobs. Construction probably won't begin until 1986 (those who respect the environment hope it never will). For a standard corporate put-down, write: Employee Relations Dept., Northwest Alaskan Pipeline Company, Box 1526, Salt Lake City, Utah 84110, USA.

A gillnetter winds in the catch off the Queen Charlotte Islands.

GOLD PANNING

Panning for gold is not only great fun, but it's also a good way to get involved in the history of the North. Besides, there's the chance you'll find a nugget which would become a lifelong souvenir. You might even strike it rich! The amount of equipment required is minimal: a 30-cm plastic gravity-trap gold pan is about all you need. Buy one at any local surplus or sporting goods store for a couple of dollars. Have tweezers and an eye dropper to separate the gold flakes, and a small vial to hold them. Ordinary rubber gloves will protect your hands from icy creek water. Once you get into it, you'll probably pick up an automobile oil dipstick bent at one end to poke into crevices, and a small garden trowel to dig out the dirt under rocks.

where to pan: Look for a gravel bar where the creek bed takes a turn. Watch for larger rocks forming eddies during high water, or for crevices in the bedrock. These are places where gold will lodge. Try your luck on any of the old gold-rush creeks; tourist offices can often suggest likely areas. Stay away from commercial mining operations and ask permission if you're obviously on someone's claim. _how to pan:_ The principle is that gold, twice as heavy as lead, will settle to the bottom of your pan. Fill the pan half full of paydirt and cover with water. Hit the rim of the pan 7 or 8 times, or shake it back and forth. Break up lumps of dirt or clay with your hands and discard any rocks after rinsing them in the pan. Shake the pan again, moving it in a circular motion. Dip the front edge of the pan in the stream and carefully wash off excess sand and gravel until only a small amount of black sand remains. If you see gold specks too small to remove with tweezers, take the black sand out and let it dry. Later dump it on a clean sheet of paper and gently blow away the sand. The gold will remain. That's the basic procedure, though there are many ways to do it. It does take practice; ask a friendly sourdough for advice.

HEALTH AND HELP

The number one killer of outdoorspeople in the North, accounting for 85 percent of all wilderness deaths, is hypothermia. Prolonged exposure to wind and cold plus general physical exhaustion can lead to persistent shivering, drowsiness, and death. The most dangerous thing about it is that you probably won't even be aware that it's happening to you. Try to stay dry while hiking; wet clothes cause you to lose body heat 200 times faster than dry clothes. A full 60 percent of body heat loss occurs through an uncovered head, so wear a waterproof or wool cap. If you experience the early-warning signs, get out of the rain and wind, make camp, remove wet clothing, and above all, do not sleep until you feel better. Be prepared for this on all overnight hikes; if making a day hike on a wet day, do not go beyond the point where you can beat a quick retreat. It's easy to become lost in forested areas once you leave the main trail. Do not blunder blindly on, but stop and look around you. Use your compass to find your way back to some known point. Panic in the wilderness is a form of culture shock which could spell your end. Another thing for hikers to keep in mind is that even clear, cold, free-running streams can be contaminated. The best way to avoid contacting parasites from beavers and muskrats upstream is to boil water for 20 minutes before drinking it. If this is not convenient, treat it with a chemical disinfectant such as chlorine or (better) iodine. Boy Scout water purification pills may also do the trick. If you're a real purist, you might take one of the water cleaning filter devices sold in camping goods stores for $35.

doctors: If you're sick or injured and can't afford the prices charged by private doctors and general hospitals, call the local welfare office and ask them to refer you to a low-cost clinic. You may have to wait in line and go during certain limited hours, but there's usually no problem about using their services.

teenagers: If you're a runaway, or are with a friend who is, and would like to send a free message to your/their parents, call one of the following toll-free numbers: 800-231-6946 in the Lower 48; 800-231-6762 in Alaska/Hawaii. An operator will answer your call and phone your folks anywhere in the U.S. with a message from you. There will be no lectures and nobody will try to find out where you are. Only one question will be asked, 'How are you and do you need anything?' Let your parents know you're alive and okay.

assault: Women travelers can protect themselves against sexual violence by wearing non-restrictive clothing which will allow you to move quickly, carrying a loud whistle, and being aware of cars and people around you. In a sexual confrontation situation, try to remain in control. Look your assailant straight in the eye and tell him to leave you alone. If this doesn't work, shout "Fire!" loudly to get attention, and try to get closer to other people. If you are being physically assaulted, a sudden clap hard over the ears or poke at the eyes can give you the chance to escape. Throw anything available in your assailant's face or scrape your foot down his shin and step hard on his instep. Measure your chances of resistance and escape, however, and do whatever is necessary to avoid getting hurt. The above is mostly for use if you have somewhere to run to or a way of escaping. Female hitchhikers put themselves in a more dangerous situation as the potential assailant is able to choose the time and place when you will be least able to get help. Lower the chances of trouble by checking the back seat before getting into a car, never getting into the back of a 2-door car, and never accepting a ride with more than one man. Memorize the license number of the car when it stops. Ask the driver where *he* is going before volunteering where you want to go. Know where the door handle is and get out if necessary—don't wait to be polite. Don't feel embarrassed about refusing a ride if you don't feel comfortable in a situation. Some women hitch everywhere, never have a problem, and find it leads to many rewarding experiences. But you must be defensive, a good judge of character, and very sure of yourself.

WILDERNESS ETIQUETTE

Make it your objective to leave no trace of your passing. Litter is pollution. Whenever you are tempted to leave bothersome garbage behind, think of how you feel when you find other people's plastic bags, tin cans, or aluminum foil in *your* yard. If you packed it in, pack it out. Burying garbage is useless as animals soon dig it up. Be a caretaker by picking up trash left by less-aware visitors. In this way you, in part, thank the land for the experiences it has given you. Along shorelines, the intertidal zone is the best for campfires and human excrement. Human wastes in other areas should be disposed of at least 30 m from any trail or water source. Bury the wastes and carefully burn the toilet paper, if possible. Try to build your campfire on sand or gravel and keep it small and under control. Extreme care should be taken during dry periods and in the forest. Refrain from doing *anything* that might cause even the smallest of accidental fires.

local people: As you explore, remember that Northerners are fiercely independent people who value their privacy. They can also be overwhelmingly hospitable if you treat them with respect. All Indian reservations are private property. You should always ask the advice of a local resident before camping on one. Never put up your tent in or near a native village without talking to someone. When visiting a native village or any small, isolated community, look people straight in the eye and be the first to say hello. Remember, you are the intruder, so you should be the one to make the effort to put them at ease.

WHAT TO TAKE

camping equipment and clothing: Even in summer, weather conditions in the North can change suddenly and you must be well prepared for rain and cold at any time! Water resistance and warmth should be your main criteria when purchasing camping equipment and clothing. Buy your pack last so you'll be able to fit everything in it. Categorize and separate all your things in plastic bags or stuff sacks; pack it that way for convenience of access and protection from moisture. Your loaded pack should not weigh more than one-quarter your body weight. Walk around the block with it a few times. Now imagine hiking 20 km into the rain with that same load on your back. Pack light. You'll still probably end up sending a few things home. Practice putting up your tent, cooking on your camp stove, etc., before you set out. A freestanding tent is best because you can pitch it on board ferries, wooden pads—even inside abandoned buildings. Just remember to anchor it down when you erect it on a windy hillside or deck. A green colored tent attracts less attention. A foam sleeping pad provides comfort, insulation, and protection from moisture—essential qualities for the North.

Down sleeping bags are useless when wet: try drying out a soggy sleeping bag in Southeast Alaska! Bags with synthetic fiber fill are preferable, but wool is best because it keeps you warm even when wet. The only consideration here is weight: wool holds 3 times its weight in water. Wearing your clothing in layers allows you to add or remove items depending on the temperature. A wool sweater and waterproof jacket are far better than a bulky coat. A pair of old tennis shoes is handy for crossing streams and muskeg. Kayakers will need rubber boots. Wear rubber thongs into public showers, around swimming pools, etc. Here's a checklist:

> pack with frame and hip belt
> day pack or shoulder bag
> nylon tent and fly
> tent patching tape
> foam sleeping pad
> wool or synthetic fiber sleeping bag
> YH sleeping sheet
> wool sweater, pants, socks
> wool or waterproof cap
> poncho or rain coat
> waterproof hiking boots
> tennis shoes
> rubber thongs

essential accessories: When using a compass, beware of large E declinations between true N and magnetic N (31 degrees at Skagway, for example). Compass declinations are marked at the bottom of topographical maps. A small pocket calculator with a clock/alarm function is always handy. Carrying a length of light-weight chain and a padlock allows you to attach the frame of your pack to something solid when you leave gear in public places. Ripoffs are rare, but they do occur. Wind and rain seem to arrive together in the North so the locals never use umbrellas. Still, a small collapsible umbrella is useful at times, even though it will brand you a *cheechako*. Take a 5-m length of rope to hang your food up out of reach of brother bruin.

    compass
    bear bells
    small flashlight
    candle
    pocket/alarm calculator
    pocket watch
    sunglasses
    padlock and 65-cm length of chain
    collapsible umbrella
    5-m length of rope
    twine for a clothes line
    mini-towel
    powdered laundry soap
    sink plug (one that fits all)
    sewing kit
    mini-scissors
    fishing line for sewing heavy gear

money and documents: Make a couple of photocopies of the information page of your passport, identification, YH card, transportation tickets, purchase receipt for travelers cheques, eyeglass and medical prescriptions, etc.—you should be able to get them all on one page. Carry these in different places and mail one home. Travelers cheques are the best way to carry money, but buy them from a well-known U.S. company such as Bank of America or American Express. European or Japanese travelers cheques are very difficult to cash in North America; even Thomas Cook and Barclay Bank cheques are sometimes refused. Get travelers cheques issued by 2 different companies; this doubles your chance of a prompt refund in case of loss. If you know you will be visiting Canada, be sure to get a few Canadian dollar travelers cheques. This is easily arranged at any large American or European bank and could save you a lot of trouble if you arrive outside banking hours (Mon. to Thurs. 1000-1500, Fri.

1000-1700). Some Canadian and U.S. cash will make your first few hours in the neighboring country more pleasant. Note that there are no exchange facilities at the borders: Canadians take U.S. dollars at a very poor rate, while Americans often refuse Canadian dollars. Any currency other than these 2 is accepted at a terrible loss (to you). Identification is usually requested when cashing travelers cheques. When changing money, do not accept bills larger than $20 (they are hard to spend), and check the rate at several banks if you're changing a lot (they do differ). A soft pouch-type money belt worn under your clothes is very safe and handy, but put the documents inside a plastic bag to protect them from perspiration and moisture. Consider becoming a life member of the YH Association, considerably more economical in the long run.

    passport or birth certificate
    youth hostel card
    photocopy of important documents
    travelers cheques
    Canadian and American cash
    money belt with plastic liner
    address book
    notebook
    envelopes
    postage stamps
    extra ballpoint
    Alaska-Yukon Handbook

food kit: A small camp stove is the only way to be assured of hot food and drink on the trail. Firewood is often wet or unavailable; other times campfires are prohibited. Look for a stove which is not only lightweight, but burns a variety of fuels. White gas stoves are best. Remember that camping fuel is not allowed on commercial aircraft. If you don't want to tie your money up in a good camp stove, consider taking a can of sterno (available at any army surplus store). Carry your food in lightweight containers. Avoid cans and bottles whenever possible. Dried or freeze-dried foods are light, easy to prepare, and less attractive to animals. Take some high protein/energy foods for hiking.

    camp stove
    tin cooking pot
    plastic plate
    Sierra Club cup
    can and bottle opener
    cork screw
    pen knife or Swiss Army knife
    spoon

tin canteen
waterproof matches
freeze-dried food
tea bags
plastic bags
litterbag
retractible fishing rod
salt

toiletries and medical kit: You'll find a plastic case in which to pack your medical kit in the dishware section of any large department or hardware store. Unscented deodorant is best for both bear and bare encounters. Mosquitos reach their peak in June and decline thereafter. They are most active at twilight and in early morning; a gentle breeze will disperse them. Strangely, mosquitos are more attracted to dark clothing than light. Calmitol ointment is good for burns, bites, and rashes. An antibiotic such as *sulfatrim apo* would be useful for serious infections (not VD), but beware of all antibiotics—know when and how to use them. For stomach cramps associated with diarrhea take a pain killer such as *imodium*. Moleskin is an effective blister preventative. Take an adequate supply of any personal prescription medicines.

soap in a plastic container
toothpaste
soft toothbrush
unscented stick deodorant
shampoo
powdered soap
white toilet paper
multiple vitamins and minerals
Cutter's insect repellent
chapstick
a motion-sickness remedy
contraceptives
iodine
water purification pills
lomotil/diarrhea remedy
Tiger Balm
vaseline
a cold remedy
Alka Seltzer
aspirins
Calmitol ointment
an antibiotic
a pain killer
bandaids

one large elastoplast or dressing
waterproof matches

free information: If you have time to write requests, an excellent selection of free maps and brochures is available from the regional tourism authorities: Tourism B.C., 1117 Wharf St., Victoria, B.C. V8W 2Z2, Canada; Division of Tourism, Pouch E, Juneau, Ak 99811, USA; Tourism Yukon, Box 2703, Whitehorse, YT Y1A 2C6, Canada; TravelArctic, Government of the Northwest Territories, Yellowknife, N.W.T. X1A 2L9, Canada. Free maps of the Tongass and Chugach national forests may be obtained from the U.S. Forest Service, Box 1628, Juneau, AK 99802, USA. A free highway map of Washington State is available from the Washington State Dept. of Transportation, Transportation Bldg., Olympia, WA 98504, USA. Get a free map of Canada from the Canadian Government Office of Tourism, 235 Queen St., O4E, Ottawa, Ont. K1A 0H6, Canada. Write for an index to maps of Alaska from the U.S.G.S. Distribution Branch, Box 25286, Federal Center, Denver, CO 80225, USA. For information on Alaska's national parks, write: National Park Service, 540 West 5th Ave., Anchorage AK 99501, USA. For a ferry timetable write: Alaska Marine Highway, Pouch R, Juneau, AK 99811, USA. A list of Alaskan YHs is available from Anchorage Youth Hostel, Inc., Box 4-1226, Anchorage, AK 99509, USA. If you are a member of the American Automobile Assn. (AAA) or Canadian Automobile Assn. (CAA), or have a friend or relative who is, get their free *TourBook* and *CampBook* covering Western Canada and Alaska, plus detailed maps. Overseas visitors who belong to an affiliated club in their home country can obtain this material free by showing their membership card at an AAA or CAA office in any large city (look in the phone book). Publishers specializing in books on the North are: Alaska Northwest Publishing Co., Box 4-EEE, Anchorage, AK 99509, USA; Alaska Natural History Assn., Box 9, McKinley Park, AK 99755, USA; The Mountaineers, 715 Pike St., Seattle, WA 98101, USA; Moon Publications, Box 1696, Chico, CA 95927, USA. Write for a free book catalog.

STATE OF WASHINGTON

SEATTLE

For Americans, Seattle is the best place to begin an Alaskan holiday. Highways and bus routes from every corner of the Lower 48, as well as major air routes from Hawaii and the Orient connect here with 3 of the largest ferry lines on the NW coast. The city is also an attraction in its own right—good for several days of adventurous sightseeing. Fascinating day trips beckon from all sides, and the beauty of Seattle's waterways complements the scenic grandeur of the Olympic Mountains to the W, the Cascades to the E, and Mount Rainier to the SE, giving one a taste of the magnificence waiting further north.

SIGHTS OF SEATTLE

downtown: Start your day with breakfast at the Pike Place Market—Lowell's Restaurant is recommended. Farmers have been bringing their produce here since before WW I; the market is one of Seattle's best free shows. A look through the fish stalls here is better than a visit to the aquarium! The market is open daily except Sun., but busiest on Saturday. After gorging yourself on the many sights, smells and tastes, take the stairs behind the market down to the waterfront. Although bounded by a noisy overhead freeway and cluttered with chintzy shops, the Seattle waterfront retains a lot of charm. Avoid the tourist traps and stroll along enjoying what is free. Vintage 1927 Aussie streetcars rumble along Alaskan Way. There are good views across Elliot Bay and the excitement of people and ships coming and going. If you haven't been on the ferries yet, go into the Washington State Ferry terminal for a look. Turn L at Yesler Way, just a little beyond the ferry terminal, to reach Pioneer Square—heart of gold rush Seattle. The totem pole and covered archway are remnants of the city of the 1890s. The old historical buildings and surrounding streets are becoming trendy with their chic shops and fancy restaurants, but the tourists and misplaced suburbanites haven't managed to drive away all the old-timers yet. Henry Yesler established his sawmill here in 1852 and the logs he slid down Yesler Way led to the naming of the original

Skid Road. The great fire of 1889 razed the area so most of what you now see was built soon after. The highlight of the historical district is the Klondike Gold Rush National Historical Park Visitor Center, 117 S. Main St., open 0900-1700 daily, admission free. Here you will hear the story of that mad summer of 1897 when thousands of men dropped what they were doing and answered the call of 'gold!' The park rangers at the Visitor Center are very helpful and will be glad to show you free movies on the gold rush in the adjoining auditorium at any time. A stop here is an absolute must for anyone headed north. For a bird's eye view of this part of the city, take the elevator to the top of the Smith Tower ($1), 2nd Ave. and Yesler Way. If you want to delve into the city a little deeper, take the highly entertaining Underground Tour ($2.50) which begins several times a day at 610 E. 1st Avenue. This is Seattle's answer to the famous Paris sewer tours. While you're waiting, the Roscoe Louie Gallery, 87 S. Washington St., has the most tubular new-wave art. *sidetrip:* On 2nd Ave. catch a no. 20 or 123 bus S to Rainier Brewery, 3100 Airport Way S, for a movie and tour of the plant followed by thirst-quenching samples of the product. Tours take place Mon. to Fri. 1300-1800. There's a 3-beer limit on the free brew.

NW of downtown: The Seattle World's Fair took place in 1962 but for the people of Seattle it never ended. The fairgrounds, now the Seattle Center, have become a local institution. Get there on a monorail which leaves from 5th Ave. and Pine downtown and costs only 35 cents OW. Entry to the grounds is free but some of the 'attractions' charge high admission prices, so once again just wander around and see what you can do gratis. The Art Museum Pavilion at the Center is free on Thurs. (regularly $2) and stays open until 2100. Spend some of the money you save on a good meal in the Center House, a large indoor pavilion with dozens of fast-food counters selling specialties from around the world. Prices are reasonable ($2-4) and the atmosphere pleasant and cheerful. Square dancing and other free events are often held in this building. When you've had your fill of the Center, walk out to 1st Ave. N and board a no. 15 or 18 bus to the S end of Ballard Bridge. The bulk of the Pacific NW fishing fleet is based at the Salmon Bay Terminal just W of the bridge. Walk down for a look. Return to the S end of the bridge and look for the no. 17 bus stop just across an access road slightly to the northeast. Bus no. 17 will take you to one of the most interesting sights of Seattle, the Government Locks. These narrow locks permit navigation between Puget Sound and Lake

This proud vendor at Seattle's Pike Place Market displays the makings of a tasty meal.

Washington. Finished in 1916, they're still very busy. The public is welcome to observe their operation and enjoy the beautiful surrounding gardens daily, admission free. The Visitor Center there is open 1100-1700 (closed Tues. and Wednesday). At the large fish ladder just on the other side of the locks you can look a salmon in the eye (in season). If you want to go to the University District, bus no. 43 will take you straight there from the entrance to the locks.

NE of downtown: Seattle's best museum and one of the finest of its kind anywhere is the Burke Memorial Museum, NE 45th St. and 17th Ave. NE in the University District (open Tues. to Fri 1100-1730, Sat. and Sun. 0900-1630, admission free). This well-arranged, colorful collection features NW Coastal Indian artifacts and will please even those who usually avoid museums. There is a very good, reasonably priced cafe downstairs. The museum is located at the N edge of the large, park-like University of Washington campus, originally the site of the 1909 Alaska-Yukon Pacific Exposition. The parking attendants in the booths on Memorial Way near the Burke Museum will give you a free map of the grounds if you ask. The Central Plaza directly S is impressive and the Suzzallo Library on its E side has a large Pacific NW collection. Away from the classroom, campus life revolves around University Way NE with many shops and restaurants catering to students. A very enjoyable day can be spent exploring the area. Numerous buses, many running N on 3rd Ave., shuttle between downtown and the University District. On your way back to town you might want to visit Volunteer Park which features a watertower with a good view, a greenhouse (open 0900:1700), and the Seattle Art Museum (open till 2100 and free on Thurs.), noted for its collection of Asian art. To get to the park from the university, take bus no. 43 to E. John St. and 15th Ave. E, then transfer to a no. 10 bus.

to the E: About the best travel deal in Seattle is the one-hour bus ride on a no. 210 bus all the way out to Snoqualmie Falls (catch it across the street from the Moore Hotel). The bus crosses the causeway over Lake Washington and passes through wooded countryside up into the foothills of the Cascades. Admission to the falls is free, and they are very impressive, especially during spring. The bus

The turbulent waters of the Snoqualmie River tumble over 82-m high Snoqualmie Falls near Seattle.

fare is just 90 cents (ask for a transfer) and if you spend only 30 min. at the falls and catch the same bus back to Seattle after it goes to North Bend to turn around, you can use your free transfer for the return journey.

STAY

hotels: The prices listed on the chart are for the cheapest category of room (bath down the hall). If you want a private bath, you pay more. Note that the weekly rates are much lower than daily rates. Seattle is well worth a week, so consider doing this. The hotels are listed in geographical sequence, beginning with those closest to Greyhound. It is recommended that you leave your luggage in a locker at the ferry terminal or Greyhound station and make the rounds in person. Ask to see the room before deciding. Don't be intimidated by the old men sitting in the lobbies — not only are they harmless, but many can spin a good yarn or two. These old hotels look a lot worse than they generally are, but single women might stay at the YMCA or YWCA to be safest. If

SEATTLE HOTELS

NAME	ADDRESS	PHONE	DAILY SINGLE	DAILY DOUBLE	WEEKLY SINGLE	WEEKLY DOUBLE
St. Regis Hotel	2nd and Stewart	622-6366	$15	$15	$45	$55
Moore Hotel	1926 2nd Ave.	622-4851	$13	$18	$45	$55
Commodore Hotel	2013 2nd Ave.	622-7535	$16	$19	$64	$70
Gatewood Hotel	1st Ave. and Pine	624-5009	$18	$25	$55	$75
Central Hotel	1516½ 5th Ave.	223-9174	$13	$14	$45	$52
YWCA (women only)	1118 5th Ave.	447-4888	$18	$22	—	—
YMCA (coed)	909 4th Ave.	382-5000	$18	$22	—	—
Pacific Hotel	317 Marion St.	622-3985	$12	$14	$53	$53
St. Charles Hotel	619 3rd Ave.	624-1674	$13	$17	$40	$47
Morrison Hotel	509 3rd Ave.	624-8323	$10	$13	$33	$40
Bush Hotel	621 S. Jackson	623-8079	$10	$12	$55	$65

you want something better than the accommodations listed on the chart, try the Windsor Hotel, 1405 6th Ave. (tel. 623-5230), more expensive, but still good value. Note that 6.5 percent sales tax is added to all room rates, restaurant meals, and purchases.

camping and hostel: If you have a tent and want to use it, take bus no. 130 (runs daily) S to S. 240th St., from which it's an easy 15 min. walk to Saltwater State Park where a site costs $5.50 (up to 2 tents and 6 people). Coming from the airport, take bus no. 174 S to S. 240th St., then walk 2 blocks W and transfer to bus no. 130 which will take you to Marine View Cr. and S. 240th Street. Since Sea Haven Youth Hostel closed in 1982, the closest hostel to Seattle is at Bothell, 30 km NE. Take bus no. 307 (runs daily) to the Exxon station at NE 190th St. and Bothell Way NE, then walk along the highway 1½ km to the YMCA Youth Hostel (tel. 483-6208). Ask about the YH accommodations at the Gatewood Hotel in Seattle ($7 for YH members).

on Skid Road: If you're broke, the Union Gospel Mission, 318 2nd Ave., has beds for men at $2, check-in at 1600, no drunks allowed. Meals ($1) are available in the adjoining cafeteria. Women can find similar accommodation at the Friendly Inn, 221 S. Washington St., just around the corner from Union Gospel. The Bread of Life Mission, 97 S. Main at 1st Ave., has beds at $2, but the first 4 nights are free. Check-in at 1800 sharp. Lunch (1130-1330) and dinner (1600-1800) are served at the Lutheran Compass Center, 77 S. Washington, for $1.25. There's a free soup line at the Salvation Army Harbor Light Center, 416 2nd Ave. at Yesler, Mon. to Fri. at 1730, Sat. at 1345, and Sun. at 1000. Note that all of the above are supported by charity and are meant for the truly needy. Don't use them unless you really have to.

FOOD

downtown: There are 5 inexpensive restaurants on 3rd Ave. between Pike and Union. All post their menus outside, so window-shop. RD's cafeteria is recommended for standard American fare and breakfast, while Bruno's across the street specializes in Italian and Mexican food. Bruno's has pizza slices for $1, if you're not too hungry. If all you want is a burger, Herfy's at 1508½ 3rd Ave. is cheaper and tastier than McDonald's and you don't have to stand in line. The Old Spaghetti Factory, Broad St. and Alaska Way near Pier 69, serves mammoth meals for about $4. There are Old Spaghetti Factories in Tacoma, Vancouver, and many Canadian cities and all are heartily recommended.

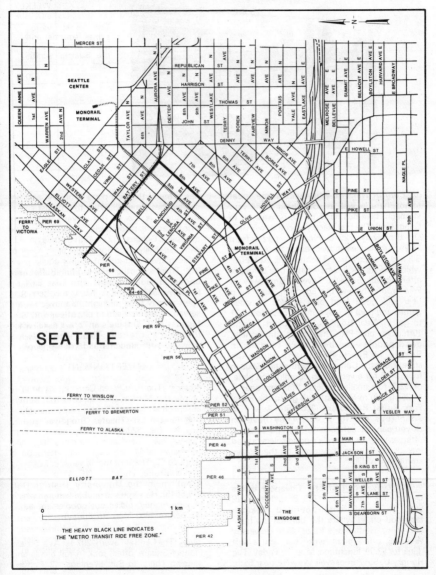

THE HEAVY BLACK LINE INDICATES
THE "METRO TRANSIT RIDE FREE ZONE."

the FRANKFURTER

The most varied sights, sounds, and smells await you on the Seattle waterfront.

on Capitol Hill: If you want some local atmosphere as well as something to fill your stomach, take bus no. 7 or 10, or walk up to Capitol Hill. The first place you come to is Bill's Off Broadway, 725 E. Pine St.; pizzas from $4.25, submarine sandwiches for $3. Adjoining Bill's is the Egyptian Theater (tel. 323-4978) which shows good films—catch one before or after dinner. Bogey's Tavern, Broadway at Pike around behind the Egyptian, has cheap beer and good food plus dozens of video games and pool tables, but you have to be 21 to get in. Near Bogey's, the Comet Tavern, 10th Ave. and Pike, has great atmosphere, good people—the best place to drink in Seattle. La Puerta Restaurant, across the street from the Comet, has authentic Mexican food, $4-5 for a very filling combination plate, or $2-3 for smaller orders; Mexican beer is $1.35. If you're really starved go to the Royal Fork Buffet Restaurant, 300 15th Ave. E at John (bus no. 10 or 43). They have an all-you-can-eat cafeteria for $4; go back as often as you like—there's a good selection and lots of it. Beware, however, of the greasy stomach overfill.

in the University District: Cheapest is the Outrageous Taco Co., 4743 Brooklyn at NE 50th St., an Oriental-operated Mexican fast-food outlet where the burritos are huge and filling. Godfather's Pizza, 4526 University Way NE, offers pizza, salad bar, and a soft drink for $3.39, lunchtime, Mon. to Friday. The Hungry U, 5517 Roosevelt Way NE near 55th,

has some of the best pizza (from $4) and hot sandwiches (from $3.50) in town. Just across the street is the Hi Hat Tavern with food, drinks and a pool table. A great Seattle cheapie is Goldies, 2121 n 45th St (bus no. 43), with especially good food and beer, rows of video games, and lots of young adults (over 21). There's another Royal Fork Buffet (see above) beside Goldies. The Last Exit on Brooklyn, 3930 Brooklyn NE, is a coffeehouse open all day until midnight. Sandwiches are served, as are a selection of coffees and teas. Monday at 2130 there's an 'open mike' when the clients entertain. This place is always crowded with students and young people.

ENTERTAINMENT

movies: The Pike Place Cinema, off an alley below the Market (ask directions), shows European art films ($4). Also recommended is the Harvard Exit Theater, Broadway and E. Roy St. (tel. 323-8986). Take bus no. 7 to Capitol Hill. There are 2 cinemas here and admission is $4, although Sat. afternoon it drops to $2. The best movie value in Seattle is the Neptune Theater, NE 45th St. and Brooklyn in the University District (tel. 633-5545). Here you see double features which change nightly, oldies but goodies for $3.50 ($2 before 1800 Mon. to Friday).

clubs: The Central Tavern, 207 1st Ave. S near Pioneer Square, offers rock 'n roll bands and dancing Thurs. to Sat. evenings, $2-3 cover.

Wednesday night it's 'open mike.' If you find the Central too trendy, take bus no. 17 or 18 to the Owl Cafe and Goodtime Music Hall, 5140 Ballard Ave. NW, which is similar but not yet known to tourists. In the University District, Jazz Alley, 4135 University Way NE (tel. 632-7414), is not especially cheap, but the only club which never has a cover charge. Monday evenings there's a lively jam session. The Eastlake East Tavern, 101 Eastlake E, is a female gay disco. The Washington drinking age is 21.

others: Friday and Sat. nights from 1930-2300 the street people gather at the Sonshine Inn Coffee House and Drop-In Center, 120 Pike Street. Just around the corner on 1st Ave. a solid row of tacky porno houses, strip joints and strolling hookers provide entertainment of another kind. Go into the back of the Scarlet Theater, 1416 1st Ave., and enter a tiny cubicle where you can peek at naked girls through a window which slides open for a minute every time you put 25 cents in the black box on the wall. The $10 special show here is a rip-off. For a change of scenery, attend the Small Claims Court at the King County Courthouse, 3rd and James. Sessions begin at 0930 and 1330 Mon. to Fri. and the public is welcome to sit in. Ask the receptionist in room 327 which courtroom is being used. Criminal cases are also heard in this building if you want something more dramatic. Every Sun. at 1630 the Hare Krishnas celebrate a love feast—call tel. 329-7011 for details. One of the best deals in Seattle is professional baseball at the Kingdome. There's a game almost every day from Apr. to Sept and 200-Level General Admission seats are only $1.50. Call tel. 628-3300 for game times.

SERVICES

medical: If you have a problem, contact the Pike Market Community Clinic, 1931 1st Avenue. The clinic is open Mon. to Fri. 0900-1600, but you must drop by to make an appointment in advance. Fees are based on your ability to pay, generally $4-10 for a brief visit. Similar medical facilities are located at 206 3rd Ave. S and at 416 Maynard Ave. South. The Community Information Line for social and health services is 447-3200. For Seattle Rape Relief call tel.632-7273. *others:* If you desperately need money go the Plasma Center, 1521 2nd Ave., where they pay blood donors $8 per pint. You may go twice a week.

There's a laundromat beside the St. Regis Hotel, convenient if you're staying downtown.

shopping: The Post Office Grocery Market, 216 Union at 3rd Ave., sells cheap canned foods. For camping gear try Federal Army and Navy Surplus, 2112 1st Ave., or Marshall's Sporting Goods, 1st Ave. at Madison. If you need some warm clothing Goodwill Industries, S. Dearborn at Ranier S (bus nos. 42, 142, 202, 210, 220, 226, 227, 235), has a huge selection of recycled garments at bargain prices.

INFORMATION

The Seattle Visitors Bureau, 1815 7th Ave., just a block away from Greyhound, has maps, brochures, and bus timetables. They open

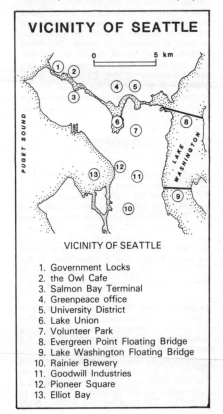

VICINITY OF SEATTLE

0   5 km

VICINITY OF SEATTLE

1. Government Locks
2. the Owl Cafe
3. Salmon Bay Terminal
4. Greenpeace office
5. University District
6. Lake Union
7. Volunteer Park
8. Evergreen Point Floating Bridge
9. Lake Washington Floating Bridge
10. Rainier Brewery
11. Goodwill Industries
12. Pioneer Square
13. Elliot Bay

0800-1700 Mon. to Friday. There's also a Tourist Information counter in the Washington State Ferry Terminal at Pier 52, open daily 0700-1900. The National Parks Information Office, 1018 1st Ave. at Spring, is open Mon. to Fri. 0745-1630. Go there for maps if you want to do some hiking in the Olympics or Cascades. For good free maps of British Columbia and Canada, visit the Canadian Government Tourist Office, 6th Ave. and Stewart, Plaza 600, 8th floor. The Youth Hostel Association office, 4730½ University Way NE (tel. 524-2844), sells memberships and has local information. They offer some excellent group trips around Washington State in the summertime. Office hours are Mon. to Fri. 1200-1600. Nearby CIEE Student Travel, 1314 NE 43rd St., Room 210, off University Way, sells cheap air tickets to Europe and Asia. No student card is required. Check out the Greenpeace office, 4649 Sunnyside Ave. N in the Good Shepherd Center near Goldies on 45th, for information on local environmental issues. The Wide World Bookshop, 401 NE 45th St. (bus no. 43), has a fine selection of travel books. Seattle's best bookstore is the Elliot Bay Book Company, S. Main at 1st Ave. S near Pioneer Square. There's a good cafe downstairs where you may sit and read for the price of a coffee.

TRANSPORT

airport: Sea-Tac International Airport (SEA) is 19 km S of downtown Seattle. Metro bus no. 174 runs from the airport into town every ½ hour Mon. to Sat., hourly on Sun., 90 cents OW. The timetable is posted at the stop. There is a very helpful Tourist Information counter on the central baggage claim level, open every day 0930-1930. The First National Bank branch on the ticketing level is open Mon. to Fri. 0900-1700. Coin lockers are available for 75 cents.

by boat: Three ferry networks originate in Seattle. The Washington State Ferries (Pier 52) run to Bremerton every 1½ hours, to Winslow every hour. Both cost $1.45 OW, but the Bremerton trip is the more scenic. No reservations are needed—just buy a ticket and get on. For 55 cents extra take your bicycle. The B.C. Steamship Company (Pier 69) has a daily sailing at 0800 for Victoria from May to September. The fares are US$18 OW, US$29

RT, and walk-on passengers do not need reservations. The Alaska Marine Highway (Pier 48) has a year-round service to Skagway with stops throughout SE Alaska. There is one ship a week and walk-on passengers *do* require reservations during the summer. Make these as soon as you arrive in Seattle if you want to use this ferry to travel north. For more information on the Alaska ferry system, see 'Southeast Alaska—Introduction'.

by bus: Greyhound Lines, 8th Ave. and Stewart, offers reliable bus service to cities all over Canada and the U.S. There are departures every couple hours (see the main "Introduction" for a discussion of fares and services). Trailways, Inc., 1936 Westlake at Virginia, is sometimes cheaper than Greyhound, but their buses are older and less punctual. If you're headed S, the cheapest way from Seattle to San Francisco is on the Green Tortoise 'magic' bus. There are 2 departures a week year-round and the fare ($49) is almost half what Greyhound charges.

Green Tortoise also has weekly buses from Seattle to Boston (via N.Y.) and on these you get to tour Yellowstone Park and do some whitewater rafting on the Snake River along the way—not exactly features of a Greyhound trans-America journey. The fare is $199 for 10 days, food kitty extra. Midsummer there's a trip to the Rainbow Peace Gathering in Idaho. If you're there at the time, go for $78 RT. For details of Green Tortoise tours to Baja California, to Mardi Gras in New Orleans, and to Alaska, and a full description of these buses, see the 'Introduction' to this book. In Seattle, call tel. 324-RIDE. Grey Rabbit Camper Tours inc. (tel. 223-0287) also has a

The *Princess Marguerite* sails daily in the summer between Seattle and Victoria.

weekly 'magic' bus to San Francisco ($49) and New York ($139).

local buses: Seattle has an excellent city bus service operating daily from 0600-0100 along the main routes. The basic fare is 50 cents, plus 10 cents at rush hours, plus 30 cents if you go outside the city limits. Exact change is required. Most of the buses used by visitors leave from the downtown area. If your entire trip is within the 'ride free zone' indicated on the city map, you pay no fare. Whenever you pay a fare, always ask the driver for a free transfer. This will allow you to take any other bus or return on the same within one hour, or by the time shown on the transfer. Saturday and Sun. All-Day Passes ($1.25) are available for unlimited Metro bus travel—a bargain. Buy from the driver.

others: Check out what opportunities are available for driveaways (see main 'Introduction' for an explanation) by looking under the travel section of the classifieds in the daily newspapers. Aaacon Transport, 1904 3rd Ave., Suite 630 (tel. 206-682-2277), has driveaway cars to all points in the Lower 48. You pay the gas and leave a $100 refundable deposit—European and Australian drivers are welcome. Hitchhiking, though prohibited on the big Interstate highways, is allowed on the access roads. If you want to go S and have a yen for adventure, take the ferry to Winslow, and hitch down the coastal route via Port Angeles, Aberdeen, Astoria, and Eureka. This could take a long time unless you're lucky, but the scenery is great and you'll have far fewer hassles with cops and kooks than on the Interstate.

PUGET SOUND AND AROUND

BREMERTON

The ferry ride from Seattle to Bremerton offers spectacular views of snow-capped mountains, pine-covered hills, shoreline cottages, and deep blue waters. The Seattle skyline recedes as you enter a long, winding inlet. The Bremerton ferry landing adjoins the naval shipyard. Around on the far side of the shipyard, 5 km from the ferry, is the final resting place of the battleship USS *Missouri,* part of the mothball fleet. The *Missouri* is famous as the vessel on which the Japanese surrendered in 1945, ending WW II. Today the Navy maintains the *Missouri* as a museum (free), open daily but closed weekday mornings during the winter. Get there on the shuttle bus ($1.50 RT) which meets the ferries from Seattle, or take a no. 3 city bus (50 cents OW), leaving hourly. There is also a free maritime museum to visit in the Bremerton ferry terminal. *stay:* The Armed Forces Services YMCA (tel. 377-3741) near the ferry wharf has rooms for men at $10 a night, $55 a week. There is camping at Illahee State Park, 5 km NE of the ferry, $5.50 per site (up to 6 people). Take a no. 5 city bus (50 cents) to Perry Ave. and Sylvan Way, then walk one km east. *from Bremerton:* If you want to do a circle trip Seattle-Bremerton-Tacoma-Seattle, Cascade Trailways has 5 buses a day between Bremerton and Tacoma ($3.25 OW). There is also a passenger ferry to Port Orchard.

TACOMA

When the Northern Pacific Railroad reached Tacoma in 1873 it seemed destined to become the metropolis of the Pacific NW. Then the 1897 to 1898 Klondike Gold Rush settled the matter in Seattle's favor. For some reason Tacoma gets left out of the guidebooks and you seldom hear anything about it, but actually the city has quite a lot to offer. *sights:* As soon as you arrive, take a no. 11 Point Defiance bus from the Transit Center, 12th and Commerce, to the boathouse in Point Defiance Park at the end of the line. Ask the driver for a timetable so you'll know when to catch the same bus back to town. Point Defiance Park has a zoo and aquarium, a restored 1830's fort (open Wed. to Sun. 1300-1600), a public beach, over 20 km of developed hiking trails through lovely forests, and excellent views of Puget Sound. You could easily spend the day here. On your way back to the city get off the bus at Wright Park to see its fine Conservatory full of plantlife. Nearby, the Washington State Historical Museum (N on N. 3rd St. from Tacoma Ave.), one of the largest and best in the Pacific NW, has a fascinating collection of Indian artifacts and old photographs. The museum is open Tues. to Sat. 0930-1700, Sun. 1400-1700, admission free. On your way back to the bus station you could have a look at the Old Tacoma City Hall, S. 7th St. and Pacific, and

In Tokyo Harbor on 2 Sept. 1945 General Douglas MacArthur presided over a ceremony aboard the battleship USS *Missouri* which ended the Second World War.

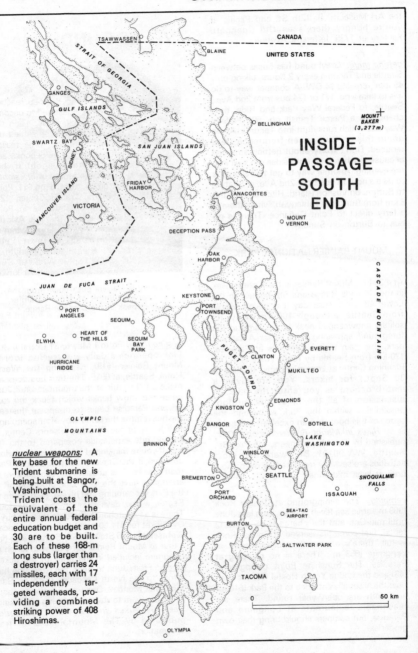

nuclear weapons: A key base for the new Trident submarine is being built at Bangor, Washington. One Trident costs the equivalent of the entire annual federal education budget and 30 are to be built. Each of these 168-m long subs (larger than a destroyer) carries 24 missiles, each with 17 independently targeted warheads, providing a combined striking power of 408 Hiroshimas.

the Art Museum, S. 12th St. and Pacific. If you're hungry there's an Old Spaghetti Factory at 1735 Jefferson Avenue.

getting there: Greyhound has buses between Seattle and Tacoma every 2 hours, taking only 45 min., costing $4 OW. A cheaper way to do it is to take a no. 171 or 174 bus from 2nd Ave., Seattle, to Federal Way Park and Ride, then change to a Pierce Transit no. 500 Federal Way bus which runs right into Tacoma. Avoid doing this on Sun. when frequencies are reduced. Don't worry about getting stranded because city buses on both sides run well into the evening. Another way to get to Tacoma is to take a no. 118 bus from 2nd Ave. in Seattle, to Burton, on Vashon Island. Hitch or walk the 8 km from Burton to Tahlequah, where there is a ferry direct to Point Defiance. There is no bus to Burton on Sunday.

MOUNT RAINIER NATIONAL PARK

At 4,394 m, Mount Rainier is the highest peak in the Cascade Range and 5th highest in the Lower 48. On a clear day it is plainly visible from Seattle, although 100 km away; its solitary snowcapped peak looms large in the foreground, appearing much closer. A national park, the main Visitor Center is at Paradise, 170 km from Seattle by road. There is a Trip Planning Center at Longmire (open 15 June to 30 Sept.) for hikers. You are given a map/brochure as you enter the park. A discussion of all the hikes and outdoor possibilities within the Park is beyond the scope of this book, but an excellent trail guide is *50 Hikes in Mount Rainier National Park,* published by The Mountaineers, 715 Pike St., Seattle, WA 98101. Be aware that most activities are severely restricted by deep snow until at least mid-June.

camping: The campground at Cougar Rock (969 m above sea level) is open from late June until mid-Oct. and the charge is $5 a site (2 tents), first-come first-served. If Cougar Rock is full, there's an overflow campground at Longmire (853 m). There is no camping at Paradise. The Sunshine Point campground ($3) and the Lodge Youth Hostel ($6) are both near the Nisqually entrance to the Park (610 m) and both are open year round. There are reasonable restaurants at Longmire and Paradise, but campers should bring their own groceries.

Numerous glaciers push down from the icecapped summit of Mount Rainier, highest peak in the Cascade Range.

getting there: From 1 May to 31 Oct. the Gray Line operates a daily sightseeing tour to Mount Rainier ($19), departing the Westin Hotel, Seattle, at 0915. The tour bus does not make a full circuit of the mountain until June when the snow banks which block the road beyond Paradise begin to disappear. Instead, the bus returns the same way after spending a few hours at the Paradise Visitors Center, a second-rate experience compared to the full trip. If you're thinking of taking this tour before July, ask if the Stevens Canyon/Cayuse Pass road is open. It is possible for backpackers to arrange to have the Gray Line drop you off in the Park for camping and hiking, then return to Seattle a few days later on the same tour. There is a $3 surcharge if you do this. Or buy a OW ticket for $14.50 and hitch out. American Sightseeing, 666 Stewart St., Seattle, also has a tour to Mount Rainier for $19, with lunch at Longmire included in the price of the ticket.

others: From June to Sept. the Gray Line has a tour to the North Cascades ($20) on Sat., Sun., and Monday. One-way tickets are about $10 if you want to stay for camping and hiking. See *101 Hikes in the North Cascades* published by The Mountaineers for trail information.

THE OLYMPIC PENINSULA

PORT ANGELES

For those who arrive on the ferry from Canada and for visitors to Olympic National Park, Port Angeles is the gateway to the peninsula. It is not a very attractive city, however, so a quick look is sufficient. Note that weekends are a particularly bad time to arrive in Port Angeles; local buses will not be running and many places will be crowded or closed. About the only thing worth seeing in the town itself is the Callam County Museum in the old Courthouse at 223 E. 4th St. (open Mon. to Fri. 1000-1600).

stay: The Pershing Hotel, Front and Laurel streets, just a block from the ferry terminal, is $10 a day single or double, $37 a week, but it's often full. *camping:* Lyre River Park, 35 km W of Port Angeles, has camping sites. Monday to Fri. there are 4 county buses (50 cents) going there daily. Call tel. 452-7831, ext. 291, for information about camping and tel. 452-4511 for the departure times of the buses. Camping is also available at Washington State Parks for $5.50 a site up to 6 people. Call tel. 800-562-0990 toll-free for information on any

of these. The closest to Port Angeles is Sequim Bay State Park (34 km) on the road from Port Angeles to Port Townsend. Monday to Fri. there is a country bus (50 cents) every hour between Port Angeles and Sequim. On Sat. the frequency drops to 4 buses and there is no service on Sunday. Monday to Fri., 4 county buses a day continue on from Sequim to the campgrounds at Sequim Bay, or you could hitch to get there.

from Port Angeles: There are 2 ferries a day in each direction between Port Angeles and Victoria (US$5 OW). Bicycles are $2 extra. Leaving Victoria on the afternoon ferry is not recommended unless you have a car or are planning on staying in Port Angeles. *by bus:* Greyhound has 3 buses a day between Port Angeles and Seattle ($11). Every afternoon there's a minibus service ($10) to Neah Bay in the Makah Indian Reservation at the NW corner of the Olympic Peninsula. Inquire at the Greyhound station. The cheapest way to get to Port Townsend is to take a county bus (50 cents) to Sequim (see above) and change there to a Jefferson Transit bus (50 cents). The Sequim-Port Townsend service operates twice daily, Mon. to Friday. Phone tel. 452-4511 in Port Angeles or tel. 385-4777 in Port Townsend for the times.

raccoons

A colonnade of massive Sitka spruce in the dense climax rainforest of Olympic National Park.

OLYMPIC NATIONAL PARK

The Olympic Mountains, a detached branch of the Coastal Mountains, fill the white heart of the Olympic Peninsula. You get a splendid view of them on the ferry ride across the Juan de Fuca Strait from Port Angeles to Victoria. Mount Olympia soars to 2,328 meters. Olympic National Park has glaciers, the only rainforest in the continental U.S., lakes, streams, hot springs, and 80 km of scenic wilderness beaches. The Visitor Center is at 600 E. Park Ave. up Race St., Port Angeles—quite a walk from the ferry terminal or bus station, but bus no. 20 (50 cents) passes nearby every ½ hour Mon. to Friday. After obtaining a map and looking at the exhibits, hitch a ride up to Hurricane Ridge (30 km) for a sweeping view. There is no camping at Hurricane Ridge itself, so you have to go halfway back to Port Angeles to the Heart of the Hills campground ($5 a site) or hike 12 km down through forest to Elwha where there is another campground, also $5 a site. Camping space in the roadside campgrounds is first-come first-served. Backcountry trail camping is free, but you must obtain a permit from a ranger. Tell one what you'd like to do and ask his advice. Again, outings in Olympic National Park are too abundant and varied to be adequately covered in this book; however the Park Service has excellent information.

PORT TOWNSEND

Port Townsend, located at the eastern tip of the Olympic Peninsula at the entrance to Puget Sound, is an attractive old town laced with many restored Victorian mansions. The local historical museum in the old city hall (closed Tues. and Wed.) is worth seeing. Climb up Jefferson Ave. to the old bell tower for a good view. Further along Jefferson Ave. are many of the old mansions mentioned above. Around the turn of the century, 3 forts were built near Port Townsend to defend this strategic passage; today they are preserved as historical sites open to the public. Fort Worden is 3 km N of the bus station, while Fort Casey is accessible every other hour on the Keystone ferry ($1.45) which leaves from the Port Townsend waterfront. Fort Flagler, on Marrowstone Island to the E, is not served by public transport.

stay: The YH (tel. 385-0655) is in Fort Worden State Park. Monday to Fri. there are 4 county buses daily to Fort Worden which accept transfers from all other buses, or you can walk to the hostel in 30 minutes. The overnight charge is $4. No stores are nearby, so bring groceries. If the hostel's full there's camping in the State Park at $8 per site, but these are often fully occupied by RVs. Camping is also available at Fort Casey State Park adjoining the Keystone Ferry Landing on Whidby Island, $5.50 per site. A third camping possibility is Dosewallips State Park S of Port Townsend near Brinnon. Monday to Fri. there's a county bus (50 cents) 3 times a day from Port Townsend to Brinnon.

transport: For the county bus service W to Sequim and Port Angeles see 'from Port Angeles' above. County buses also connect with the Greyhound service to Seattle ($5.50). All county buses charge 50 cents and give free transfers. You can rent a bicylce from Shining Star Cycle, 220 Taylor St. in Port Townsend.

THE SAN JUAN ISLANDS

The 172 islands in the San Juan Archipelago are peaks of a submerged mountain range which once linked Vancouver Island with the mainland. The San Juans offer coastal scenery, picturesque settlements, and historic sites, all very accessible and convenient for a stopover. San Juan Island is the best known and most visited of the group, but the Washington State Ferries also call at Orcas, Shaw, and Lopez. These are less populated and developed than San Juan (perhaps an advantage!). Unless you have a car or a bicycle, be prepared to rough it.

GETTING THERE

from Seattle: The Evergreen Trailways bus to Anacortes ($7.65 OW) leaves Seattle's Greyhound terminal twice a day. One service goes via Mukilteo at the S end of Whidby Island, the other up the freeway to Mount Vernon and across to Anacortes. The Mukilteo route is by far the more scenic, so try for it. Just before reaching Mukilteo you'll pass the Everett Boeing plant where the 747s are made. Call Evergreen Trailways toll free number, (tel.

800-542-7802) for departure times. If you want to hitch from Seattle, take Metro bus no. 6 to Aurora Village, where you'll change to an F7 blue bus to Mukilteo (no service on Sunday). The total fare for this is about $1—call tel. 778-2185 for details. You can also go via Everett by taking Metro bus no. 403 or 406 ($2) from Seattle to Everett, then catch an Everett Transit bus no. 10 (25 cents) to Mukilteo. There is a ferry every ½ hour from Mukilteo to Clinton (90 cents), from where you must hitch. From Port Townsend take the ferry to Keystone ($1.45), then hitch to Anacortes. There's talk of discontinuing the Evergreen Trailways bus due to lack of business, in which case there won't be any choice but to hitch. _camping:_ There's a big campground in Deception Pass State Park ($5.50 a site) in a stunning location between Oak Harbor and Anacortes. If you get into Anacortes late they won't mind your camping on the grass beside the parking lot at the ferry terminal.

by ferry: There are 6 ferries a day in each direction between Anacortes and Friday Harbor on San Juan Island. All call at Lopez, Shaw, and Orcas Is. before reaching Friday Harbor, and one ferry goes on to Sidney, B.C.

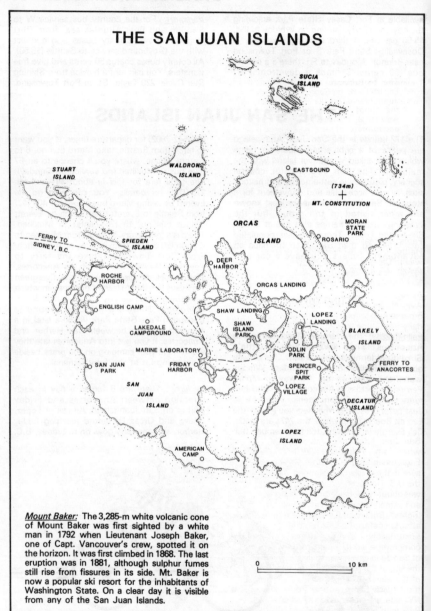

THE SAN JUAN ISLANDS

SUCIA ISLAND

EASTSOUND

(734m)
+
MT. CONSTITUTION

WALDRON ISLAND

STUART ISLAND

ORCAS ISLAND

MORAN STATE PARK

ROSARIO

FERRY TO SIDNEY, B.C.

SPIEDEN ISLAND

DEER HARBOR

ORCAS LANDING

ROCHE HARBOR

ENGLISH CAMP

SHAW LANDING

LOPEZ LANDING

BLAKELY ISLAND

LAKEDALE CAMPGROUND

SHAW ISLAND PARK

MARINE LABORATORY

SAN JUAN PARK

FRIDAY HARBOR

ODLIN PARK

SPENCER SPIT PARK

FERRY TO ANACORTES

SAN JUAN ISLAND

LOPEZ VILLAGE

DECATUR ISLAND

AMERICAN CAMP

LOPEZ ISLAND

Mount Baker: The 3,285-m white volcanic cone of Mount Baker was first sighted by a white man in 1792 when Lieutenant Joseph Baker, one of Capt. Vancouver's crew, spotted it on the horizon. It was first climbed in 1868. The last eruption was in 1881, although sulphur fumes still rise from fissures in its side. Mt. Baker is now a popular ski resort for the inhabitants of Washington State. On a clear day it is visible from any of the San Juan Islands.

0   10 km

The blockhouse at English Camp on San Juan Island recalls the joint Anglo-American military occupation of the island from 1859 to 1872.

Fares are reasonable: Anacortes to Friday Harbor is $2.20, while $5.25 takes you all the way to Canada. There's an hourly bus service ($1.40) from Sidney to downtown Victoria.

by air: Lake Union Air Service, 1100 Westlake Ave. N, Seattle, (bus no. 26 or 28) flies a 5-passenger seaplane to Friday Harbor twice daily from June to Aug., $36 OW. In Seattle, call tel. 284-0300 for details. San Juan Airlines has several flights a day from Sea-Tac Airport, S of Seattle, to Friday Harbor ($39). The airstrip at Friday Harbor (FRD) is just a 15-min. walk from town.

SAN JUAN ISLAND

San Juan found its place in history in 1859 when an American settler shot an Englishman's pig. Up to that point no one was sure if these islands belonged to England or the U.S. However, when the guilty marksman was about to be hauled off to court in Victoria and American troops landed to protect his 'rights,' Britain and the United States were almost catapulted into the 'Pig War.' Fortunately, sanity prevailed and a compromise led to a joint military occupation of San Juan which was to last 12 years. Today the site of the American Camp near the SE tip of the island, 13 km from Friday Harbor, and the English Camp, 16 km from town on the NW side, are preserved as a National Historical Park with plaques and exhibits which tell the full story. If you only have time for one,

American Camp has a better display, more striking scenery, and is easier to get to; however, both parks are well worth visiting. Incidentally, in 1872 the German Kaiser, Wilhelm I, was asked to mediate the hot dispute over ownership and he decided in favor of the U.S.

sights near town: Friday Harbor is small enough that you soon learn where everything is. The Whale Museum ($2 admission, closed Tues.) is unique in that it is dedicated to the whales themselves, instead of to whaling. Orcas and Minke whales are often seen in these waters. The University of Washington maintains a large marine biology laboratory just NW of Friday Harbor, an easy walk from town. During July and Aug. there are free guided tours of the facility from 1400-1600 Wed. and Saturday. Go anytime for a look at the aquarium (below the stairs in the main buiding) and walk further down to take in the view from the wharf.

stay and eat: The Elite Hotel, only 2 blocks from the ferry wharf, has dormitory accommodations at $8 pp, double rooms for $19. There's a $1 discount if you show a YH card. Downstairs there's a pleasant European-style cafe. Saturday afternoons there's a jazz band playing strong at the Electric Co. Tavern (no cover charge). Although it tends to be a little touristy, it's still good fun. The same tavern has rock bands Fri. and Sat. nights, and pizza anytime. *camping:* There are 2 good campgrounds on San Juan,

jumping orca (killer whale)

there are also hourly rates of $2-3. San Juan Island does have its ups and downs so if cycling's not your thing, rent a moped at the Friday Harbor Motor Inn for $5 an hour or $25 a day (gas included).

OTHER ISLANDS

Orcas: Orcas (148 sq km), the largest of the San Juans, has some facilities, but these tend to be expensive. The campground at Moran State Park ($5.50 a site) is 30 km from the ferry with no way to get there but walking, thumbing or cycling. Orcas is hilly, so you need to be a hardy peddler. There's a highway right up to the top of Mount Constitution (734 m), which takes some of the challenge out of climbing it. The Alive-Polarity Institute, with its new-age outlook on self-improvement, has a living community on this island. Their programs are very expensive but include exercise, diet, massage, group therapy, etc. on a 24-hour basis for allotted periods of time.

Shaw: Shaw Island is recommended if you want to get away from people. It's also small enough to make foot travel a possibility. Shaw Island County Park with its campground ($1.50 pp) is about 5 km from the ferry. *Lopez:* Lopez Island is still largely dedicated to farming and the people are friendly. There's good camping at Odlin Country Park ($1.50 pp), just a 20-min. walk from the ferry, or go to Spencer Spit State Park, 6 km from the ferry, which charges $5.50 a site. Inquire at the ferry landing about bicycle rentals. Lopez is the easiest of the islands for cyclists.

neither convenient to the ferry. Lakedale Campground, 7 km down the road to Roche Harbor, is beautifully set among lakes and pine forests; $2 pp (showers 75 cents) and there's always plenty of room. San Juan County Park ($1.50 pp), on the W side of the island, looks directly across to Victoria. If the sign on the highway says they're full, ask at the office because they usually make room for cyclists and hikers (or call tel. 378-2992). There's no bus service on the island so you must walk, hitch or cycle to these.

transport: In Friday Harbor, rent a bike from Island Bicycles across from the Elite Hotel. Three-speeds are $10 a day, 10-speeds $12.50;

BRITISH COLUMBIA

VICTORIA

Victoria, at the southern tip of Vancouver Island, was established in 1843 as a Hudson Bay Company fort. Agricultural lands were soon developed nearby, but the little settlement didn't gain momentum until 1858 when a gold rush on the Fraser River brought a flood of American miners through the town. In 1868, Victoria was made capital of the crown colony of British Columbia. Today, half the people on Vancouver Island live in this city of a quarter million and on the adjacent Saanich Peninsula. Tourist promoters play up the town's British flavor for the benefit of visiting Americans. The many historic sites, parks and gardens make Victoria a pleasant place to spend a couple of days, a recommended stop on the way north.

SIGHTS OF VICTORIA

<u>top sights:</u> Most walking tours begin at the Parliament Buildings (1898) which dominate Victoria's Inner Harbor and, together with the Empress Hotel (1908), lend the city a monumental air. The free tours of the buildings leave regularly every day from in front of Parliament and are well worth taking. Just to the E is the ultra-modern Provincial Museum (open daily, free), the largest in Western Canada. Although many sections are still closed, the rich collection on the top floor envelops the visitor in the history of British Columbia. Allow a couple hours here. The old photos of B.C. coastal Indians are especially gripping. Thunderbird Park, beside the museum, has totem poles and replicas of large NW Indian houses. Helmcken House (1852), just behind the totem poles, is one of the oldest houses in the province still at its original location (open daily except Mon., free). Just a block S on Douglas St. is the entrance to Beacon Hill Park. This century-old reserve extends all the way to the Juan de Fuca Strait. From the shore there is a splendid view of the Olympic Mountains. A 39-m-high totem pole, numerous ponds, and flower gardens for relaxing add to the park's allure.

A statue of Queen Victoria stands before the Parliament Buildings in Victoria, built during her reign in a city named for her.

downtown: Bastion Square, heart of the 1890s city, gets its name from a bastion of old Fort Victoria (1843) which once stood here. Today the old courthouse (1889) is a Maritime Museum ($2), and the square with its trees and park benches is a perfect picnicking or people-watching place. Market Square, a few blocks N at 560 Johnson St., is similar but trendy. Victoria's colorful Chinatown is just N of here at Government and Fisgard Streets. Take note that Victoria is full of bizarre side-show 'attractions' ranging from a fairy tale cottage to a wax chamber of horrors. Give them all a miss and stick to the places which are free or cheap.

sidetrip E: Walk up Courtenay St. to the impressive facade of Christ Church Anglican Cathedral. Many old tombstones from Victoria's first cemetery may be perused in the park beside the church. Continue E on Rockland Ave. for 15 min. through a peaceful residential area to Government House, home of the Lieutenant-Governor. The beautiful gardens surrounding the estate are open to the public daily (free). Leave the gardens through the second gateway and head N on Juan Cres. to Craigdarroch Castle at no. 1050. This towering Victorian mansion, built by coal magnate Robert Dunsmuir in 1890, is now open daily ($1). There is a good view of Victoria from the upstairs windows. If it's Thurs. afternoon, go S on Moss from Fort St. to the Victoria Art Gallery which is free that day from 1700-2100 (regularly $2). Walk back to town along Fort St. past many antique shops.

sidetrip W: If you're into history and scenery there's a good excursion to several places W of downtown, and all of the admissions are free. Begin by taking the no. 15 Craigflower bus from Yates and Douglas to Pleasant St. just before the Pt. Ellice Bridge. Point Ellice House (open Tues. to Sun. 1000-1700) is just N on Pleasant Street. Built in 1861, it's full of mid-Victorian artifacts which belonged to the original family. Also, have a look at the Upper Harbor behind the house. Return to the bus stop and continue on a no. 15 bus to Admirals Road. Craigflower Manor (1856), on the corner of Admirals Rd. and Craigflower Rd., typifies the life of an early pioneer family. Closed Monday. Catch a no. 60 Admirals bus from here to Western Exchange. Fort Rodd Hill National Historic Park is a 15-min. walk SE of the Exchange. In 1896, coastal batteries were set up here to protect the naval base at Esquimalt. You get splendid views of the coastline from the old bunkers and fortifications, which are open daily. Just a few km SW of Fort Rodd is the Royal Roads Military College with some of the finest Japanese, Italian, and rose gardens in Canada. Forget the much advertised Butchart Gardens ($6) and get an eyeful of these. An impressive English-style manor (1908) built for James Dunsmuir, son of Robert Dunsmuir mentioned above, completes the scene. The gardens are open daily 1000-1600—take bus nos. 52, 53, 54, 55, 61 from Western Exchange. To return to Victoria take the same buses back to the Exchange and transfer to no. 50 for downtown.

STAY

hotels: In the summer there is a shortage of inexpensive accommodations in Victoria, so be prepared to look a little harder and pay a little more than you might expect. If you're only staying a day or 2 consider the large and decent James Bay Inn, 270 Government St., tel. 384-7151, $19 s, $24 d. There is a convivial pub downstairs where you can get burgers and hot sandwiches for $3. The Cherry Bank Hotel, 825 Burdett Ave., tel. 385-5380, is similar though it costs less, at $16 s, $19 d. Try for rooms 10 or 11, which are the quietest and cheapest. For better security, women could stay at the modern YWCA, 880 Courtney St., tel. 386-7511, $13 s, $20 d. No men are accepted at the YWCA. If these are full, try the Ritz Hotel, 710 Fort St., tel. 383-1021, at $20 s, $25 d, or $75 s, $95 d weekly. The Hotel Yates, 712 Yates St., tel. 384-7187, about the same price as the Ritz, is somewhat nicer. Another possibility is the Fairfield Hotel, 710 Cormorant St., tel. 386-1621, at $22 s, $25 d. English-style bed and breakfast is available at the Craigmyle Guest House, 1037 Craigdarroch Road beside Craigdarroch Castle, tel. 595-5411. Rates are $22 s, $30 d (minimum stay 2 nights) but a huge breakfast is included in the price. Add 6 percent room tax to all of the above.

hostels: Cool Aid Youth Hostel, 1900 Fernwood Road (bus no. 10 Haultrain from Fort and Douglas), is $7 for bed, breakfast (at 0700), and dinner (at 1730). There are separate dormitories for men and women—check-in at 1630 and be out by 0900. Note that this hostel is not connected with the Canadian Hosteling Assn. and is not up to their standards. If you can't afford $7 go to the Salvation Army Harbor Light Center, Wharf and Johnson Sts., where 3 nights free food and accommodation are offered to those in need. Check in at 1600.

camping: The closest official campground to downtown Victoria is Fort Victoria Camping, 340 Island Highway 1A, tel. 479-8112, $8 for two people. Take bus no. 15 Craigflower which runs every 15 min. Mon. to Sat., every 30 min. Sunday. More attractive is the campground at Goldstream Provincial Park, 20 km W of Victoria on the Trans-Canada Hwy., $6 a site. Bus no. 50 Goldstream ($1.40) stops at Humpback Rd. and Sooke Lake Rd., just 400 m from the campground. Note that not all no. 50 buses come out this far and that there is no service on Sunday. Call tel. 382-6161 for bus times. There are many excellent nature trails through the rain forest at Goldstream Park and these alone are reason enough for coming. Another campground to keep in mind is McDonald Provincial Park, midway between the Sidney and Swartz Bay ferry terminals. Bus no. 70 connects both terminals to the park and goes into Victoria daily. Camping is $4 a site—very convenient if you arrive late from Vancouver, the Gulf Islands, or Friday Harbor. Camping is not allowed in Beacon Hill Park, back in mid-city, but, if desperate, you might get away with it if you arrive after dark, choose an inconspicuous site, and leave early in the morning.

FOOD AND ENTERTAINMENT

restaurants: The YWCA Cafeteria, Broughton and Quadra Sts. (open Mon. to Fri.

The Japanese garden at Hatley Castle is among the best Victoria has to offer.

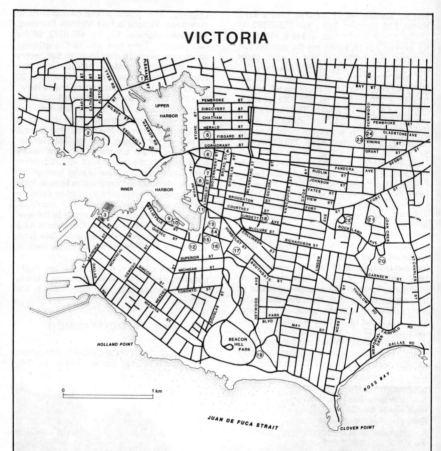

VICTORIA

VICTORIA

1. Point Ellice House
2. railway station
3. fishing fleet
4. City Hall
5. Chinatown
6. Market Square
7. post office
8. Bastion Square
9. Seattle ferry
10. Port Angeles ferry
11. Tourist Information Center
12. Parliament Buildings
13. Empress Hotel
14. bus station
15. Provincial Museum
16. Helmcken House
17. general hospital
18. Christ Church Cathedral
19. totem pole
20. Government House
21. Craigdarroch Castle
22. Victoria Art Gallery
23. Cool Aid Youth Hostel
24. Prancing Pony Restaurant

0800-1600), has good breakfast and lunch specials. Viteway Cafeteria, 753 View St. (open Mon. to Fri. 0830-1600), has cheap soup-and-salad combinations at lunchtime. There's a good organic foods store adjoining the Viteway where you might stock up for hiking. The Dutch Bakery and Coffee Shop, 718 Fort St., is good for lunch with homemade soup ($1). Try a Flying Dutchman sandwich ($2.10)! Great pastries to choose from in the front window. Mr. Mike's, 1740 Douglas St., has good steaks and salad at very affordable prices. McDonald's Townhouse, Douglas at Fort, serves the standard fare at the usual prices. If you want to splash out a little try Pagliacci's, 1011 Broad St. off Fort, which has lunch for $5, dinner from $9, or just come in for the homemade cheesecake and coffee. Tuesday, Wed., and Thurs. from 2130-2400 and Sun. from 2000-2300 there's live jazz at Pagliacci's—no cover charge and great atmosphere and character. In the same price range is the Prancing Pony Vegetarian Restaurant, 1309 Gladstone Ave. (bus no. 10 Haultrain).

bars: Harpo's Cabaret on Wharf St. at Bastion Square is the local pick-up spot for singles. There's live rock music and dancing, $4 cover, $2 drinks. The Sunset Rock 'n Roll Cabaret across the street is similar, but slightly cheaper. Both are very popular with young locals. The street people and unemployed hang out at The Square Tavern, downstairs in the Bastion Hotel at 1140 Government Street. Native Indians patronize the beverage room at the Kings Hotel, 568 Yates Street. The Century Club on Government between Johnson and Pandora specializes in striptease. Hookers work along Government from here to Yates and up Yates to Douglas.

others: The best free shows in town are the debates of the Provincial Legislature seen from the public gallery in the Parliament Buildings. The Legislature meets Mon. to Thurs. 1400-1800, Tues. and Thurs. 1000-1200, and Fri. 1000-1300. Ask one of the uniformed guides in front of the building if the members are in session. There is no hassle about getting in and the proceedings can be highly informative and entertaining. The National Film Board, 811 Wharf St. opposite the Tourist Information Center, allows you to preview documentary films free in their office Mon. to Fri. 0830-1700. There's always something doing at the Fernwood Neighborhood Center

Dan the Man operates his Magical Music Machine on Victoria's Inner Harbor.

across the street from Cool Aid Youth Hostel. Check out the notices in the window if you're staying at the hostel.

SERVICES AND INFORMATION

The Visitor Information Center, 812 Wharf St. on the Inner Harbor (open daily) has stacks of maps and brochures on Victoria and the surrounding area. Tourism B.C., 1117 Wharf St. (closed Sun.) has information on the whole province. There are medical and dental clinics at 1291 Gladstone Ave., tel. 384-2043, to help the less affluent. Those interested in finding out about local ecology issues should visit Greenpeace, 620 View St., Suite 312. Have a look at the notice board outside Self-Heal Herbs and Foods, 1221 Wharf St., for rides, classes, and happenings. The Pack and Boots Shop, in the rear of the arcade at 720 Yates St., sells camping equipment, trail guides, and YH cards. The best bookstore in Victoria is Munro's Books, 671 Fort Street. Everywoman's Books, 641 Johnson St., is a women's collective providing feminist literature.

TRANSPORT

by boat: The Port Angeles and Seattle ferries dock at adjoining wharfs in Victoria's Inner Harbor. The Port Angeles ferry leaves several times daily, CDN$6.40 OW. Clear U.S. Immigration before embarking. The *Princess Marguerite,* launched in Scotland in 1948, sails for Seattle daily at 1730 from May to Sept., CDN$21 OW, CDN$2.50 extra for a bike. The Anacortes ferry to Friday Harbor, San Juan I., (US$3) leaves Sidney daily at 1230. There are 12 ferries daily between Swartz Bay (Vancouver Island) and Tsawwassen (Lower Mainland), $3.50 OW.

bus connections: Bus no. 70 to Pat Bay Hwy. ($1.40) runs from Douglas St. in downtown Victoria, right to the Swartz Bay Ferry Terminal hourly every day. This same bus passes within a block of the Sidney Ferry Terminal for the Washington State Ferry to Anacortes. At Tsawwassen, catch the no. 640 Valley-to-Sea bus (75 cents), also hourly every day, to Ladner Exchange where you transfer to the bus to downtown Vancouver. If you're going to the Vancouver YH hang onto your transfer and ask the driver where you change to the Fourth Ave. bus.

long-distance buses and trains: Pacific Coach Lines, 710 Douglas St., Victoria, has a bus

every 2 hours to Vancouver, $10 weekdays, $11 weekends. This is double the cost of doing the trip on local buses as described above. There are 6 P.C.L. buses a day from Victoria to Campbell River ($16) on the E, mid-island, and one a day all the way to Port Hardy ($37), near the N end of Vancouver Island. Stopovers are allowed. For your bicycle to accompany you on the bus it must be boxed (ask for a box at a cycle shop) and you must pay extra freight charges (about $11 for Victoria-Port Hardy). There are handy coin lockers (50 cents) at the P.C.L. depot behind the Empress Hotel if you need a place to leave your luggage for the day. If you prefer trains there's a diesel rail car from Esquimalt to Courtenay daily at 0815, $16 OW. No bicycles are carried. Take bus nos. 23, 24, 25, to the station.

local buses and hitching: Urban transit buses have 2 fare zones: 70 cents for most trips, $1.40 for very long trips. A Daily Bus Pass ($2) is sold by drivers in the summer, but it is only good on Routes 1 to 28, 60, and the 900 series. To hitch N to Nanaimo, take bus no. 50 Goldstream to Brock and Jacklin, which is very close to the Trans-Canada Highway. To hitch to Port Renfrew for the West Coast Trail, take a no. 61 Sooke bus from Western Exchange to Sooke ($1.40) which is on Hwy. 14 on the way to the trail head. The Sooke bus only runs every couple hours, so call tel. 382-6161 for the schedule before leaving.

Montague Harbor Provincial Park on Galiano Island has the most convenient campground for visitors to the Gulf Islands.

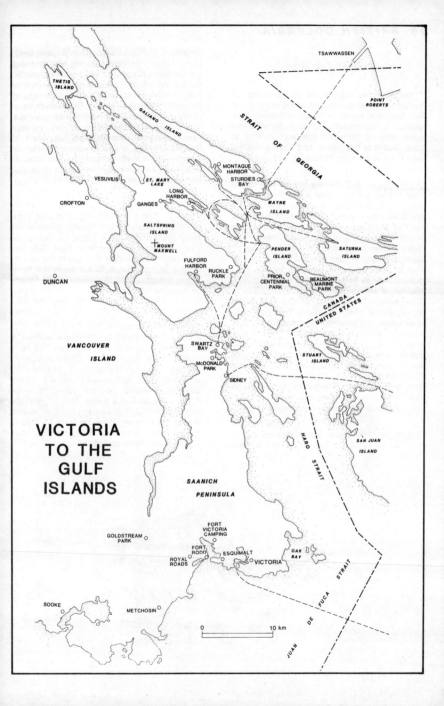

THETIS
ISLAND

GALIANO ISLAND

TSAWWASSEN

POINT
ROBERTS

STRAIT OF GEORGIA

VESUVIUS

ST. MARY
LAKE

MONTAGUE
HARBOR

STURDIES
BAY

CROFTON

LONG
HARBOR

GANGES

MAYNE
ISLAND

SALTSPRING
ISLAND

MOUNT
MAXWELL

SATURNA
ISLAND

FULFORD
HARBOR

PENDER
ISLAND

RUCKLE
PARK

DUNCAN

PRIOR
CENTENNIAL
PARK

BEAUMONT
MARINE
PARK

CANADA
UNITED STATES

VANCOUVER
ISLAND

SWARTZ
BAY

McDONALD
PARK

STUART
ISLAND

SIDNEY

HARO
STRAIT

VICTORIA
TO THE
GULF
ISLANDS

SAANICH

PENINSULA

SAN JUAN
ISLAND

GOLDSTREAM
PARK

FORT
VICTORIA
CAMPING

FORT
RODD

ESQUIMALT

ROYAL
ROADS

VICTORIA

OAK
BAY

SOOKE

METCHOSIN

DE FUCA STRAIT

JUAN

0   10 km

THE GULF ISLANDS

These 100-plus islands off the E coast of Vancouver I. were once part of the main island but became separated by glaciation. The scenery is magnificent, with long channels and inlets flowing between hillsides covered in pine. But it is the peace and easy-going life which most attracts droves of city people.

getting there: B.C. Ferries has service to the Gulf Islands several times a day from Swartz Bay and Tsawwassen. Study a timetable for the best connections. The Swartz Bay ferry calls at Montague Harbor on Galiano, and at Pender, Mayne and Saturna Islands. The Tsawwassen ferry stops at Sturdies Bay on Galiano, Long Harbor on Saltspring, and at Pender and Mayne. A separate service links Swartz Bay to Fulford Harbor on Saltspring. Instead of sailing directly from Swartz Bay to Tsawwassen ($3.50), stop off at a Gulf Island at no extra cost. If you're not going to Vancouver, the morning run from Swartz Bay around the islands is an excellent, inexpensive scenic cruise ($1.75 RT). Ferries from one Gulf Island to another are free. For information on local buses to the Swartz Bay and Tsawwassen ferry terminals, see 'bus connections' above. There is no bus service on the Gulf Islands themselves. Hitchhiking on the islands is very easy—everybody stops.

Saltspring: The largest and most populous of the islands is Saltspring. There are 3 ferry landings: Fulford Harbor (for Swartz Bay), Long Harbor (for Tsawwassen), and Vesuvius (for Crofton). None are close to campgrounds. Ruckle Provincial Park, 10 km from Fulford Harbor, has camping at $4 a site. Mouat Provincial Park near Ganges, the main town, is midway between Long Harbor and Vesuvius. There are also a number of private campgrounds around St. Mary Lake, NW of Ganges. There's a small farmers' market in Centennial Park at Ganges on Saturday. A nice view can be had by hitching or driving to the top of Mount Maxwell (589 m).

Pender: There are actually 2 islands here, North Pender and South Pender, joined in the middle by a bridge. Both official campgrounds, Prior Centennial Provincial Park ($4) and Beaumont Marine Park ($6) are in the vicinity of this bridge, about 10 km from the ferry. There are no official campgrounds on Mayne or Saturna Islands.

Galiano: Montague Harbor Provincial Park is the most expedient for campers without a vehicle as it is only one km from the ferry landing from Swartz Bay. There is a small grocery store near the wharf. Campsites ($6), on a first-come first-served basis, are usually taken on weekends, so come during the week if you want to find a place. This is generally true of all the campgrounds in the Gulf Islands during the summer. It's 8 km from Montague Harbor to Sturdies Bay, where the Tsawwassen ferry comes in.

VANCOUVER

Canadians consider Vancouver their most beautiful city and certainly no other in North America is so spectacularly located. A wall of snowcapped mountains faces Vancouver on the N; wide bays and inlets encircle it on the N, W, and south. Abundant parklands and beaches offer unforgettable vistas of clean modern buildings clustered against the forested hillsides. Vancouver is a young city. Although Capt. George Vancouver sailed into Burrard Inlet in 1792 and made the area known to the world, permanent white settlers did not arrive until 70 years later. A rough-and-tumble shantytown of lumbermen and timber millers established itself on the site about that time, but it was the settlements along the Fraser River which received early official attention and benefited from the 1858 Cariboo gold rush. All this changed in 1887 when Canada's first transcontinental railway reached Vancouver and the city became the country's major Pacific port. Today Vancouver is Canada's third largest city, its half-million people comprising a third of the province's population. It is an exciting city to visit and, for Canadians, the gateway to the Pacific coast.

SIGHTS OF VANCOUVER

the West End: For many, the highlight of the city is Stanley Park (bus no. 11 from W. Pender St.). This beautiful park occupies a large peninsula jutting out into Burrard Inlet. A walk along the seawall promenade offers totem poles, beaches, honking geese, and a series of splendid views. If you only have a couple of hours, spend them here. Stanley Park also has a free zoo, an expensive ($3.50) aquarium, snack bars spread out at intervals, and lots of lawns and scenic spots where you can sit and watch the world go by. If you like your action a little faster, rent a bicycle from the shop at the foot of Alberni St. across from the bus loop. Five-speeds go for $3.50 an hour, $12 a day, or try the tandems which are a lark. The Manhattan-like residential area between Stanley Park and downtown is a checkerboard of highrise apartments slowly swallowing the last of the old family houses. Walk back to town along Robson St. for Vancouver's best

On the daily excursion to Squamish the "Royal Hudson" passes this scenic wilderness in Vancouver's backyard.

window-shopping. Locally known as Robsonstrasse, there are many delicatessens, tearooms, and small shops with a European air. In the summer the restaurants move some of their tables into the open air.

downtown: The big redevelopment news in downtown Vancouver is Robson Square, filling 3 city blocks along Howe, S from Georgia Street. Features include the restored old courthouse (now the Vancouver Art Gallery), the central Plaza to one side with its excellent Food Fair, and the sloping glass roof of the Provincial Law Courts. Landscaping and a balance between open spaces and offices help make Robson Square the architectural show place of the city. Robson Square is also a magnet for its soft seats and numerous washrooms (bureaucrats look after themselves). Walk through Eatons Department Store, on the E side of Robson Square, out into the Granville Mall and down to the waterfront. Take a quick look in the old Canadian Pacific Railway Station, now the Sea Bus Terminal (see 'North Vancouver' below), and continue E hugging the waterfront into Gastown. Vancouver got its start near the corner of Water and Carrall Sts. where there's now a statue of notorious saloon and hotel keeper, Gassy Jack Deighton, for whom Gastown was named. Today, Water St. is lined with art galleries, boutiques, and fancy restaurants crowded with chic people and tourists. All of the original buildings from

Gassy Jack's time disappeared in the building boom which followed the arrival of the railway and in the great fire of 1886, but the restored old warehouses and hotels from the 1890s and early years of this century offer an evocative glimpse into history. This makes Gastown well worth a stroll. Continue along Carrall St. to Pender. At 8 W. Pender is the "narrowest building in the world." Chinatown runs along Pender St. for 3 blocks from Carrall to Gore. Vancouver's Chinatown is the 2nd largest in North America (San Francisco's is bigger). The many restaurants, markets, and emporia are good for a leisurely look.

North Vancouver: Take the Sea Bus from the old CPR station at the foot of Seymour across Burrard Inlet to North Vancouver. On the other side transfer to bus no. 228 or 229 to Lynn Canyon Park. The park has a free suspension bridge, forests, and trails, and a river where you can swim. The highlight of the park is the Ecology Center with films and exhibits on all aspects of the local environment. The Center opens from 1000-1700 daily, admission 75 cents (25 cents if you show a YH or student card). Take bus no. 228 or 229 back to Lonsdale Ave. where you can transfer to a no. 232 Queens bus to the Grouse Mountain Skyride. The cable car ($6) to the ski resort on Grouse Mountain operates in the summer for sightseers and daytrippers. It's a memorable ride if you can spare the money, but look up the hill before buying a ticket. If the trees disappear into the clouds there will be zero visibility on top. Much of the forest has been cleared for ski runs and the area available to hikers is limited. From the skyride take a no. 232 bus or walk 2 km down to Cleveland Dam (1954) and Lake Capilano. This is the source of Vancouver's water supply. The dam is impressive in itself, but be sure to take the dirt road below the dam to the S and look for the signposted trail to the fish hatchery on the right. The Capilano Salmon Hatchery (free) is worth a visit anytime for its informative displays and striking setting, but it's at its best from July to Oct. when you can watch the returning fish fighting their way up a fishladder into the holding tanks. There is an excellent 30-min. walk along the river here—consult the trail guide sign opposite the hatchery. This lovely area along the Capilano River should not be missed, but beware of the much-touted "Capilano Suspension Bridge" ($2.50) further S which is a tourist trap. After the hatchery, it's a 15 min. walk up a paved road to the highway. Walk S on Capilano Road to Ridgewood Dr. where you can get a no. 246 Highland bus running across the Lions Gate Bridge back to Vancouver. Note that bus routes in North Vancouver can be a little confusing, so tell the driver where you are going each time and ask him to let you know when to get off.

museums and parks: Take a no. 10 Tenth Ave. bus from Granville St. out to the University of British Columbia (UBC). There's a map of the campus by the bus stop at the end of the line. Go via the clock tower and rose garden (in bloom from June to Sept.) to the Museum of Anthropology (Tues. to Sun., 1200-1900; $1.50, free Tues.). This museum has a fantastic display of NW Coastal Indian sculpture and a large research collection open to visitors. Find your way around the E side of the building to the back where there's a great view of the Strait of Georgia from the adjacent cliff. Just to the L is a steep stairway down to the beach. Walk S along Wreck Beach, where nude sunbathing is the norm, to another stairway leading back up to the UBC campus. Wreck Beach, with its huge driftwood logs and high wooded cliffs, is so wild that you hardly know you're on the edge of a big city. When you get up to the top of the stairs turn L and walk between the red brick residences to the Nitobe Japanese Garden (50 cents) on campus. The UBC campus covers a large, beautifully-landscaped area with many buildings worth looking into. Wander at will. If you're weary and hungry, try the Student Union Building with its large cafeteria (The Subway) and pub (The Pit). Both are cheap and the public is welcome. From UBC take a no. 14 Hastings bus back along Broadway to MacDonald where you transfer to a no. 22 Knight bus to go as far as Cypress Street. Walk due N on Cypress to the totem pole flanking a group of museums on the S side of English Bay at the entrance to False Creek. The Centennial Museum is good on Vancouver history and has a pleasant cafeteria

The arrival of the first train into Vancouver on 23 May 1887 opened an era which saw the city eventually grow into the metropolis of Western Canada.

with a fine view. The $2.50 admission includes a small Maritime Museum nearby; the main museum is free on Tues. (take note!). The RCMP ship *St. Roch*, the first to traverse the difficult NW Passage between the Pacific and Atlantic oceans in both directions (during the 1940s), can be seen at no charge every day in the same building as the Maritime Museum. All these facilities open daily, 1000-1700. The unusual mushroom dome over the Centennial Museum contains a planetarium. If the sun is shining, walk W along the shore to Kitsilano Beach to join the local sun worshippers. There's also an outdoor saltwater swimming pool here which you may use for a buck.

along Howe Sound: A good day trip from Vancouver and one which no rail buff will want to miss is on the Royal Hudson, an authentic 1930s steam locomotive. This is a 6-hour RT excursion from North Vancouver station to the logging town of Squamish. From May to Sept., Wed. to Sun., the train pulls out at 1000 for the 2-hour journey past Horseshoe Bay and up the side of Howe Sound to Squamish. In Squamish there is ample time for lunch and a visit to the local pioneer museum in the park near the station. Although the trip may be a little touristy, at $9.50 RT it's still a good value and the scenery is hard to beat. Tickets are available from Tourism B.C. at Robson Square; the seller will explain where to catch the city bus to the station.

up Indian Arm: Harbor Ferries Ltd. on Coal Harbor just beyond the Bayshore Inn offers a 6-hour day trip up and down Indian Arm, 90 km to the Wigwam Inn. The boat leaves daily at 1000 ($14 RT) and reservations are not necessary. The 2-hour journey up the fjord gives you a taste of what to expect on the Inside Passage cruise to Skagway —snowcapped mountains, thick forests, eagles and seals. You also get to see Vancouver Harbor from end to end with a knowledgeable commentary from the captain. There's a 2-hour stopover at the Wigwam Inn but the food sold is expensive, so bring along a picnic lunch. A short trail behind the lodge leads straight up to a waterfall viewpoint. You could extend your trip by hiking for 2 days along a logging road from Wigwam to Squamish. There's a high pass to cross, so do this only from mid-June on. An alternative way of getting to the trail head is to call Jim Patterson (tel. 929-3911 or 929-1520) and arrange to have his water taxi take you from Deep Cove (bus no. 211 or 212 from Phibbs Exchange) to the top of Indian Arm for about $8 pp.

to the Fraser River: To see the Fraser River take a no. 820 Canada Way bus from Hastings St. to New Westminster. Stay on till you come down the hill and see the river in front of you. The waterfront is undergoing development and it may be hard to get to the riverside. A

A ride on the MV *Hollyburn* from Vancouver to the Wigwam Inn is a fine way to get acquainted with the city's scenic waterways.

VANCOUVER

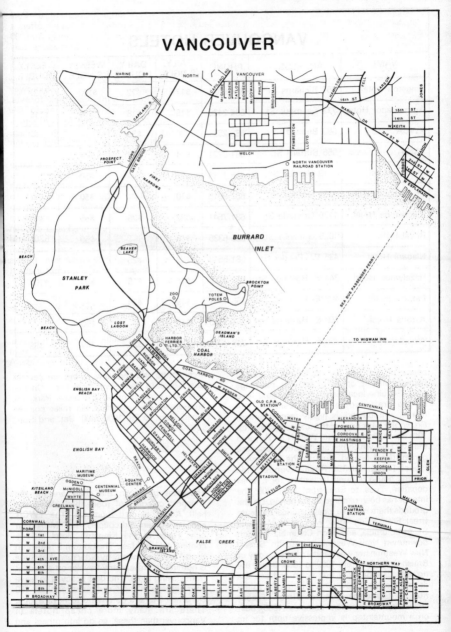

VANCOUVER HOTELS

NAME	ADDRESS	PHONE	DAILY SINGLE	DAILY DOUBLE	WEEKLY SINGLE	WEEKLY DOUBLE
Kingston Hotel	757 Richards St.	684-9024	$17	$22	$102	$132
Ambassador Hotel	773 Seymour St.	684-2436	$15	$18	$95	$115
YWCA	580 Burrard St.	683-2531	$20	$30	—	—
YMCA	955 Burrard St.	681-0221	$14	$24	—	—
Murray Hotel	1119 Hornby St.	685-1733	$12	—	$50	—
Bon Accord Hotel	1235 Hornby St.	682-9919	$10	—	$50	—
Blackstone Hotel	1176 Granville St.	681-7541	$22	$25	$55	$72
Royal Hotel	1025 Granville St.	685-5335	$15	—	$50	—
Niagara Hotel	435 W. Pender St.	681-5548	$22	$25	—	—
Hazelwood Hotel	344 E. Hastings St.	687-9126	$14	$16	$90	$100
Patricia Hotel	403 E. Hastings St.	255-4301	$19	$23	—	—
Astoria Hotel	769 E. Hastings St.	254-3355	$10	—	$50	—
Woodbine Hotel	786 E. Hastings St.	253-3244	$15	$20	$69	$89

couple blocks S at 1051 Columbia St. is the Farmers Market, open Fri. and Sat. mornings only. Genuine local handicrafts are sold here by the craftspeople themselves and the market, untouristed, is highly recommended. Go out the back door of the market hall and up 10th St. to Royal Avenue. Walk N on Royal to the City Hall, which has an attractive Japanese garden (free) behind. Just to the N is Irving House (1862), at 302 Royal Avenue. This historic house is open to visitors for a small donation, Tues. to Sun. from 1100-1700; the interior has been restored to the period. On the grounds there is also a local historical museum (free). From Irving House walk down Merrivale St. to Columbia, and S on Columbia through downtown New Westminster to 8th Street. New Westminster was capital of the Colony of British Columbia from 1859 to 1868. Board the no. 820 Canada Way bus again and ask the driver to let you know where to transfer to the no. 58 Edmonds bus to Simon Fraser University. This modern complex (1965) built on a mountaintop is impressive both for its architecture and the view. There are several buses back to Vancouver from here. On the way you might stop at Exhibition Park, an amusement center with a big roller coaster (open Tues. to Fri. 1900-2400, Sat. and Sun. 1300-2400).

STAY

The rates given on the chart are for the cheapest category of room (bath down the hall). Add 6 percent room tax. The YWCA accepts women and couples; the YMCA men only. Rates at the Kingston Hotel include continental breakfast. The bottom 9 hotels on the list are used mostly by older men, but there is nothing to prevent any traveler on a budget from staying there. The best policy is to leave your luggage at the Greyhound terminal, 150 Dunsmuir St., and go around to have a look. There are many more cheap hotels in Vancouver than these, so go into others and ask to see a room. Avoid the hotels on E. Hastings between Columbia and Main; these are used for prostitution. There are no official campgrounds near downtown Vancouver.

youth hostel: If you're alone, or want to meet other travelers, the best place to stay if you're only going to be in Vancouver a couple of days is the Vancouver Youth Hostel in Jericho Park (no. 4 Fourth Ave. bus from Granville St.). This is the largest hostel in Canada and has excellent facilities, including a members' kitchen, laundromat, lockers, left-luggage service ($1 per week), and restaurant (dinner, $4). There is a great view of the city from the park. The overnight charge is $6.50 for YH members, $8.50 for non-members, and the hostel closes from 1000-1600 (tel. 224-3208). Highly recommended.

FOOD

As might be expected, the best restaurants in Vancouver are in or near Chinatown. Of these, the Kwantung Restaurant, 137 E. Pender St., is recommended for its great prices ($3 for a full meal with soup and tea). Foo's Restaurant, 72 E. Pender, is a little more expensive and a little better. Also try the Vietnamese Garden, 6 E. Hastings Street. Nearby is the Only Sea Foods, 20 E. Hastings St., a Vancouver institution with Coney Island clam chowder at $2 a bowl (closed Sunday). Often a line forms to get in here. If you're starved, head for the Old Spaghetti Factory, 53 Water St. in Gastown, where the cheapest meal is still $3.50, including salad, bread, spaghetti, coffee, and Spumoni ice cream. There's a 1910 streetcar parked in the middle of the dining room, but it's not going anywhere. Baskin-Robbins, Carrall and Water Sts., has the best ice cream in town. Downtown, check out Mr. Mike's, 921 Granville St., for steak and salad, or the Papaya Gardens, 948 Granville St., for sandwiches and salads. They have tables out on the Mall. If you want a taste of West End life, head for the Fresgo Inn, 1138 Davie St., which operates cafeteria-style, but the meals are good, the portions large and the prices reasonable. Try the clubhouse sandwich ($4) or pot pie. The place is always crowded with local apartment dwellers. If you don't want to spend that much, Harvey's, 1157 Davie St., is cheaper but still good. For that special occasion, repair to Carlos'n Bud's Tex-Mex Restaurant, 555 Pacific at Seymour, in a converted garage with Texas border

SORRY WE'RE FULL ...
BUT THERE'S AN ELKS CLUB IN TOWN

Noontime events at Robson Square draw crowds to this futuristic complex.

decor. Count on at least $10 pp here, but at night there's 'foot-stompin' music' and fun. Out towards the YH only the fast-food places are cheap, but Sidhu's Kitchen, 2953a W. 4th Ave. at Bayswater, has Indian food (dinner only) and prices are reasonable if you stick to the vegetarian specialties. Also, check the menu posted outside the Saigon Restaurant, 2394 W. 4th Avenue.

ENTERTAINMENT

movies: Vancouver has 3 movie houses which specialize in double features and change their programs frequently: the Hollywood Theater, 3123 W. Broadway (tel. 738-3211); the Ridge Theatre, 3131 Arbutus at 16th Ave. (tel. 738-6311); and the Savoy Cinema, 2321 Main St. at 7th Ave. (tel. 872-2124). Showtime is usually 1930 and admission $4. See old favorite movies for a buck on Fri. at 1900 at the Carnegie Center, 401 Main St. at Hastings. At the National Film Board, 1161 W. Georgia St., preview any of their documentary films for free at their office, Mon. to Fri. 0830-1630. There is a large selection indexed in a card catalog.

music and dancing: If you're looking for action and want live rock 'n roll to dance to, head for Outlaws, 1136 W. Georgia St., the local meet market. Go Mon. to Thurs.; women get in free, men pay $1. Weekends the cover is $5. Gandydancer, 1222 Hamilton St., is a gay disco. There's never a cover charge at the Spinning Wheel, 212 Carrall St. in Gastown, where you can hear Irish folk music. The pub

closest to the YH is Jerry's Cove, 3681 W. 4th Ave. at Alma. If it's too crowded downstairs, have a look upstairs by the dart board. Read the _Georgia Strait_ (50 cents) for a complete rundown on what's happening in town. The drinking age in B.C. is 19, but you'll have a hard time getting a beer on Sunday. _coffee houses:_ Two of the best places to hear live music in Vancouver are coffee houses, which is fortunate if you don't want alcohol or if it's Sunday. The Soft Rock Cafe, 1925 W. 4th Ave. (tel. 734-2822), has a cover from $3 to $14 depending on who's appearing, but Tues. (audition night) is usually free. Good atmosphere, good people; the music starts at 2030. For jazz it's the Classical Joint Coffee House, 231 Carrall St. (Tues. to Sun. 2030-0200), a Bohemian institution. Single women will feel comfortable in both these places.

cultural events: Sunday mornings at 1100 there are 'coffee concerts' at the Q.E. Playhouse, 630 Hamilton St. at W. Georgia. Top classical performers appear and tickets are only $1.50, available at the door on the day of the concert. There's a Hari Krishna love feast at 4574 Belmont St., just a block from the YH, Sun. at 1630. Visiting writers and anyone into literature should drop by the Literary Storefront, 314 W. Cordova St. (tel. 688-9737), open Mon. to Fri. 1300-1700. The Storefront organizes poetry and fiction readings, authors' nights, workshops and special events. There's always something happening and well-known authors such as Edward Albee and Czeslaw Milosz sometimes participate.

free shows: See capitalism in action from the Visitors Gallery of the Vancouver Stock Exchange, 2nd fl. 609 Granville St., Mon. to Fri. 0700-1400. Sit in on a trial at the new Law Courts at Robson Square. The proceedings are usually open to the public from 1000-1200 and 1400-1600. The criminal jury courtrooms (nos. 62-67 on Level 6) are the most fun. Have a look at the county court trial list behind the information desk near the entrance. If you find yourself in here as a defendent instead of an observer (no fun), Gedye and Guenther, Lawyers, 245 Main St. (tel. 683-1321) are recommended.

VANCOUVER AND VICINITY

VANCOUVER AND VICINITY

1. Horseshoe Bay
2. University of British Columbia
3. Vancouver Youth Hostel
4. Pack and Boots Store
5. Centennial Museum
6. English Bay
7. Stanley Park
8. Lions Gate Bridge
9. Capilano Salmon Hatchery
10. Cleveland Dam
11. Grouse Mountain Skyride
12. Lynn Canyon Park
13. North Vancouver
14. Burrard Inlet
15. Exhibition Park
16. Deep Cove
17. Indian Arm
18. Simon Fraser University
19. Port Moody
20. Port Mann Bridge
21. Fraser River
22. New Westminster
23. Burnaby
24. to Tsawwassen and U.S. border
25. Vancouver International Airport
26. downtown Vancouver

SERVICES

Everyone but Canadians needs a visa to visit the U.S. If you don't already have one, apply to the U.S. Consulate, 1199 W. Hastings St., Mon. to Fri. 0800-1200. Check several banks before changing money as all offer a different rate of exchange. Avoid changing money at shops, hotels, and foreign exchange dealers where you always lose. The Pine Free Clinic, 1985 W. 4th Ave., offers free medical care Mon. to Fri. 0900-1200/1400-1630 (closed Wed. afternoons). Run by the City Health Dept., this clinic operates on a first-come first-served basis, so arrive early. The Ministry of Human Resources, 575 Drake St., operates a free clinic evenings Mon. to Fri. from 2000-2300 for infections, rashes, infestations, VD, and other similar problems. For the Provincial VD Clinic, call tel. 874-2331. For the Rape Relief Line, call tel. 732-1613. If you have a specific medical or social problem and don't know where to turn, call the Vancouver Information and Referral Service, tel. 736-3661 (answered Mon. to Friday). When your spirits are down or you want a change of pace, visit the Vancouver Aquatic Center, 1050 Beach Ave., which features a large, indoor, heated, saltwater swimming pool. You may use the pool for $1.60, or pay $2.85 to have the run of the pool, sauna, whirlpool, and gym. These new facilities are most refreshing. The Aquatic Center opens daily year round, but call tel. 689-7156 for times. A 10-min. walk W of here along the shore is English Bay, Vancouver's most popular sunbathing beach (washrooms and dressing rooms). The most knowledgeable travel agency in Vancouver is WestCan Treks, 3415 W. Broadway (tel. 734-1066). Haircuts go for $1.50 at the Ferry Barber Shop, 227 Carrall Street. If you're planning to be in Vancouver a couple of weeks and would like to get involved in some unpaid community service work, call the Volunteer Center, tel. 731-6168. They will be able to direct you to a charitable organization that needs your help. This is an excellent way of learning about Canadian life and should be seriously considered by European visitors.

INFORMATION

The Vancouver Visitors Bureau in the Pacific Center Mall, Howe and Georgia Sts. (daily 0830-1700), has maps of the city, brochures on local attractions, and bus timetables. Tourism B.C., downstairs by the Plaza at Robson Square, Howe and Robson Sts., hands out maps and information on the whole province. Detailed topographical maps for hikers are available from the Government Agent, Room 222, Robson Square. For free maps of Alaska and all other U.S. destinations, go to Travel USA, Rm. 84 in the old CPR station at the foot of Seymour St. (Mon. to Fri. 0900-1700). Greenpeace, 2623 W. 4th Ave., publishes information sheets on local environmental issues. The Vancouver Public Library, Robson and Burrard Sts., is open Mon. to Thurs. 0930-2130, Fri. and Sat. 0930-1800. Duthie Books, Robson and Hornby Sts., is the best bookstore in the city. The Pack and Boots Store, 3425 W. Broadway, sells camping equipment, guide books, and YH cards.

TRANSPORT

airport: Vancouver International Airport (YVR) is 20 km S of downtown Vancouver. Transit bus no. 100/800 leaves from outside the terminal's upper level (departures) to the right. Pay 75 cents exact change and ask for a transfer. Just after the large bridge change to the no. 25 Victoria bus which runs straight up Granville into town. The no. 100/800 bus leaves the airport every 30 min. Mon. to Sat., hourly on Sun., and there is service until after midnight. The Tourism British Columbia counter on the lower level (arrivals) is open daily 0800-2300 and is very helpful with maps and brochures. There is no bank, but a currency exchange booth opens 0600-2230 daily, which gives about 2 percent less than the banks downtown. Coin lockers are plentiful and cost 50 cents a day. The airport is open 24 hours a day so crash here if you're arriving or leaving in the wee hours. Don't feel badly about stretching out your sleeping bag because they charge $12.50 airport tax on international flights. On domestic flights the charge is 8 percent of the ticket price, or $23, whichever is lower. If you bought your ticket abroad and weren't charged, Air Canada collects the money when you check in.

by boat: B.C. Ferries has frequent service throughout the day from Tsawwassen, S of Vancouver, to the Gulf Islands and Swartz Bay (for Victoria). The ferry to Nanaimo on Vancouver Island leaves frequently from Horseshoe Bay, NW of Vancouver, as does the ferry to Langdale (for the Sunshine Coast).

Ferry services to Nanaimo, Langdale, and Bowen Island
connect with buses to Vancouver and Powell River at
Horseshoe Bay at the mouth of Howe Sound.

The fare on all of the above services is $3.50.
bus connection: To get to the Tsawwassen
ferry terminal, take bus no. 601 South Delta
from Howe St. to Ladner Exchange where you
transfer to a no. 640 bus to the ferry. West
Vancouver transit has frequent service, usually
every 30 min. daily, to Horseshoe Bay. Look
for the blue bus (65 cents) in front of the
Hudson Bay Co. at Georgia and Seymour
Streets. *local ferry:* The Sea Bus crosses
Burrard Inlet to North Vancouver from the old
RR station at the foot of Seymour Street.
There is service every 15 min. weekdays, every
30 min. evenings and weekends. The fare is 75
cents and city bus transfers are both given and
accepted.

by bus: Greyhound Lines, 150 Dunsmuir St.,
sells tickets to Beaver Creek, Yukon, or to
Montreal for $99; $132 all the way to Sydney,
Nova Scotia. You have 60 days to finish the
trip and may stop off anywhere along the way.
Pacific Coach Lines has a service every 2 hours
from the Greyhound terminal to Victoria ($11),
but this costs double what you'll pay by doing

it in stages on local buses. Maverick Coach
Lines has a bus from the same terminal twice a
day to Powell River. The early, 0800, bus is the
one to take if you want to be able to see
anything. The fare, $16.25, includes both
ferries. *local buses:* All Vancouver city buses
charge a flat rate of 75 cents regardless of
distance traveled, and all give a transfer valid
for stopovers and RTs for up to 1½ hours. A
Sun. bus pass is available from drivers for
$1.50.

other travel options: Auto Driveaway, 211 W.
1st St., North Vancouver (3 blocks from the
Sea Bus terminal), has driveaway cars to
Toronto, Montreal, and Los Angeles. You
must put up a $250 refundable deposit and pay
the gas, but otherwise it's free transportation.
Europeans should have an International
Drivers License. Call tel. 985-0936 for
information. Many other such agencies are
listed in the yellow pages of the phone book
under "Automobile Transporters and
Driveaway Companies." *hitching:*
Hitchhiking is prohibited on the Trans-Canada

Highway E out of Vancouver. However, if you're determined, take bus no. 330 Ferguson (no Sun. service) from Hastings St. and get off at the first stop after the Port Mann Bridge. Walk back to the highway and smile. To reach the White Rock/Blaine border crossing into the U.S.A., take bus no. 351 North Bluff from Howe St. to Johnston and King George Highway. From there it's easy to hitch to the border.

THE SUNSHINE COAST

The Sunshine Coast, part of the mainland just W of Vancouver, stretches 150 km along the NE shore of the Strait of Georgia from Howe Sound in the E to Desolation Sound in the west. For anyone headed to Port Hardy with an extra day to spare, the route via the mill town of Powell River offers an alternative to the beaten track through Nanaimo.

getting there: The 6-hour, 140-km bus ride from Vancouver to Powell River ($16.25)

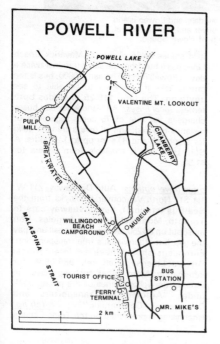

includes 2 scenic ferry rides, the first across Howe Sound, the 2nd down Jervis Inlet. The Maverick Coach Lines terminal in Powell River is on Duncan St., a km straight up from the Comox ferry landing. If you don't want to spend money on a bus ticket, take the West Vancouver Transit bus (65 cents) from Georgia St., Vancouver, to Horseshoe Bay. Catch the ferry to Langdale ($3.50 — 13 services a day). Save your ferry ticket as it is also valid for the second crossing.

camping and hosteling: If you'd like to stop off on the way to Powell River, there's a youth hostel (8 beds) at Grantham's Landing just a couple km from the Langdale ferry terminal. At low tide you can walk along the beach to the hostel (tel. 886-9146 - $8 pp). Several provincial parks along the Sunshine Coast offer camping. Roberts Creek Park ($3 a site) is 14 km W of Gibsons, right on the highway. Porpoise Bay Park ($5) is probably the best in the area with its broad, sandy beach and view of Sechelt Inlet. It's 5 km NE of Sechelt on a side road. Saltery Bay Park ($6) is a 10-min. walk beyond the 2nd ferry terminal.

Powell River amenities: The Willingdon Beach Municipal Campground ($5 a tent) is just a km N along Marine Drive from the ferry terminal in Powell River. It has hot showers and a laundromat, but can fill up. If you call tel. 604-485-2242 they'll reserve a spot for you. The next closest official campground is Garnet Rock Park (tel. 487-9535), 5 km south. There's a good tourist information office just 100 m up from the ferry terminal, where you can pick up a free map of the town.

sights of Powell River: The local museum is across the highway from Willingdon Creek Nature Trail, off the highway to the right. Powell River's most unusual sight is a breakwater of 10 WW II liberty ships sunk in a semi-circle beside the pulp mill to provide a storage area for logs. Get there along a 2-km beach trail N from Willingdon Beach, then a short distance down a dirt road. The MacMillan-Bloedel pulp mill, opened in 1912, is still one of the largest of its kind in the world. Ask at the tourist office near the ferry terminal if there are tours. The best view of the area is to be had from Valentine Mountain Lookout (243 m). Every hour on the hour Mon. to Sat. bus no. 1 (45 cents) leaves the Powell River Plaza, Joyce and Alberni, for the corner of

Crown Ave. and Cranberry Street. It's an easy walk up Crown Ave. to the foot of the trail.

from Powell River: The Powell River-Comox ferry ($3.50) runs 4 times a day in each direction. The ferry terminal in Powell River is convenient to the bus station, restaurants,

campground, etc., while the Comox terminal is at Little River, 8 km from Comox and 11 km from Courtenay. The only public transportation available at Little River is a shared taxi ($3 a seat) which leaves for Courtenay at 1420. It isn't hard to hitch a ride into town.

VANCOUVER ISLAND

Vancouver is the largest island off the W coast of North America. Lying parallel (NW-SE) to the mainland of B.C., it is 454 km long and an average of 97 km wide. The island was discovered by Capt. Cook in 1776, but it was Capt. George Vancouver who, by entering Discovery Passage near Campbell River and sailing on through Johnstone Strait, proved it was not connected to the mainland. Today, 350,000 people live on the island, mostly around Victoria and along the E coast. Logging is the main industry, followed by fishing and tourism, with mining in the Strathcona Provincial Park (!) and near Port Hardy. A spine of snowcapped mountains runs down the center of the island, isolating the wild, rugged W coast. Though much of this coast is inaccessible, Pacific Rim National Park is becoming a haven for backpackers.

buses and rides: Pacific Coach Lines will stop anywhere along the highway to pick up or drop off passengers. If you get tired of hitching, just flag down a bus. Stopovers are permitted if you buy a through ticket. Consider getting a bus ticket as far as Campbell River, then hitching on to Port Hardy. Hitchhiking is possible all over Vancouver Island, but is not especially easy. The really adventuresome should try hitching rides on fishing boats. There's always someone going and if you offer to pay the equivalent of about half what it would cost by ferry, they'll be interested. Women often get free rides this way.

NANAIMO AND VICINITY

Nanaimo: Founded in 1852 as a coal-mining settlement, downtown Nanaimo and its small boat harbor are very quaint and attractive, with excellent views of the mainland and other offshore islands. Don't judge the city by the jumble of parking lots, shopping centers, and string suburbia you find on the outskirts. Old Nanaimo is worth a stopover.

sights of Nanaimo: Just beyond the anchorage and up the hill from the bus station is the tourist office and museum. The museum (50 cents) has informative exhibits on the early English and Chinese coal miners who settled the area. Just along the waterfront from the museum is the Bastion, an old wooden fort built in 1853 by the Hudson Bay Company to protect the coal-mining families against Indian attack. Fort or no fort, the Indians remained friendly and today the Bastion can be visited Tues. to Sat. for a small donation. Continue along the same way a few blocks further to

Captain George Vancouver was the first to circumnavigate Vancouver Island. His negotiations with the Spaniard, Quadra, at Nootka Sound in 1792 laid the groundwork for British domination of this coast. From 1792 to 1794 he explored and charted the entire Inside Passage from Puget Sound to Glacier Bay.

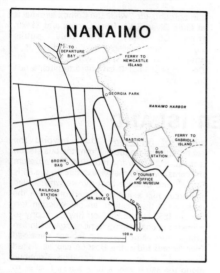

Georgia Park with its 2 totem poles and Squamish canoe.

stay and eat: The tourist office keeps a list of private families who offer bed and breakfast for about $15 s, $25 d. The best camping spots nearby are on Newcastle and Gabriola Islands (see below). The Brown Bag Alternative Restaurant at the W end of the Bastion Bridge has good healthy sandwiches for $2-3.

Newcastle Island: There is excellent hiking and camping ($4) on Newcastle Island, the green, wooded island just offshore from downtown Nanaimo. A self-guide folder for the 9-km nature trail is available free from the Nanaimo tourist office. June to Aug. there's an hourly passenger ferry (daily except Tues.) from Nanaimo to the island ($2.50 RT). The entire island is a provincial park; there are no cars to contend with.

Gabriola Island: The Gabriola ferry (75 cents RT) leaves approx. every hour from the landing adjoining the bus station in downtown Nanaimo. Even if you don't get off to visit the island, the return trip is a cheap scenic cruise. Campsites ($6) without shower are available at Taylor Bay Lodge (tel. 247-9211), an easy 3-km walk from the ferry (a phone call from Nanaimo for reservations is not long distance).

There's a splendid view of the Strait of Georgia from the lawn in front of the lodge. At low tide walk W along the shore a couple of hundred meters to Malaspina Point to see the deeply-cut galleries of weathered sandstone. A similar walk E from the lodge brings one to Gabriola Sands Provincial Park (no camping), with a view of the mountains of the mainland. B & K Grocery Store is just S, up the road from Gabriola Sands. There's a restaurant/bar at the Taylor Bay Lodge (open Tues. to Saturday).

from Nanaimo: The ferry to Horseshoe Bay (Vancouver) leaves from Departure Bay, about 3 km N of downtown Nanaimo. Every hour, Mon. to Sat., bus no. 2 passes Stewart Ave. and Brechlin Road, the closest stop to the B.C. Ferries terminal. Pacific Coach Lines has 3 buses daily to Port Alberni ($5), 6 daily to Campbell River ($9), and 9 daily to Victoria (109 km — $7). There are coin lockers (50 cents) in the bus station. _hitching:_ If you want to hitch N, take bus nos. 1 or 2 (55 cents) from

The old Hudson Bay Company bastion still stands watch over Nanaimo's picturesque harbor.

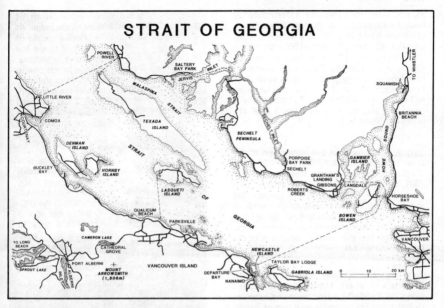

STRAIT OF GEORGIA

the downtown bus station to Woodgrove Mall, which is well out of town on the Island Highway. To hitch S, take bus no. 7 from the bus station and ask the driver to drop you at Cranberry and Trans-Canada Highway. None of these buses run on Sunday.

PORT ALBERNI TO THE WEST COAST

across the island: The road from Parksville to Port Alberni traverses superb forested countryside along the N slope of Mt. Arrowsmith (1,806 m), which dominates this part of Vancouver Island. Just beyond lovely Cameron Lake is MacMillan Provincial Park (Cathedral Grove) with its 850-year-old Douglas firs. The cross-island highway cuts right through the middle of this ancient forest.

Port Alberni: There isn't much to see in Port Alberni itself; generally it's only a place you come to catch the boat down Alberni Inlet. If you have some time on your hands, take any city bus (50 cents) out to the Echo Center which has an indoor swimming pool ($1), sauna ($1), public library, and museum (free). There are sporadic tours of the big pulp mill in Port Alberni. Call tel. 723-2161 if you're

interested. _stay:_ The Dry Creek Municipal Campground, at the end of Napier st. off 3rd Ave. near the Dairy Queen, charges $4. It's an easy walk from the bus station or harbor and there's plenty of room. If the weather's bad, the King Edward Hotel, 1st and Argyle (tel. 724-3544), has rooms for $15 s or d.

from Port Alberni: The MV _Lady Rose,_ a passenger-carrying cargo boat built in Scotland in 1937, leaves from the wharf at the bottom of Argyle St. for 4-hour runs down Alberni Inlet. Tuesday, Thurs. and Sat. at 0800 the _Lady Rose_ leaves for Bamfield ($12 OW) near the start of the West Coast Trail, and on Wed. and Fri. at 0800 to Ucluelet ($15 OW). Be there a little early as accommodation on the boat is first-come first-served, and after the first 100 passengers show up no more are allowed on board. Check departure days at any tourist information office in B.C. On the Ucluelet trip the ship sails between the Broken Group Islands, now part of Pacific Rim National Park. Upon request you can be let off at Gibraltar Island for camping, but for the most part the island is a favorite destination for canoeists and kayakers. There are no facilities on Gibraltar and fresh water is scarce. Bald eagles can be spotted on their treetop roosts as you pass through the extraordinarily beautiful Broken Group. *by bus:* Orient Stage Lines has a bus at 1230 daily except Sat. to Ucluelet ($8), Long Beach ($8.50), and Tofino ($9). There are no coin lockers in the bus station at 3rd and Mar Streets in downtown Port Alberni. *hitching:* If you want to hitch to Long Beach, bus no. 3 will take you out as far as Falls St. and River Road. To hitch to the E coast take bus no. 1 to the Alberni Mall. No buses on Sunday.

Ucluelet: The name of this fishing and tourist town is pronounced YOO-CLOO-LET. The *Canadian Princess,* a large steamship built in 1932, is permanently moored at Ucluelet as a floating hotel ($29 s, $36 d) — touristy but quaint. There are no official campgrounds in Ucluelet itself so it's best to push on to Long Beach after a quick look. If you came in on the *Lady Rose,* you can usually connect with the bus to Tofino ($3).

Long Beach: Certainly the best beach on Canada's W coast, Long Beach stretches along the middle 11 km of the coast between Ucluelet and Tofino and is now part of Pacific Rim National Park. The brown sands court naked feet and the water is cool but invigorating. Sea lions and grey whales can sometimes be seen swimming offshore. Camping is restricted to 2 designated areas. Green Point Campground ($5), just off the main road, is often full of camper vans. To get to the Schooner Cove Campsite ($3) at the N end of Long Beach you must walk 800 m, which eliminates most of the motorists. Since you camp right on the beach itself there is usually no problem about finding a place, although it too can get crowded. Drinking water is available, but bring all the food you'll need; the nearest store is 15 km away in Tofino. Schooner Cove is unquestionably the choice of backpackers (but no showers). Pacific Rim Campground ($8), just outside the National Park on the road to Tofino, is popular with the motor and mobile home sets.

Tofino: Tofino, 126 km from Port Alberni, is a very picturesque small community with many small islands in the deep blue bay and lovely snow-mantled mountains in the distance. *from Tofino:* Pacific Rim Airlines will take you N from Tofino to Tahsis in a float plane (2 passenger minimum) for $88. The MV *Solander* sails from Tofino to the Indian

A campsite on Long Beach at Schooner Cove on Vancouver Island's wild west coast.

village of Ahousat on Wed. and Fri. at 1700. They don't usually carry passengers, but the captain may take you for free if you ask him nicely. At Ahousat get permission from Jack Dale to cross his land to White Sands Beach where you may camp on crown land. There is a bus from Tofino to Port Alberni every afternoon but Saturday. The fantastically beautiful road winds between mountains, forests, and lakes. If you're hitching be prepared to wait awhile as there are often more hitchhikers than cars. Sometimes you can count as many as a dozen people waiting for a ride.

the West Coast Trail: The West Coast Trail from Bamfield to Port Renfrew was originally built in 1907-1912 as a lifesaving trail for shipwrecked seamen from ships which often foundered on this windswept coast. Today, a favorite of intrepid backpackers, it forms part of Pacific Rim National Park. Be prepared, however, as this is no Sunday outing. Six days is the minimum required to do the trail and most hikers take eight. Rain and fog are possible anytime and no supplies are sold anywhere along the route. Beach hiking and camping are the most popular activities and there is plenty of driftwood for campfires. Be aware of tidal conditions and of being cut off below cliffs by rising waters. The Sierra Club puts out an excellent trail guide. Copies can be purchased at the Pack and Boots Stores in Vancouver and Victoria. Pick up a copy of the tide tables for Tofino, B.C., while you're at it. *the route:* The trail begins at Pachena Bay, 5 km from the village of Bamfield, which is accessible on the *Lady Rose* ($12) 3 times a week from Port Alberni. There is also a 90-km logging road between Port Alberni and Bamfield along which you could try to hitch. The 47-km stretch from Pachena Bay to Carmanah Point is the easiest part of the trail. On the 30-km walk from Carmanah to Port Renfrew you must cross deep gullies on fallen trees, climb steep slopes on rough ladders and stairways, and traverse high cliffs on a slippery trail. Local Indians ferry hikers across the Nitimat Narrows, midway on the trail, for a

nominal amount. A similar crossing must be made for $3 pp just before Port Renfrew. After a backcountry experience such as this, there is little to detain you in Port Renfrew so hitch the 71 km to the Sooke Regional Museum (free) where there are city buses into Victoria.

CENTRAL VANCOUVER ISLAND

Courtenay: Courtenay is a communications and supply center half way up the E coast. Fifth St. is downtown Courtenay. The Civic Center is at 5th and Cliffe, and just 2 blocks N is the Native Sons Museum (open daily 1300-1700, 50 cents). A Bailey bridge crosses the Courtenay River E from 5th St. to Lewis Park. *stay:* The Maple Pool Campsite, a 15 min. walk NE from town, has pleasant sites ($5) along the river. From Lewis Park follow the highway towards Campbell River, then turn L on Headquarters Road (the first turn) and continue along around the bend. The Hotel Courtenay opposite Lewis park has

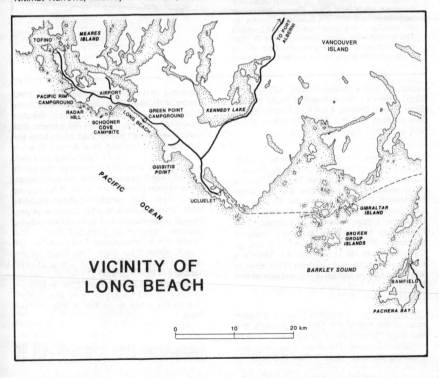

VICINITY OF
LONG BEACH

0   10   20 km

VANCOUVER ISLAND

Nootka Sound: Captain Cook's landing at Friendly Cove in 1778 was the first by a European in this part of North America. Fourteen years later Capt. George Vancouver negotiated here with the Spaniard, Quadra, for the transfer of this coast from Spain to England. The Nootka tribe, which dominated the W coast of Vancouver I., at first grew rich from the fur trade until the white man's diseases decimated them.

rooms for $13 s (without bath), $22 d (with bath). There's a home hostel (2 beds) at 1660 Robb Ave. in Comox, 4 km E of Courtenay (no bus service). Call tel. 339-3763 before going and you must have a YH card.

from Courtenay: The Powell River ferry lands at Little River, 11 km NE of Courtenay. There is no bus service, but Comox Taxi Ltd. runs a jitney service ($3 a seat) from the Courtenay bus station, Cumberland and 8th St., daily at 1400. There's a large Canadian Air Force base between Little River and Comox. The Courtenay bus station has coin lockers accessible 24 hours a day and the bus to Campbell River (45 km) is only $2. There's a train from Courtenay to Victoria ($16), daily at 1300. The railway station is at Cumberland and McPhee, a 10-min. walk.

Campbell River: Campbell River is a boom town at the top of the Strait of Georgia, the last large settlement of Vancouver Island's populated E coast. The town is so new, and growing so fast, that it has the look of

suburbia, with the Tyee Plaza Shopping Center at its heart. The downtown area faces Discovery Passage, which Capt. George Vancouver sailed through in 1792, proving that Vancouver was an island. Just down from the Quadra ferry landing is a Kwakiutl-style longhouse constructed of giant logs in a park with a superb view of the passage. On the W side of Tyee Plaza is a small yet surprisingly good regional museum (closed Sun. and Mon.—free). The excellent 236-km highway from Campbell River to Port Hardy is largely though undeveloped and uninhabited logging country. _services at Campbell River:_ The closest offical campground is Elk Falls Park ($6 a site), about 6 km from Tyee Plaza on the road to Gold River. There are a salmon hatchery (4 km), waterfall (2 km), and canyon to visit near the campground. Coin lockers are available at the Campbell River bus station. The tourist office is on the N side of Tyee Plaza.

Quadra Island: There is an hourly ferry (50 cents RT) across Discovery Passage to Quadra

Island, leaving from the E side of Tyee Plaza. The Kwakiutl Museum in Cape Mudge village, 4 km S of the ferry landing on Quadra, has an excellent collection of Potlatch regalia. Notice the petroglyphs on the rocks in the park across from the museum.

Gold River: The paved road to Gold River follows the S shore of Upper Campbell Lake near Strathcona Provincial Park, affording some splendid views of the mountains, forests, and rivers of central Vancouver Island. There are numerous trails in the park and backcountry camping is permitted anywhere over 800 m off the main roads. The Butte Lake Campground ($6) is near the bridge at the S end of Upper Campbell Lake. Heavy ore trucks rumble along the highway to Campbell River from mines in the southern portion of Strathcona, B.C.'s oldest provincial park. Gold River is a modern bedroom community for the employees of the big pulp mill on Muchalat Inlet, 16 km SW by the wharf at the end of the road. There is a direct road from Gold River to the logging camp at Tahsis.

to and from Gold River: The MV _Uchuck III,_ a passenger-carrying freighter, provides service to Tahsis ($13 OW) twice a week. In July and Aug. there are afternoon trips Mon. and Wed. to Friendly Cove on Nootka Sound ($20 RT). Note however that the _Uchuck III_ is primarily in the business of servicing logging operations and schedules can change suddenly without notice. The printed timetable is often inaccurate and even the driver running the minibus service from Campbell River may give misleading information. Call tel. 283-2325 for confirmation or just go to Gold River for the scenery and consider the boat trip a bonus if you connect. Information on the minibus to Gold River ($7) can be obtained at the Campbell River bus station.

ON BROUGHTON STRAIT

Port McNeill: Just 2 km off the Island Highway, Port McNeill itself has little to offer but is useful as a gateway to several offshore islands. The bus from Campbell River to Port Hardy calls at Port McNeill daily. There's a free, unserviced campsite on the waterfront opposite the ballpark, 2 blocks W of the shopping center. Since there are no official campgounds on the islands, it might be better to make day trips from here. Throughout the

Maquinna, chief of the Nootka: When Captain Cook visited Nootka Sound in 1778 he was so well received by Maquinna that he named the bay facing the Indian village Friendly Cove. Ten years later Maquinna sold a small strip of land here to trader John Meares for 2 pistols. This transaction became the basis of the British claim to this entire coast. In 1792, Maquinna hosted captains Vancouver and Quadra at a great feast. By 1803, however, the Nootka had become a little tired of the double-dealings of white men; after a supposed insult from the captain of the American brig _Boston,_ Maquinna captured the ship and killed all of the crew but two. The Europeanized-likeness of Maquinna above was engraved in Madrid in 1802.

day a ferry crosses Broughton Strait to Sointula and Alert Bay, $1.50 RT. There is no charge for the ferry between Sointula and Alert Bay. All 3 ferry landings are in the center of town. Killer whales are often seen in this strait.

Sointula: On Malcolm Island, this is a friendly little community descended from Finnish settlers who came looking for utopia in the early years of this century. Many still speak Finnish and the blond heads and Nordic landscape make it easy to imagine you're in Scandinavia. The names on the tombstones in the graveyard, 500 m to the R from the ferry, are mostly Finnish. There's a rocky but attractive beach just beyond where you can sit on a log and watch for your ferry.

Alert Bay: Alert Bay, on 5-km-long Cormorant Island near the mouth of the Nimpkish River, was established in 1870 when a salmon saltery

The Victorian influence of English missionaries is seen in Christ Church near the Indian village at Alert Bay.

was set up. In 1878 the Kwakiutl Indian mission was moved from Fort Rupert near Port Hardy to Alert Bay. Today the population of 1,800 is half native Indian, half white. The picturesque town with its large, frame houses and fishing boats winds along the water's edge; the Indian village is to the L of the ferry landing, the white man's town to the right. Alert Bay is probably the most interesting coastal town in northern B.C., but you won't see much about it in the offical tourist brochures because the locals want to keep it to themselves.

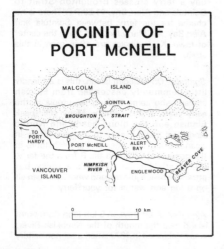

VICINITY OF PORT McNEILL

MALCOLM   ISLAND

SOINTULA

BROUGHTON   STRAIT

TO PORT HARDY

PORT McNEILL

ALERT BAY

VANCOUVER ISLAND

NIMPKISH RIVER

ENGLEWOOD

BEAVER COVE

0   10 km

sights of Alert Bay: The large white building you see at the N end of the waterfront is the former mission school (1929), now the Namgis Band Administration Building. Beside this is the U'mista Cultural Center ($2), open Tues. to Fri. 1000-1700, Sat. 1300-1700. The Center houses the Potlatch Collection, a large assortment of ceremonial objects seized by the Indian agent at Alert Bay in 1921 in an attempt to destroy Indian culture so the natives would be more amenable for missionaries and officials. Many of these objects were returned to the Indians by a more enlightened government in 1980. Back up the hill from the Center, on the N side of the village, is what is said to be "the world's largest totem pole" (53 m), erected in 1973, and a Big House where Indian ceremonies once more take place. On the waterfront between the Cultural Center and the ferry is Christ Church (1879), a premier gingerbread specimen of Victorian architecture. The Nimpkish Burial Grounds are 500 m SE of the ferry, on the waterfront just beyond St. George's Hospital. Twelve large totem poles stand here; a small library and museum (free) are nearby. Several craft shops along the main street sell contemporary Indian art at reasonable prices. A boardwalk has been constructed through the marsh at Alert Bay Ecological Park, locally known as "the swamp." From the waterfront head up the road beside the RCMP, turn first L then right. Follow the road towards the airstrip past the large wireless tower and look for a dirt road turning in on the left. There's a lot to see in Alert Bay, so allow as much time as you can.

PORT HARDY AND VICINITY

Port Hardy, near the N end of Vancouver Island 485 km from Victoria, lives on logging, tourism, and the big Utah copper mine on Rupert Inlet. It's actually just a big village with everything of interest to visitors along a 4-block stretch of Market St. near the fishing wharf. The helpful tourist office in the middle of town has a small museum (free) in back.

stay and eat: The closest official camping area to Port Hardy is the Quaste Municipal Campsite ($6), 4 km from town on the road to Coal Harbor. There are nature trails behind the Pioneer Inn nearby. Wildwoods Campsite ($6) is off the road to Bear Cove, about 3 km from the ferry. There's a Dept. of Highways roadside park near the Bear Cove ferry terminal itself where you could camp in a pinch. The Seagate Hotel beside the wharf downtown has some rooms over the bar in the older building at $22 s, $30 d with bath. Careful planning would eliminate the need for a stop in Port Hardy altogether. Of the restaurants downtown, Han's has Chinese and Vietnamese food. There's also a Mr. Mike's and a couple of fast food places.

from Port Hardy: You can see the new Bear Cove ferry terminal from the waterfront at Port Hardy, but it's 8 km around by road. A minibus ($2) leaves the bus station on Market St. 90 min. prior to all ferry sailings, a convenient connection. If you call tel. 949-6300, they will pick you up from the Quaste Campsite at no extra cost. This minibus and the big Pacific Coach Lines buses to Port McNeill ($4), Campbell River ($21) and Victoria ($37) also meet most arrivals of the ferry from Prince Rupert. The B.C. Ferries service from Port Hardy to Prince Rupert ($45) runs almost daily in the summer, a beautiful trip up the almost uninhabited middle Inside Passage. Once a week they stop at Ocean Falls and Bella Bella ($30 OW). Any tourist office in B.C. will have a schedule of sailings; there's always room for walk-on passengers. The ferries are large and clean, with plenty of space to spread out a sleeping bag. They are far less crowded than the better-known Alaska Marine Highway ships, yet the journey is equally as gratifying. Prices for food on board are not unreasonable. Try the clam chowder in the cafeteria! Air B.C. has a flight to Bella Bella ($86 OW) Mon. to Friday.

Cape Scott: Cape Scott Provincial Park, 60 km W of Port Hardy by road at the NW tip of Vancouver Island, can only be entered on foot. A trail leads 20 km to Nels Bight Beach on the N, the best in the park. Cape Scott itself is 28 km from the end of the road. Wilderness camping is permitted anywhere in the park, but be prepared for wet weather and winds. Bring all you'll need.

Hamatsa raven mask: The Kwakiutl Indians of coastal B.C. painted these huge, 1½-m-long dance masks black, red, and white. Shredded cedar bark fell to the shoulders; a long cape covered the body. The spectacle of a line of squatting dancers, masks swinging from side to side, hinged beaks opening and clapping shut to the beat of their batons, must have been overwhelming.

PRINCE RUPERT AND THE NORTH COAST

THE NORTH COAST

the middle Inside Passage: The 400-km ferry ride from Port Hardy to Prince Rupert takes about 20 hours; the northern half of the journey is the more spectacular. Try to pick a departure that travels during daylight. This part of the Inside Passage is still unequivocal wilderness. There are no cottages, logging, roads, or people. Some of the ferries stop at Ocean Falls and Bella Bella, but it is impractical to get off as you might have to wait a week for another boat. Ocean Falls, which gets its name from the impressive waterfalls draining Link Lake into Cousins Inlet, once had a large papermill. Bella Bella is a large Indian village which all of the coastal ferries pass. Watch for the cannery at Namu, the first settlement you see on the way north.

Port Simpson: This small Coast Tsimshian settlement 30 km N of Prince Rupert was founded as a Hudson Bay Company trading post in 1834. William Duncan, of Metlakatla fame (see below), served as the missionary here until 1862. The Grand Trunk Railway terminus was to have been here until it was decided that a better harbor was situated at Kaien Island. Today the town lives on government handouts and a fish processing plant which is owned by the Indians. Basic food and accommodations are available at Mrs. Clausen's store. *getting there:* A small passenger boat leaves the wharf just N of Prince Rupert railway station Mon. and Fri. at

0900, leaving Port Simpson to return at 1130, $3.50 OW. North Coast Air Services (tel. 627-1351) at Seal Cove in Prince Rupert has a seaplane service to Port Simpson ($20 OW) 4 times a day, allowing you to take the ferry up, sightsee, and fly back for a reasonable price.

others: The boat up Portland Inlet to the Indian village of Kincolith ($7 OW) leaves from the wharf just N of Prince Rupert railway station, Mon. to Fri. at 0800. Call tel. 624-9627 for reservations. After unloading passengers, the boat returns to Prince Rupert immediately. There is no longer any ferry up the spectacular Portland Canal to Stewart. 200 km NE of Stewart is Spatsizi Plateau Wilderness Provincial Park where jet-set head hunters are helicoptered in to shoot the increasingly rare stone sheep.

PRINCE RUPERT

Prince Rupert is a medium-sized city at the N end of the Canadian portion of the Inside Passage where ferry, road, and rail routes converge. Many Alaska-bound travelers pass through the city, which is also a gateway to the Queen Charlotte Islands, Vancouver Island, and the Canadian interior. In 1906, this site on Kaien Island near the mouth of the Skeena River was selected as the terminus of Canada's second trans-continental railroad, the Grand Trunk Pacific, which arrived in 1914. Prince Rupert's role as a transportation hub has spawned numerous canneries, a monstrous pulp mill, and trans-shipment terminals for much of Canada's grain and coal. Fortunately for sightseers, most of the industrial installations are far from the downtown area.

sights of Prince Rupert: Start with a visit to the Museum of Northern B.C. (free) which features Indian artifacts, old photos of Metlakatla, and displays relating to the early history of Prince Rupert. The tourist information office in the same building is very helpful. Walk right around the courthouse beside the museum to enjoy the attractive gardens and scenic views. The "sunken gardens" behind the courthouse were an ammunition dump during WW II. Nearby in the Pride O' The North Mall is the North Coast Fishing Exhibit (free) which tells you everything you'd ever want to know about the subject—and then some. There are sometimes free movies and slide shows here (closed Sunday). From the city hall in the center of town, make your way up the hill towards Roosevelt Park. Prince Rupert was an important Allied transportation base during WW II and at one time 7,000 U.S. soldiers slept in the barracks on this hill. On a clear day there are good views of the city and harbor from the park. The totem poles you see all over Prince Rupert are mostly copies of old poles now lost or in museums.

to the seaplane base: Take the no. 51 Seal Cove bus (40 cents) from 2nd Ave. W and 3rd St. (every 30 min. Mon. to Sat.) to the seaplane base at the end of the line. The road SE from the bus stop leads past a series of abandoned WW II ammunition bunkers to the Dept. of Fisheries wharf. After a look at the seaplanes, walk back to the corner where the bus turns, and continue straight ahead past a PRIVATE PROPERTY sign along an abandoned railway line. This line follows the shoreline below a high, wooded bluff, back past the small boat harbor to Cow Bay and cannery row.

up Mount Hays: The best day hike near Prince Rupert is to the top of Mount Hays (732 m) along a dirt road beginning beside the new Civic Center swimming pool (open daily, $2). The easy way to do it is to take the cable car ($5), then follow the T-bar lift up to the road which leads to the radio towers on top of the mountain. The cable car only operates during July and Aug., or when a cruise ship is in. The tourist office will know about this. If you

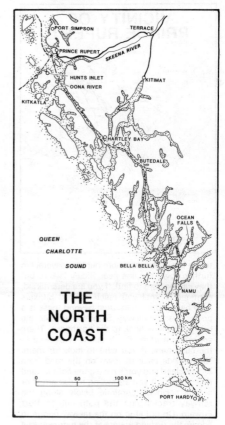

decide to walk both ways, allow at least 4 hours and have a good breakfast. On a clear day there are unsurpassed views in every direction from viewpoints all along the way. To really appreciate it you have to do this walk on foot. The city dump, just below the cable car terminal, is the best place in town to see bald eagles.

around Kaien Island: About 2 km S of the Alaska/B.C. ferries terminal is an overgrown concrete bunker and gun emplacement built during WW II to protect Prince Rupert from a Japanese naval strike. A hike this way also offers excellent views of Chatham Sound and the surrounding waterways. Follow the railway tracks S past 2 NO TRESPASSING signs and keep going until you see the bunker above you

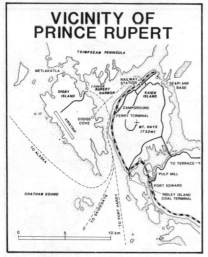

VICINITY OF PRINCE RUPERT

TSIMPSEAN PENINSULA

METLAKATLA

DIGBY ISLAND

PRINCE RUPERT HARBOR

RAILWAY STATION

SEAPLANE BASE

KAIEN ISLAND

CAMPGROUND

FERRY TERMINAL

DODGE COVE

MT. HAYS (732m)

TO TERRACE →

TO ALASKA

CHATHAM SOUND

PULP MILL

PORT EDWARD

RIDLEY ISLAND COAL TERMINAL

TO SKIDEGATE

TO PORT HARDY

0   5   10 km

to the left. There are more bunkers several km further down the line near Ridley Island, but they can be hard to find. If you are determined, continue S until you reach 3 small bunkers right beside the tracks. Just beyond these is a bridge over the railway. Scramble up onto the bridge and look back to the northwest. There are many wartime fortifications swallowed in the bush here, if you care to look for them. Hitch a ride back to town on the road from Ridley island and you'll have gone right around Kaien Island. If you are willing to risk arrest or a fatal accident, continue boldly along the railway tracks past the pulp mill to Port Edward. Do not stop on the railway bridge to admire the rushing waters at the narrows, as a sudden train could spell your end. The old canneries at Port Edward have now closed, but the fishing fleet still ties up here for lack of alternative facilities.

Digby Island: The island you see to the L as your ferry arrives in Prince Rupert is Digby Island, site of an old Norwegian settlement. Many of the old houses remain, as does Wahl's Boatyard (now closed) at Dodge Cove, where wooden fishing boats were once built. There's an old wharf and more dilapidated buildings at Casey Cove, the next bay over. *getting there:* A small ferry leaves from the wharf just N of Prince Rupert railway station Tues. at 1200, Fri. at 1000, and Sat. at 1030, $1 OW. There is an afternoon sailing for the return trip to Prince Rupert.

Metlakatla: The small Indian village of Metlakatla, 8 km W of Prince Rupert by boat, was founded in 1862 by Anglican missionary William Duncan on an ancient Tsimshian site. A sawmill and trading post were set up and these native people became prosperous and self supporting. The church Duncan built in 1874 seated 1,200 people and, at the time, was the largest W of Chicago and N of San Francisco. In later years Duncan came into conflict with Church authorities who wanted to impose the elaborate Episcopalian ritual on the Indians. When Duncan demurred, the Episcopal bishop had local officials seize the land on which the mission was built in an attempt to force Duncan to obey. Instead, Duncan traveled to Washington D.C. and asked permission for the Tsimshians to homestead in Alaska. In 1887, Duncan led 823 Indians to Annette Island, Alaska, where they founded a new Metlakatla (see "Metlakatla" in the "Southeast Alaska" chapter for details). Metlakatla, B.C. burned in 1901 and today there are no structures remaining from Duncan's time. *getting there:* The only scheduled service from Prince Rupert to Metlakatla is on the *Sisayda Lady* which leaves the Standard Oil (Chevron) wharf Mon. to Fri. at 1130. The boat returns immediately after unloading passengers at Metlakatla, so there

Missionary William Duncan converted the Tsimshians into model Christians, but obliterated all trace of Indian culture in the process.

The Alaska and B.C. ferries meet at the terminal in the lower foreground; the road to the right leads 5 km to the city of Prince Rupert.

won't be any time to walk around. Still, at $3 RT it's an enjoyable quick glimpse of the village and its inhabitants. Note that the *Sisayda Lady* has only 35 seats and that schoolchildren and village residents get priority over tourists on this government-subsidized run.

stay: The only official place to put up a tent is the Park Ave. Municipal Campground, a 10-min. walk from the ferry terminal up the road into town. The cost is $8 per tent—on the expensive side. There are several inexpensive hotels if you'd like a roof over your head. Your first choice should be Pioneer Rooms, 167 3rd Ave. E, (tel. 624-2334), which is homey and friendly. Rates are $15 s, $20 d. The Commercial Hotel, 901 1st Ave. W (tel. 624-6142), is clean and comfortable, but can get a little noisy. Similar accommodations are available at the Ocean View Hotel, 950 1st Ave. W (tel. 624-6259), the Islander Hotel, 830 2nd Ave. W (tel. 624-4027), and the Savoy

Hotel, 316 5th St. (tel. 624-6751). Rooms at these 4 cost $16-19 s, $16-28 d, and all have weekly rates which are the equivalent of about 3 nights at the daily rate.

eats and entertainment: Two of the better fast-food chains have branches in Pride 'O The North Mall: Smitty's Pancake House is good for breakfast (try the buckwheat pancakes with the fancy topping); Mr. Mike's for lunch or dinner. Vimar Delicatessen beside Mr. Mike's has good sandwiches at lunchtime. All 3 above offer a bottomless cup of coffee. Also try the cafe in the Islander Hotel. The pub in the Commercial Hotel serves pizza. The most popular drinking spot is the lounge in the Prince Rupert Hotel, where there is also dancing. Don't have too many beers before catching the 2030 bus to Prince George or the driver won't let you on. Across the street at 703 2nd Ave. W is TJ's, which has live rock bands weekends. For movies it's the Capitol Theater, 515 3rd Ave. W, nightly at 1900 and

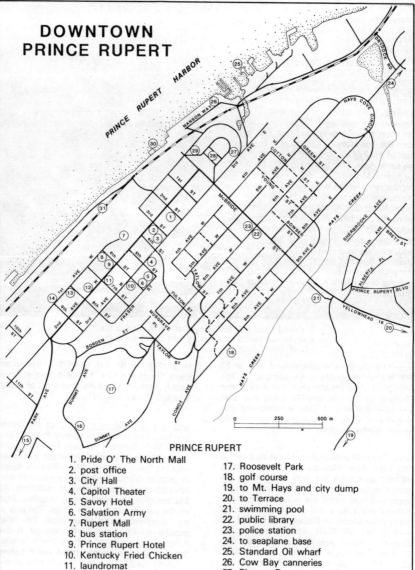

DOWNTOWN PRINCE RUPERT

PRINCE RUPERT

1. Pride O' The North Mall
2. post office
3. City Hall
4. Capitol Theater
5. Savoy Hotel
6. Salvation Army
7. Rupert Mall
8. bus station
9. Prince Rupert Hotel
10. Kentucky Fried Chicken
11. laundromat
12. Islander Hotel
13. Commercial Hotel
14. Ocean View Hotel
15. to Alaska/B.C. ferries
16. hospital
17. Roosevelt Park
18. golf course
19. to Mt. Hays and city dump
20. to Terrace
21. swimming pool
22. public library
23. police station
24. to seaplane base
25. Standard Oil wharf
26. Cow Bay canneries
27. Pioneer Rooms
28. courthouse
29. museum/tourist office
30. local ferry wharf
31. railway station

2100 ($5). There are free movies at the public library Mon. to Fri. at 1300 and 1900, Sat. at 1300.

FROM PRINCE RUPERT

by air: CP Air has jet service from the airport (YPR) on Digby Island. The ferry to the airport, leaving from beside the Alaska Marine Highway terminal, is a bit of a ripoff at $6 for the short trip. Actually, you can take a bus from the downtown air terminal in the lower level of the Rupert Mall right to the airport for the same price. This bus connects with all CP Air flights. More adventurous than the jets are the seaplanes which leave from Seal Cove (see "to the seaplane base" above for bus service). Trans Provincial Airlines (tel. 627-1341) has service to Ketchikan ($55), Masset ($48), and Bella Bella ($114). The Masset service operates twice daily, permitting you to combine sea, land, and air travel on a visit to the Queen Charlotte Islands (ferry to Skidegate, hitch to Masset, seaplane back to Prince Rupert). For information on North Coast Air Services see "Port Simpson" above.

by sea: B.C. Ferries has almost daily service in the summer to Port Hardy ($45), and weekly to Ocean Falls and Bella Bella ($30). The ferry to Skidegate in the Queen Charlotte Islands ($10.50) runs 3 times a week. The Alaska Marine Highway has daily ferry service in the summer to Ketchikan and all SE Alaska points. Alaska ferry passengers clear U.S. Customs and Immigration in Prince Rupert before boarding. Get a timetable and study up a little before going to the ticket office at the terminal. Buy a ticket from Prince Rupert to your furthest destination and request free stopover coupons for all the ports you wish to visit along the way. If you want them all, request Prince Rupert-Ketchikan-Wrangell-Petersburg-Sitka-Juneau-Haines-Skagway. If you'd like to visit Metlakatla, Alaska, buy a ticket Prince Rupert-Metlakatla, then Metlakatla-Skagway (for example). This would be US$11 cheaper than Prince Rupert-Skagway (US$90) with a sidetrip to Metlakatla. The B.C. and Alaska ferry landings are side-by-side at Fairview, 5 km SW of downtown Prince Rupert. A shuttle bus ($1) meets all B.C. Ferries arrivals, but not arrivals from Alaska. City bus service to the ferry is erratic, although bus nos. 52 and 54 (no service Sun.) go as far as Pillsbury Ave. which is near. Ask at the cafe opposite the ferry terminal about bus times. There are coin lockers in the B.C. Ferries terminal.

by rail and road: Via Rail (tel. 112-800-665-8630) has a train from Prince Rupert to Prince George, B.C. ($34), 3 times a week. You leave in the morning and travel during daylight along the historic Skeena River route. Get a window seat on the R for the best views. Greyhound Lines, 1st Ave. W and 6th St., has 2 buses daily to Prince George, B.C., with connections to any point in Canada and the U.S. Bus fares in Canada are generally lower than U.S. fares, so if your destination is New York, for example, buy a ticket to Montreal ($99) and another to New York when you get to Montreal. Incidentally, the ticket to Beaver Creek, Yukon, is also $99. There are no coin lockers in the bus station, but there are many just across the parking lot opposite in the CP Air terminal at the Rupert Mall.

Tsimshian eagle crest

Haida village at Skidegate (1878)

THE QUEEN CHARLOTTE ISLANDS

The once-remote Queen Charlotte Islands form a chain 300 km long, 80 km off the Canadian mainland at the western edge of the Continental Shelf. Although there are 150 islands in all, the 2 largest, Graham and Moresby, account for most of the groups's land area. Narrow Skidegate Channel slices these 2 apart near the middle of the group. Snowcapped mountains run down the W coast of the archipelago, with a wide area of lowland and rolling hillside on the E towards the middle and top. For the most part, the Queen Charlotte Islands are an empty, wild, natural land where eagles and deer still outnumber people, and where it is still possible to find plenty of untouched wilderness. If you are looking for a unique experience, this is the place.

history: Juan Perez, the European discoverer, first sighted the islands in 1774; however, the Charlottes have been the homeland of the Haida Indians for centuries. The Haidas built the largest canoes on the Pacific coast, which they used for whaling and raiding. Missionaries and white officials proscribed the art and customs of the Haidas; by 1915 cultural degeneration and European diseases had reduced their numbers from 8,000 to 588. Today their descendants live in Haida village, near Masset, and in Skidegate. 5,000 whites also inhabit the group, mostly along Skidegate and Masset inlets.

SIGHTS OF THE QUEEN CHARLOTTES

near the ferry: The Queen Charlotte Islands Museum ($2), just 500 m E of the ferry landing, is open 1300-1700 daily. The museum has a good collection of Haida argillite carvings, century-old totem poles, and stuffed birds. 350 Haida Indians live in Skidegate village, 2½ km beyond the museum. The new Band Administrative Building (open Mon. to Fri. 1400-1600) on the waterfront, built in the form of a traditional longhouse, is totally modern inside. One old totem pole stands alongside. Queen Charlotte City, a focal point for tourists and bureaucrats, is 7 km W of the ferry.

Sandspit: The Ministry of Highways ferry to Moresby Island (50 cents OW) leaves hourly from the Skidegate ferry terminal. It's 13 km by paved road from the landing on Moresby to Sandspit, a logging town with good beaches. If you arrive in the Charlottes in the late afternoon, spend your first night camping on a beach on Moresby. Sandspit also boasts the only airstrip (YZP) in the group. The protected lower E side of Moresby is a still unknown paradise for canoeists and kayakers. On Anthony Island, off the SW coast of Moresby, standing Haida totems rot.

Naikoon Park: Naikoon Provincial Park covers a large flat area in the NE corner of Graham Island. The easiest way to get the feel of the park is to hitch N to the Tlell River bridge, then hike 4 km along the N shore of the river to the beach. Camping is permitted but there are no stores at Tlell or near the ferry landing, so bring everything you'll need from Prince Rupert. A couple of km up the beach is the wreck of the *Pesuta,* a log barge grounded during a fierce storm in 1928. It is possible to hike up the beach from Tlell River to Tow Hill in about 5 days. It's unlikely you'll meet anyone along the way. Tow Hill is 26 km E of Masset along a gravel road. Three trails begin by the Heillen River bridge at the base of the hill. The hardest is the Cape Fife Trail (10 km) which cuts across to the E side of the island. The Blowhole Trail (1 km) leads down to fantastic rock formations by the shore and a view of the spectacular basalt cliff on the N side of Tow Hill (109 m). The 3rd trail leads up to the top of Tow Hill for a view of the grey sandy beaches which arch in both directions along the N coast of Graham Island for as far as you can see. *camping:* There is an established campground (windy) beside the road just W of Tow Hill, but backcountry camping is allowed anywhere in Naikoon Park.

other towns: Masset, 113 km N of Queen Charlotte City by paved road, lives on fishing and income from a Canadian military base here. Three km N of Masset at the mouth of Masset Sound is Haida village, with 500 Indians and a couple of totem poles. Port Clements is a bustling little logging town with a long pier out into Masset Inlet.

PRACTICALITIES

stay and eat: There are several hotels and restaurants in Queen Charlotte City which cater to tourists, but these tend to be expensive. You could camp among the trees

QUEEN CHARLOTTE ISLANDS

Queen Charlotte Islands: Captain George Dixon named these islands in 1787. In expectation of an influx of American miners following local gold discoveries, James Douglas was appointed first Lieutenant-Governor of the Queen Charlottes in 1852. Six years later the islands were annexed to the mainland colony of British Columbia.

just before the cemetery at the end of the paved road beyond Queen Charlotte City, 10 km W of the ferry landing, or on the beach beside the highway N of the Skidegate Indian reservation. Go at least 2 km beyond the village. Elsewhere on the islands campsites are easier to find. There are small grocery stores in Sandspit, Queen Charlotte City, Skidegate village, Port Clements, and Masset.

transport: There is no public transportation. The locals are good about picking up hitchhikers, but cars can be few. Tilden Car

Rental, 200 m E of the Skidegate ferry landing, has Datsuns for $28 a day, plus 10 cents a km, plus $5 insurance, plus 6 percent tax. Check the spare tire to make sure it's not flat. *getting there:* Trans Provincial Airlines has a seaplane service from Prince Rupert to Masset ($48) twice daily. Most people arrive on the excellent B.C. Ferries service from Prince Rupert to Skidegate landing ($10.50) which runs 3 times a week. The ferries make a 6-hour stopover at Skidegate, enough time to see the museum and Indian village if you don't want to stay. While a quick RT is certainly better than nothing, campers and naturalists will want to spend longer in the islands.

Kwakiutl ceremonial design

above, clockwise: Ron Brockman at Wiseman, AK (National Park Service photo by Joe Standart); kayaker on the Noatak River, AK (National Park Service photo by M. Woodbridge Williams); Eskimo women at Shishmauf, AK (National Park Service photo by Robert Belous); ferry passengers at Auke Bay, AK (Alaska Marine Highway); Rocky at Ketchikan, AK (Division of Tourism)

above, clockwise: Vancouver, BC (Greater Vancouver Convention and Visitors Bureau photo by Al Harvey); Creek St., Ketchikan, AK (U.S. Forest Service); Parliament Buildings, Victoria, BC (Tourism B.C.); Russian Orthodox church, St. Paul, Pribilof Islands, AK (ATMS photo by Bob Giersdorf); Broadway, Skagway, AK (National Park Service)

above, clockwise: west coast of Vancouver Island N of Tofino, BC (Tourism B.C.); purse seiner at Hoonah, AK (Larry K. Lowie); canoeists in the Kenai National Wildlife Refuge, AK (U.S. Fish and Wildlife Service); Trans-Provincial Airlines amphibians (Prince Rupert Visitors Bureau photo by L. Reid); Craig, AK (U.S. Forest Service)

above, clockwise: brown bear (U.S. Fish and Wildlife Service photo by Jon Nickles); horned puffin (U.S. Fish and Wildlife Service photo by Art Sowls); musk ox (U.S. Fish and Wildlife Service); Dall sheep rams (Division of Tourism); hummingbird in its nest, Queen Charlotte Islands (Tourism B.C.)

SOUTHEAST ALASKA

INTRODUCTION

The long tongue of Alaska stretching down the western coast of North America almost all the way to Prince Rupert, B.C., was once known as the Alaskan Panhandle. Now it is simply called 'Southeast.' This is a land of spectacular natural beauty: deep fjords drive up between snowcapped mountains; waterfalls plummet hundreds of meters through the evergreen forests to feed waters rich in salmon and whales; bald eagles perch on the treetops beside the rugged, rocky coastline; great blue glaciers push down toward the sea. Not quite surrounded by British Columbia, 60 percent of Southeast consists of precarious, much indented mainland, 40 percent islands. The Islands are known collectively as the Alexander Archipelago. Over 1,000 of them are named, the largest being Revillagigedo, Prince of Wales, Kupreanof, Baranof, Chichagof, and Admiralty. The names reflect the Spaniards, Englishmen, and Russians who explored the area. Southeast corresponds almost exactly to the ancestral homeland of the Tlingit (pronounced KLINK-IT) Indians, and signs of their culture, both authentic and visitor-oriented, are common. Today, a full 95 percent of Southeast is federally owned, much of it included in the Tongass National Forest (6.9 million ha.). This is the largest national forest in the U.S. (the Chugach National Forest with 2.5 million ha. in Southcentral Alaska is second). The lush, ever-present rainforests abound in Sitka spruce, hemlock, and some cedar. Alpine tundra begins above tree line at the 1,200-m level. The whole region is bathed in an almost continuous rainfall; the locals call it 'liquid sunshine.' Ketchikan gets 3,941 mm of it a year, but it decreases as you travel N to only 660 mm annually at Skagway. You can always tell a local by his/her red rubber boots. The people live in isolated towns and villages squeezed between the narrow waterways and high, forested hillsides. The main industries are fishing and lumbering. Every summer the area is flooded with young Americans looking for jobs in canneries and on fishing boats. Accommodations are tight. Once you forsake camping and youth hostels, expect to pay a minimum of $30 s, $35 d for a stark room with shared bath and no discounts or weekly rates.

Erecting your own nylon stateroom on deck in the heated solarium is common practice on the long journey north from Seattle to Alaska.

There are almost no exceptions to this rule. Fortunately, campgrounds are plentiful and youth hostels exist in the main towns. Camping is freely allowed anywhere in the national forest, except day-use areas. Camping on public land within city limits is usually prohibited, so keep out of sight.

getting there: Since only Haines and Skagway are connected to the North American road network, travel within Southeast is by sea or air. The lack of roads (hopefully they will never be built) has led to an efficient public ferry system, the best in the Western Hemisphere and longest in the world. The Alaska Marine Highway services 7 major ports in Southeast, Ketchikan, Wrangell, Petersburg, Sitka, Juneau, Haines and Skagway, and 7 minor ports, Metlakatla, Hollis, Kake, Angoon, Tenakee Springs, Hoonah and Pelican. Most of the ferries sail between Prince Rupert, B.C., and Skagway, although there is a weekly service from Seattle to Skagway. The larger towns enjoy almost daily service during the summer. Fares are reasonable. For example, a foot passenger will pay US$155 Seattle-Skagway, or US$90 Prince Rupert-Skagway. Stopovers are free, but you must acquire stopover passes for each port you wish to visit. If in doubt, ask for all 7

major ports when you buy your ticket. Ferries out of Seattle require reservations and are much more crowded than those which begin in Prince Rupert. If you find you can't get on in Seattle, take a ferry to Victoria, bus to Port Hardy, and ferry to Prince Rupert. This will cost slightly more, but will be far more exciting. (See 'British Columbia' for other options). Foot passengers do not require reservations out of Prince Rupert or within Southeast. Bicycles are carried on the ferries at no extra charge.

life onboard: The ferry route through Southeast Alaska is one of the most spectacular of its kind in the world and the Alaska Marine Highway is one of the best travel bargains anywhere. Most young travelers and backpackers think of the ferry as a 'floating motel'—a place to dry off, wash up, relax, sleep, and meet other travelers, while at the same time moving on to new sights, new adventures. Services are excellent. There are free hot showers and reasonably-priced (for Alaska) cafeterias and bars on the ferries. There is plenty of space to stretch out a sleeping bag in the recliner lounge, an inside area with airline-type seats, and solarium. The solarium is a more open area on the top deck, complete with deck chairs for sunning and

SOUTHEAST ALASKA

ATLIN

SKAGWAY

BEN-MY-CHREE

HAINES

GLACIER BAY
NATIONAL
PARK

LYNN CANAL

MENDENHALL
GLACIER

GUSTAVUS

ICY BAY

JUNEAU

PELICAN

HOONAH

TENAKEE
SPRINGS

ADMIRALTY
ISLAND
NATIONAL
MONUMENT

CHICHAGOF
ISLAND

ANGOON

TRACY
ARM

STEPHENS PASSAGE

TELEGRAPH
CREEK

COAST

CANADA
UNITED STATES

MT. EDGECUMBE

SITKA

BARANOF
ISLAND

CHATHAM STRAIT

FREDERICK SOUND

KAKE

KUPREANOF
ISLAND

LE CONTE
GLACIER

PETERSBURG

MOUNTAINS

GULF
OF
ALASKA

SUMNER STRAIT

WRANGELL

CLARENCE STRAIT

PRINCE
OF WALES
IS.

THORNE
BAY

KLAWOCK

CRAIG
HOLLIS

HYDER

STEWART

MISTY
FJORDS
NATIONAL
MONUMENT

REVILLAGIGEDO
ISLAND

BEHM CANAL

PORTLAND CANAL

KETCHIKAN

HYDABURG

METLAKATLA

KINCOLITH

PORT
SIMPSON

the Inside Passage: This sheltered waterway stretches 1,750 km N from Seattle, Washington, to Skagway, Alaska. The deep, protected channel allows smooth sailing, although strong tidal currents build up in the narrows. The entire route is flanked by a chain of mountainous islands which complement the icecapped peaks seen inland. Prevailing winds drop a deluge of rainfall on these mountains, creating lush forests and primeval beauty. Two efficient ferry lines service the Inside Passage, making this whole marvelous region easily accessible to travelers.

ALASKA MARINE HIGHWAY

M/V COLUMBIA	
M/V TUSTUMENA	M/V MALASPINA
M/V BARTLETT	M/V MATANUSKA
M/V CHILKAT	M/V TAKU
M/V LE CONTE	

0   100   200 km

sleeping (a stateroom is unnecessary). Most young backpackers head straight for the solarium which is heated when it's cold out. Enjoy fresh air and good views of the scenery and wildlife from up here. Tents may be erected in the solarium for the long journey up from Seattle. In the recliner lounge, avoid sitting near the TV sets as the purser may decide to put on a loud, inane movie or cartoon which you'll have to bear. Besides the purser providing 'entertainment,' a shipboard naturalist from the U.S. Forest Service

conducts an educational program (talks and films) on all ferries during the summer. The naturalists have free maps and brochures on the area and are storehouses of information. About the only hassle in the whole scene is the lack of coin lockers in most terminals. However, you can often leave luggage in a hotel lobby or at a taxi stand (if you ask nicely), or under a chair in the ferry terminal (at your own risk). A chain and padlock come in handy here. A heartfelt gratuity for anyone especially helpful never does any harm.

Tlingit rattle

KETCHIKAN

Ketchikan (pop. 7,189 in 1980) is built on a steep slope along the Tongass Narrows on Revillagigedo (RAY-VEE-YA-HE-HAY-DO) Island, 145 km N of Prince Rupert. Forty hours out of Seattle, this is the first stop in the 49th State, and its busy frontier flavor will satisfy most travelers' Alaskan expectations. The town is a narrow continuous strip along the waterfront from the ferry terminal over 4 km to beyond Thomas Basin. Much of Ketchikan is built on piles over the water, or is perched on the hillside with wooden ramps for streets. Downtown is on a flat area at the mouth of Ketchikan Creek, a rich salmon stream that drew fishermen to establish a cannery here in 1885. Fishing boats jam the Small Boat Harbor and the canneries are still at full throttle during the season. There is a large pulp mill 12 km N where spruce are processed and shipped out to Japan. Today, a hilltop above Ketchikan owned by the Cape Fox Indian Corporation is being ripped apart for a luxury hotel and condominium housing for the rich. Ketchikan and vicinity has more totem poles than anywhere else in the world, symbols of an enduring native culture. The area is also one of

the rainiest places in Alaska. Luckily, May to Aug. are the driest months, but expect to get wet!

SIGHTS OF KETCHIKAN

downtown: Begin at the Forest Service Visitor Center in the Federal Building (open Mon. to Fri. 0730-1700) which has a small display on the Tongass National Forest and gives out maps and brochures. The local historical museum (free) in the library building nearby is open Mon., Tues., Thurs., and Fri. 1100-1700, Sat. and Sun. 1300-1600. From the parking lot beside the museum, cross the footbridge over Ketchikan Creek and find your way along the picturesque trestle boardwalk that is Creek Street. This was once a thriving red-light district, the only place in Alaska 'where both fishermen and fish went upstream to spawn,' but the city has now cleaned up the area for tourists. There's even a brothel museum, Dolly's House ($2), which memorializes the era. For something spicier, continue on a little further to the Shamrock Bar (Chapel by the

Sea) on Stedman Street. Plenty of nude dancers and hot action at the Shamrock, day and night. The Small Boat Harbor is just across the street. Turn R on Thomas St. just beyond the Salvation Army and go out to the end of the boardwalk for a good view of the fishing boats and spruce mill behind. Further down Stedman St. notice the colorful mural on the side of Ketchikan Community College. A short walk up Deermount St. is the Totem Heritage Center (open 0900-1700, Sun. 1300-1700, closed Wed., admission $1 but free on Sunday). This novel center preserves old totem poles brought in from abandoned Indian village sites. Unlike most of the other poles around Ketchikan which are restorations or copies, these totems were carved long ago to record the events and legends of the Haida and Tlingit peoples. Ask to see the video programs which tell the story. Just across a footbridge from the Heritage Center is Deer Mountain Hatchery where the process of breeding and rearing salmon is clearly explained and illustrated. The salmon arrive from the Pacific Ocean to spawn at the hatchery up Ketchikan Creek late in the summer. A fish ladder to help them get past the rapids is visible from the Park Ave. bridge.

VICINITY OF KETCHIKAN

Saxman Totem Park

Deer Mountain: The best hike from Ketchikan is up to the summit of Deer Mountain (915 m). Allow a minimum of 2 hours for the ascent, one hour for the descent (although you'll probably take longer). Begin by following the dirt road up towards the city dump from Deermount and Fair streets. The trail begins near the point where the road divides. (The road to the L goes on 2 km to the Ketchikan Lakes, source of the town's drinking water.) You'll see the trailhead. There is an incredible view in all directions from the top of Deer Mountain, but right into July you'll have to cross snow banks to reach the summit. Just before the final climb to the peak, a trail to the L leads around the N slope and on to Blue Lake (808 m) and John Mountain (987 m). There are Forest Service A-frame cabins at Deer Mountain (below the N slope beyond the fork) and at Blue Lake. Up to 8 hikers may stay in each free of charge on a first-come first-served basis. There are also places to camp near the summit of Deer Mountain and at Blue Lake. Although a lot of people make it to the top of Deer Mountain on a clear summer day, very few go on to Blue Lake as this is a strenuous full day RT from Ketchikan.

totem viewing: A collection of 25 large standing totem poles can be seen at Saxman Totem Park (free), 4 km SE of town. One of the poles is surmounted by a woody likeness of Abraham Lincoln! Totem Bight State

KETCHIKAN

KETCHIKAN

1. Bed of Rose's Hostel
2. Arctic Bar
3. Outdoor Alaska
4. totem pole
5. youth hostel
6. bus stop
7. Gilmore Hotel
8. tourist office
9. Pioneer Cafe
10. branch post office
11. Alaska World Travel
12. Voyageur Bookstore
13. Knickerbocker Hotel
14. fish ladder
15. library/museum
16. Forest Service Visitor Center
17. Shamrock Bar
18. Ketchikan Community College
19. supermarket
20. The Drift In
21. Totem Heritage Center
22. Deer Mountain Hatchery

Historical Park, 16 km NW of town, has 15 Haida and Tlingit totems, plus an authentic replica of a clan house complete with a brightly painted facade. The totems, carved from 1938 to 1941, are replicas of old poles; several are very well done. There's also an attractive hemlock forest and a scenic view of the Tongass Narrows. Open daily 0600-2200, free. *note:* There is no bus service to either of these sites, so you must walk or hitch.

Ward Lake area: There's an enjoyable nature trail around Ward Lake, 12 km NW of town, which anyone can do in less than an hour. The Perseverance Trail is a 4-km boardwalk leading up to Perseverance Lake. The trail begins to the R of the road, just beyond Ward Lake. Allow 2 hours for the RT. About 3½ km further up a road to the R is Connell Lake with a swampy trail along the N shore from the dam to Talbot Lake.

And don't forget the Shamrock Bar, mentioned earlier, for a hot night on the town.

PRACTICALITIES

stay: The First Methodist Church Youth Hostel, Grant and Main, provides sleeping space for $2.25. You must do a housekeeping chore. The hostel closes from 0830-1900 and is only open 1 June to 1 September. Very friendly, with free coffee and hot chocolate, it's a good place to meet other travelers. No one is ever turned away. The Bed of Roses Hostel just before the tunnel offers similar accommodations for $10 pp. There's an acute housing shortage in Ketchikan, so most of the cheaper hotels are permanently full of tenants who pay by the month. You could try the Knickerbocker Hotel, 421 Dock Street. The manager lives in room four. The only old hotel where you won't have trouble getting a room is the Gilmore, which charges $32 s, $40 d plus 7 percent tax (bath down the hall). Weekly rates start at $187.

camping: The Forest Service has 4 campgrounds near Ketchikan. The Settlers Cove Campground is on the coast 26 km N of the ferry terminal, the last 5 km on a dirt road. The other 3 are near Ward Lake. Get to these by hitching or walking along the main highway NW from the ferry terminal to the pulp mill (7 km), then following a dirt road one km to Signal Creek Campground which is right beside Ward Lake. If Signal Creek is full, the CCC Campground is only 500 m further down the road. The Last Chance Campground is 2 km beyond that. All charge $4 per site per day, and you must have exact change with you. A night or two in this area is recommended for the many hikes which are available. Consider going up and spending your first night in Ketchikan at one of these campgrounds, right after you get off the ferry. Some travelers camp in the bush at the foot of Deer Mountain. There would be a lot less damage to the environment here if the Forest Service created an official backpackers' campground in the area.

eats and entertainment: There are no real stand-outs here, but you might try the places in the mall beside the Gilmore Hotel for good pastries, soup and salad. The Drift Inn, Stedman and Deermount, has tasty takeaway fries. The Arctic Bar near the tunnel is recommended for cheap beer and snacks.

transport: The ferry terminal is 4 km NW of the town center. You can buy ferry tickets at Alaska World Travel downtown. The city bus ($1) runs from town out to the ferry terminal every half hour Mon. to Sat. 0730-1700; catch it at the corner of Front and Grant in town. There is no other bus route. There are no coin lockers at the ferry terminal, but they let you leave bags in their office. Ketchikan Airport (KTN) is on Gravina Island, directly across the narrows from the ferry. The airport ferry charges $1.75 RT. All the seaplane operators (Revilla Flying Service, SEA Airlines, Taquan Air Service, Tyee Airlines) land in the narrows beside Tongass Ave., between the ferry terminal and downtown.

PLACES NEAR KETCHIKAN

Misty Fjords National Monument: Misty Fjords is a remote wilderness park, 65 km E of Ketchikan by air. It consists of the E side of Revillagigedo Island, the adjacent mainland all the way to the Canadian border, and long narrow Behm Canal which separates the two. The Monument includes rugged mountain ranges, numerous bays, coves, and rivers, most often shrouded in fog, as the name implies. There are several Forest Service cabins clustered around Walker Cove and Rudyerd Bay, one of the most scenic areas, where granite cliffs rise starkly from the water. A 2-km trail climbs from Punchbowl Cove on Rudyerd Bay to Punchbowl Lake. Now U.S. Borax plans a huge molybdenum mine inside the Monument. _getting there:_ Outdoor Alaska, 501 Water St., runs cruises to Misty Fjords from June to September. Prices begin at $99 (lunch included) for a 12-hour trip, or

$139 for a faster trip in which you fly one way. They'll give you a 30 percent discount if you take your chances and book standby the day before. These boat trips are preferable to the flightseeing tours offered by other companies.

Prince of Wales Island: This huge, accessible, yet nearly unpopulated island is a good place to leave it all behind. There is ferry service Ketchikan-Hollis ($11 OW) almost daily in the summer, and if you timed it right, you could catch the Hollis-Wrangell ($18) ferry which travels once a week. There are no facilities in Hollis, but finding a place to camp is no problem. Sadly, clearcut logging, a practice which destroys the habitat of most animals, is common here. A minibus ($10) runs 50 km to Klawock, which has a totem park and a cannery. Another possibility is to fly to Craig, walk or hitch 10 km to Klawock, then fly back to Ketchikan. SEA Airlines has 5 floatplane flights a day Ketchikan-Craig-Klawock ($45 RT). Hydaberg, 35 km SE of Craig, is a Haida Indian village with a good collection of restored totem poles. Access is usually by air.

METLAKATLA

Metlakatla (pop. 1,100 in 1980) is a small, prosperous community S of Ketchikan on Annette Island, one of Alaska's only Indian reservations. The town still has the air of a pioneer vilage with large, frame houses occupying big corner lots, and it also boasts a flourishing cannery, cold storage facility, and

sawmill. Metlakatla was founded in 1887 when missionary William Duncan arrived from Canada with 823 native Tsimshian Indian followers and began clearing a townsite. (For the story of Duncan's activities in Canada, see 'Prince Rupert'). At Metlakatla, Alaska, Duncan established a sawmill to provide lumber for the construction of houses and the first cannery. The most ambitious building to be erected was a 1,000-seat church which unfortunately burned in 1948. In 1891, the U.S. Congress granted the Tsimshian Indians the entire island as a reservation, a right they jealously guard to this day. Duncan maintained his paternal hold over most aspects of Indian life here until 1913 when a government school opened. Duncan opposed the school, preferring that education remain in the hands of the church. The ensuing conflict led to the intervention of the U.S. Dept. of the Interior in 1915 which seized the sawmill, cannery, and other facilities which had been under Duncan's personal control. Duncan was only to live 3 years longer, but his memory is still revered by many, and his influence can be seen in the healthy little Indian settlement of today.

sights: Father Duncan's cottage, where the missionary lived from 1894 until his death in 1918, is now open as a museum Mon. to Fri.—donation. The fascinating assortment of personal items owned by Duncan and the old photographs of Metlakatla make a stop here a must. Ask for Mrs. Laverne Welcome, the curator, who is always delighted to talk to visitors about the history of Metlakatla. Also visit the Small Boat Harbor where a traditional-style longhouse is being erected to stimulate local arts and crafts. There's a short trail from the corner of Milton St. and Airport Rd. on the SE edge of town which runs along the side of Skaters Lake, a large pond where native plants and waterfowl can be observed.

hiking: A good hike is up Yellow Hill (165 m) along a boardwalk which begins to the R of Airport Road, about 2½ km from town. The rounded hill, which is clearly visible behind Metlakatla, is striking in itself and from the summit the entire W side of Annette Island is visible. The walk up is easy. _others:_ A zigzag waterfall tumbles down between 2 bald mountains from Chester Lake above the ferry landing E of town. If you're really ambitious, hike up there.

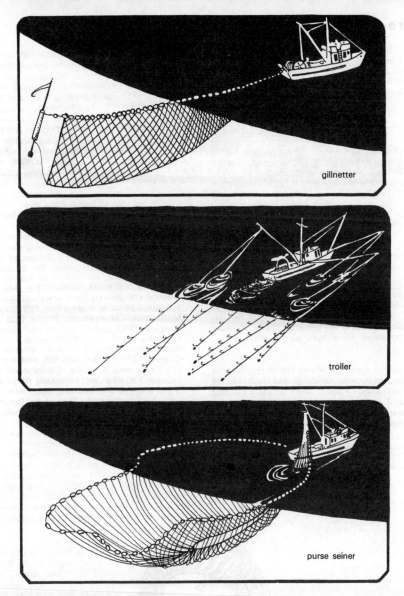

gillnetter

troller

purse seiner

commercial salmon fishing: Three types of salmon-fishing boats are commonly seen along the Pacific coast. The gillnetter is easily recognized by the large drum at the back of the boat. Fish are caught by the gills in the long nylon net played out from the drum and removed by hand as the net is wound back in. A troller catches fish by using up to 6 stainless-steel lines at a time. The hooked fish are pulled in either hydraulically or by hand. The purse seiner is the largest of the types. A net with floats along the top edge and weights at the bottom is pulled out around a school of fish by a man in a skiff. When the fish are surrounded, the bottom is closed like a purse and the net is pulled out by a block on a mast at the rear of the boat.

An old photo of William Duncan's cannery at
Metlakatla, with a Seattle steamer loading canned
salmon from the wharf. The cannery burned down in
1916, but has been rebuilt.

stay and eat: Rooms at the Taquan Inn in
town are $20 pp; call Mrs. Duncan at tel.
886-7090 for reservations. There's a small cafe
overlooking the cannery in back of the Inn.
Several stores sell groceries but no alcoholic
beverages are allowed on the island.

getting there: The Alaska Marine Highway has
service between Ketchikan and Metlakatla ($8
OW) 4 days a week. There is both a morning
and an afternoon ferry on these days,
permitting an excellent day trip from
Ketchikan. If you know in advance that you'll
be visiting Metlakatla, compare the cost of
breaking your journey there as against buying
a through ticket with an added side trip to
Metlakatla. For example, Prince Rupert-
Skagway ($90) and Ketchikan-Metlakatla-
Ketchikan ($16) total $106, while Prince
Rupert-Metlakatla ($24) and Metlakatla-
Skagway ($71) come to only $95, a saving of
$11. Study your timetable. Seaplane service
between Ketchikan and Metlakatla ($20 OW)
is also available with frequent flights made by
both Tyee Airlines and Taquan Air Service.
These 2 airlines sometimes have price wars, so
compare before you buy.

WRANGELL

At the N tip of Wrangell Island near the mouth of the Stikine River, Wrangell (pop. 2,184 in 1980) is a friendly little town, its inner harbor alive with shrimp and salmon processing plants, fishing boats, seaplanes and totem poles. The surrounding old buildings on piles, wooded hillsides, and snowcapped mountains add even more to its appeal. Wrangell was founded by the Russians in 1834 (Fort St. Dionysius), then leased to the Hudson Bay Company in 1840 (Fort Stikine). In 1867 it became a U.S. possession (Fort Wrangell) along with the rest of Alaska. During a gold rush in 1873, thousands of miners passed through Wrangell on their way up the Stikine River to the interior Cassiar region of B.C. Today, forestry is the main source of income, followed by fishing.

sights: Petroglyphs (ancient stone carvings) abound in this charismatic seaport and are found along the shoreline N from the ferry terminal. The closest is on a flat rock between the 4th and 5th buildings to the L of the ferry. Many more may be seen by walking one km N from the ferry, 200 m beyond Dick Stough's Mobile Home Park. A boardwalk (signposted) leads down to the shore; the petroglyphs are to the right. Most are submerged at high tide.

Precisely who carved the petroglyphs or when is uncertain. Back in town visit the Wrangell Museum ($1) which is open Mon. to Thurs. 1300-1600, Fri. 1900-2100, Sat. 1300-1600, or whenever a ferry or cruise ship is in port. The museum building (1906) was Wrangell's first schoolhouse. Petroglyphs, old photographs, and local relics are kept in this crowded and provocative museum. There are several (new) totem poles in front of the adjoining library. Chief Shakes Island, in the middle of Wrangell harbor, is the town's most picturesque sight. A footbridge at the bottom of Front St. near Wrangell's 2 canneries gives access to the island (free), where Chief Shakes Community House and 9 large totem poles, replicas of older poles from the area, are to be seen. The poles, carved during a CCC project in 1939 and 1940 are quite impressive. Chief Shakes gravesite is around on Case Ave. opposite the Hansen Boat Shop. Two carved killer whales watch over the site.

hiking: A soggy 1½-km trail leads in to Rainbow Falls from a point just before the old Wrangell Insititute, 7-1/2 km S of town. Closer to town, an overgrown trail winds up Mt. Dewey from near the end of 3rd St. (see the

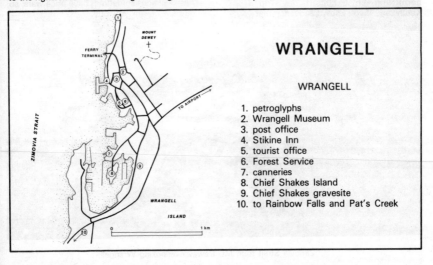

WRANGELL

WRANGELL

1. petroglyphs
2. Wrangell Museum
3. post office
4. Stikine Inn
5. tourist office
6. Forest Service
7. canneries
8. Chief Shakes Island
9. Chief Shakes gravesite
10. to Rainbow Falls and Pat's Creek

map). It's an easy 15-min. climb up to this viewpoint over Wrangell once you get on the trail. You could probably find a place to camp up here in a pinch.

camping: Camping is allowed (free) in the City Park just beyond the old cemetery and ball park, 3 km S of the ferry on the water side of the main highway. You could also sleep in the bleachers at the ball park. There is more free camping at Pat's Creek Wayside, 17 km S of town.

information: The tourist office is in an A-frame beside the 20-m-high Kiksadi totem pole, adjoining the city hall in the center of town. The Forest Service office is upstairs in the Yamasaki Mall opposite. *from Wrangell:* The ferry terminal is right in town. It's only 2 km from the ferry terminal to the airport (WRG).

THE STIKINE RIVER

Wrangell is only 11 km from the mouth of the Stikine River, one of the 10 top wild rivers of Canada and the fastest navigable river in North America. The Grand Canyon of the Stikine, just above Telegraph Creek, B.C., has 300-m walls enclosing fierce white water. River travel is easier below Telegraph Creek, all the way to Wrangell, between mountains, past glaciers and rainforest. Well-prepared, intrepid riverrunners with rafts might put in off the Cassiar Highway; canoeists and kayakers would be best to begin at Telegraph Creek. On a visit to the Stikine in 1879, John Muir described it as 'Yosemite 100 miles long.' Now B.C. Hydro plans a destructive CDN$8 billion series of monster dams on the Stikine to feed a proposed industrial site or generate power to sell to the U.S. Don't wait too long to come.

tours: Alaska Discovery (Box 26, Gustavus, AK 99826, USA) offers river trips from Telegraph Creek to Wrangell. The cost is US$975 for 9 days, including the flight from Wrangell to Telegraph Creek. Raft trips on the upper end of the river from Spatsizi Wilderness Park to the beginning of (but not through) the Stikine Grand Canyon are offered by Iskut Trail and River Adventures (Iskut, B.C. VOJ 2KO, Canada). Groups are

Zimovia Strait from Mt. Dewey overlooking Wrangell

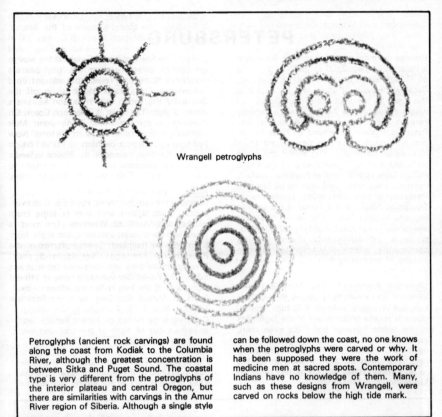

Wrangell petroglyphs

Petroglyphs (ancient rock carvings) are found along the coast from Kodiak to the Columbia River, although the greatest concentration is between Sitka and Puget Sound. The coastal type is very different from the petroglyphs of the interior plateau and central Oregon, but there are similarities with carvings in the Amur River region of Siberia. Although a single style can be followed down the coast, no one knows when the petroglyphs were carved or why. It has been supposed they were the work of medicine men at sacred spots. Contemporary Indians have no knowledge of them. Many, such as these designs from Wrangell, were carved on rocks below the high tide mark.

accompanied by native Indian guides of the Tahltan people; costs average CDN$100 pp a day.

on your own: Telegraph Creek is accessible by road from the rest of B.C. or you can charter a small plane from Wrangell. If you arrive in Wrangell from Canada in your own vessel, report at once to U.S. Customs on the 2nd floor of the post office building. Only one person should go; other members of the party should remain by the boat. After 1700 and on Sun. an overtime fee is charged for Customs inspections.

PETERSBURG

Perhaps the most attractive town in Southeast is Petersburg (pop. 2,821 in 1980), at the N tip of Mitkof Island on the Wrangell Narrows. Great white walls of snow and ice backdrop the town to the east. Peter Buschman, for whom Petersburg is named, built a cannery here in 1897. The business prospered and Petersburg grew up around it. Most of the present inhabitants are descended from Norwegian fishermen, who found the place reminded them of their native land. Fishing is still the main activity here with salmon, halibut, herring, king crab, and shrimp all landed. Petersburg has the most canneries in Southeast Alaska and is home to the world's biggest halibut fleet. The world's largest salmon (57 ½ kg) was caught in nearby waters. It is a self-sufficient, inward-looking community, which only tolerates tourism instead of promoting it.

Wrangell Narrows: The ferry between Wrangell and Petersburg passes through the tortuous Wrangell Narrows, a 46-turn nautical obstacle course which is one of the highlights of the Inside Passage trip. It's even more exciting at night when the zigzag course is lit up like a Christmas tree. Be up front to see it. *note:* The luxury-class cruise ships are too big to go through these shallow waters between Kupreanof and Mitkof islands.

sights: The Sons of Norway Hall (1911), built on pilings over Hammer Slough, bears traditional Norwegian rosemaling designs on the exterior. The Clausen Memorial Museum, 2nd and F Sts. (open 1300-1600, donation), is worth a visit. The 'Fisk' fountain ouside the museum was erected in 1967. Free tours of the cannery and cold storage at Petersburg Fisheries Inc. are possible Mon. to Fri. at 1400, one of the few canneries in Alaska where visitors are welcome.

hiking: The trail to Raven's Roost Cabin begins at the rock quarry on the SE side of the airport, 2 km from town. After crossing the muskeg on a boardwalk, climb steeply through forest and open country to the cabin at 610 m, 5 km from the trailhead. Spectacular views of Petersburg, Frederick Sound, and the Wrangell Narrows are obtained from this ridge. The Forest Service cabin rents at $10 a night (ask at the Forest Service office in the Bank of Alaska Building, or write Forest Service, Box 1328, Petersburg, AK 99833). Camping is permitted on Forest Service land anywhere out of sight of the trail and well away from the cabin.

practicalities: The Mitkof Hotel, an old frame building (1905) in the center of town, charges $30 s, $35 d (plus tax) for rooms with shared

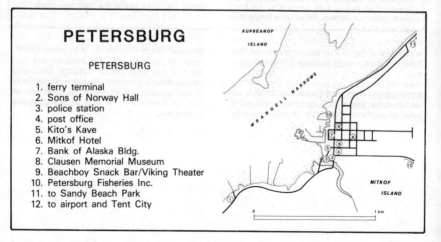

PETERSBURG

PETERSBURG

1. ferry terminal
2. Sons of Norway Hall
3. police station
4. post office
5. Kito's Kave
6. Mitkof Hotel
7. Bank of Alaska Bldg.
8. Clausen Memorial Museum
9. Beachboy Snack Bar/Viking Theater
10. Petersburg Fisheries Inc.
11. to Sandy Beach Park
12. to airport and Tent City

KUPREANOF ISLAND

WRANGELL NARROWS

MITKOF ISLAND

0   1 km

Campers at Tent City near Petersburg share crowded wooden pads over the muskeg with young cannery workers.

bath. The tourist office (closed Sun.) adjoins. There are sometimes dormitory accommodations ($10) at the Beachcomber Inn (tel. 772-3215), 5 km S of the ferry wharf. Kito's Cave is the liveliest place in town to have a beer.

camping: The Forest Service has built 3 free campgrounds near the S end of Mitkof Island: Blind Slough (28 km from Petersburg), Ohmer Creek (35 km), and Sumner Strait (38 km). Unless you have a vehicle there's no way to get there except to try to hitch a ride with elderly RV drivers who never stop. The only designated camping area anywhere close to town is Tent City, about 3 km from town between the airport and Sandy Cove. Actually, this city-operated facility, meant to accommodate migrant workers who provide a labor pool for the canneries, is not suitable for travelers. The charge is $2.50 pp, but a $42.50 deposit must be paid in advance; the balance is refunded when you leave. The manager is only present during business hours, but a sign warns that those not paying their deposit will have their tent seized by the police. Check-out time is 0800. Due to muskeg in the area, tents must be erected on wooden pads, and as many are jammed on a pad as will fit. A long list of rules greets newcomers. Rule #13 informs you that TENT CAMPING WITHIN CITY LIMITS IS PROHIBITED ON PUBLIC PROPERTY EXCEPT AT PETERSBURG CAMPGROUND. Rule #17 reads: THE CITY OF PETERSBURG WELCOMES YOU AND HOPES YOUR VISIT WITH US IS A PLEASANT ONE.

PLACES NEAR PETERSBURG

Le Conte Glacier: Le Conte Glacier dips into Le Conte Bay only 40 km E of Petersburg across Frederick Sound on the mainland. It is part of the vast Stikine Icefield and the southernmost glacier in Alaska to drop icebergs into salt water. Ice from the glacier was once used by local fishermen to keep their catches cool on the way to market in Seattle. Today the locals use it to cool their drinks. Le Conte Bay is home to 2,000 harbor seals. There are no boat trips to the glacier but amphibian flightseeing is offered. You could also rent a 5½-m outboard motor boat from Tongass Marine (tel. 772-3905) for $65 (one day) or $100 (2 days) and drive yourself over.

Kake: Between Petersburg and Sitka the ferry *Le Conte* calls at the Tlingit Indian village of Kake on Kupreanof Island. A 38-m-high totem pole stands in the village.

SITKA

Sitka (pop. 7,803 in 1980), on the W side of Baranof Island facing Sitka Sound, was founded in 1799 by Alexander Baranof, head of the Russian American Company under a charter from the Czar. Baranof built his settlement at Old Sitka near the present Alaska ferry terminal, but this was destroyed by an Indian attack in 1802. The Russians returned in 1804 and defeated the Tlingits. Baranof then rebuilt the town on the present site. A stockade ran from where the Sheffield Hotel is now to Swan Lake, separating Russians from Indians. From 1806 to 1867 they coexisted, though uneasily, and Sitka, then called New Archangel, was the capital of Russian America and an important center for the sea otter trade. An emotional ceremony at Sitka in 1867 marked the passage of Alaska from Russian to American hands. During WW II Sitka was a major link in the defense of Alaska. Hangars remaining from the large amphibious air base are just across the bridge on Japonski Island. Today the Japanese own the big pulp mill on Silver Bay, 8 km E, which is the mainstay of the local economy. Aside from its rich history, Sitka offers some of the best scenery and hiking in Southeast, if you're lucky enough to be there in good weather.

Sergius Narrows: The Sergius Narrows, which the ferry must pass at slack tide, is the highlight of the ferry trip to Sitka. Bald eagles are very often spotted in the treetops along this very narrow, treacherous body of water. Fierce currents prevent the ferries from going through while the tide is changing; they must time their passage to coincide with a high or low tide. Often passengers will have to wait at Sitka 3 hours (allowing you to take the excellent, though rushed, bus tour), or they will turn around immediately, in which case you will see nothing of the town unless you stop over.

SIGHTS OF SITKA

downtown: One of the best views of Sitka is from the bridge across Sitka harbor to Japonski Island airport. On a clear day, the mountains of Baranof Island behind the town and the perfect volcanic cone of Mt. Edgecumbe (976 m) on Kruzof Island are in full view. Beside the post office a stairway leads up to Castle Hill, a public park commemorating the spot where Alaska was transferred to the U.S. in 1867. The Kiksadi Indian clan inhabited this hill for many generations prior to the Russian arrival. After defeating the Indians, Baranof built his house here, but the building burned in 1894. The many historical markers and splendid view make Castle Hill a must. The most prominent feature of the downtown area is the large yellow Alaska Pioneers Home (1934), where seniors with 15 or more years state residence may stay. The famous Prospector statue in front of the Home was modeled from a photo of George Carmack, one of the discoverers of gold in the Klondike. Across the road is a totem pole bearing the

Russián coat of arms. On a hill just W of the Pioneer Home stands a reconstructed blockhouse of the stockade that kept the Indians restricted to the area along Katian St. to the west. Some remains from the old Russian graveyard are nearby. There are more graves at the end of Princess Way, just to the north. The most striking symbol of Russian influence in Sitka is St. Michael's Cathedral

(1848), which unfortunately burned in 1966 but was replaced by a replica in 1976 (open 1100-1500, admission $1). The original Russian icons, including the miraculous healing Sitka Madonna, were saved from the fire and have been returned to their original setting in this, the mother church for all of Alaska's 20,000 Russian Orthodox members.

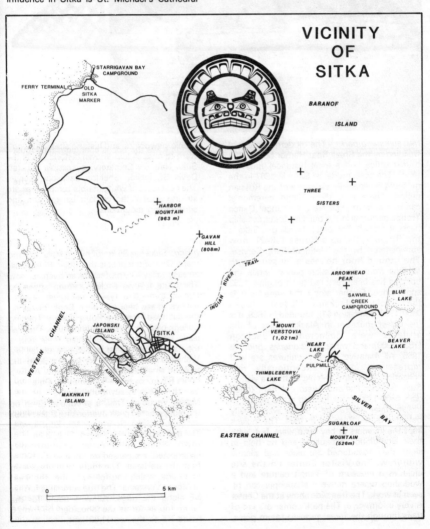

VICINITY OF SITKA

Sitka

museums and parks: The modern Centennial Building by the Small Boat Harbor houses the tourist office and a local historical museum (free). The scale model of Sitka in 1867 in the museum is especially evocative of the Russian period. There is a 15-m Tlingit ceremonial canoe out front. The New Archangel Dance Troupe performs in the building for cruise ship passengers ($2). The oldest building in Sitka is the Russian Bishop's House (1842), now administered by the National Park Service. The ground floor houses a museum with exhibits from the Russian period, while the upstairs has been restored to its original 1853 appearance. Further along the waterfront is the Sheldon Jackson Museum (open 0900-1700, admission $1); founded in 1888, it is the oldest museum in Alaska. Most of the artifacts were collected by Jackson (1834-1909) and other missionaries prior to 1895. All 4 native Alaskan cultures are well represented in this exceptionally rich collection. For many, the highlight of a visit to Sitka is Sitka National Historical Park (open daily 0800-1800, free), located at the mouth of Indian River where the Tlingits were finally defeated by the Russians in 1804. The Indians kept the invaders at bay for a week but, with their ammunition exhausted and no help in sight, they abandoned the place and silently withdrew. The Visitor Center on the site includes a museum of Tlingit culture and a workshop where native craftspeople can be seen at work. The free slide show at the Center is very informative. The park contains 3 km of trails through the forest passing totem poles,

scenic viewpoints, and historic sites you won't want to miss. A less-known historic site is the Sitka National Cemetery, accessible via Jeff Davis St. beside Sheldon Jackson College. The neat rows of white marble tombstones are striking against the verdant background and surrounding mountains.

hiking: Sitka has 65 km of hiking trails (see the map). One of the best is the Indian River Trail, an easy valley hike perfect for an overcast day. The route follows a clear salmon spawning stream through a typical rainforest, with a chance to see bear and deer. Begin by taking the dirt road from the Public Safety Training College back to the city pumphouse. The trail leads from here up the Indian River and a tributary to the R as far as a 25-m waterfall in a V-shaped valley. Watch for berries along the trail and small water life in the stream. Allow 5 hours RT to cover the 9 kilometers. On a clear day there are spectacular views from the Mount Verstovia Trail, a strenuous climb up the high, pointed peak overlooking Sitka. Look out across Sitka Sound to Mt. Edgecumbe. The trail begins at the Kiksadi Club, 3 km E of town. Some old Russian charcoal pits (signposted) are passed on the way up, 500 m from the trailhead. The route switchbacks up to a ridge, which you follow to the 'shoulder' of Mount Verstovia. The true summit is further NE along the ridge. Allow 4 hours for the return trip as far as the 'shoulder' (777 m), 6 hours RT to the top (1,021 m).

SITKA

1. to airport
2. Native Brotherhood Hall
3. Pioneer Bar
4. The Observatory Rare Books
5. Sheffield Hotel
6. totem pole
7. post office/Forest Service
8. Castle Hill
9. Sitka Hotel
10. Island Taxi
11. Tilson Building
12. St. Michael's Cathedral
13. Old Harbor Books
14. Pioneer Home
15. blockhouse
16. Russian graves
17. Centennial Building
18. Kentucky Fried Chicken
19. Russian Bishops House
20. Sheldon Jackson College
21. Sheldon Jackson Museum
22. Visitor Center
23. to pulp mill
24. to Indian River Trail
25. Public Safety Academy
26. Sitka National Cemetery
27. youth hostel
28. Gavan Hill Trail
29. to ferry terminal

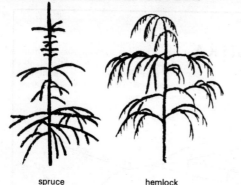

spruce   hemlock

conifers: The Sitka spruce is the largest tree found throughout Southeast Alaska. Its bark is divided into scaly plates. Spruce is one of the first trees to colonize areas uncovered by glaciers. Hemlock is more tolerant of shade than spruce and eventually comes to dominate the climax rainforest. Hemlock bark is divided into vertical ridges. It's easy to differentiate hemlock from spruce by their tops.

PRACTICALITIES

stay: The Sitka Youth Hostel (open 1 June to 1 Sept. only) in the United Presbyterian Church at the corner of Sawmill Creek Blvd. and Baranof St. is $2.50 for members, $3.50 for non-members. The hostel does fill up, but members are guaranteed a place. During the day hostelers must remove their luggage from the premises, but the warden will suggest somewhere in town where you may leave it. Be up and out by 0730; doors open again at 1800. The Sitka Hotel, an old concrete building in the center of town, charges $29 s, $33 d (plus tax) without bath.

camping: There are no campgrounds near downtown Sitka, but the Forest Service provides free camping each end of the road. The Starrigavan Bay Campground is NW of town, just a km beyond the ferry terminal (bring water). A plaque marks the site of Old Sitka (burned by the Tlingits in 1802) between the ferry and campground. Sawmill Creek Campground is up Blue Lake Road beyond the pulp mill (which gives off a distinctive smell), 10 km E of town. There is an excellent 1-km trail up to Beaver Lake from the bridge at this campground.

eats and entertainment: The cafe downstairs in the Sitka Hotel is reasonable. Get ice-cream cones at Dip 'n Sip beside the Russian Orthodox Church. The Pioneer Bar is the favorite local drinking place. **books:** If you're in the market for old maps and prints, check out The Observatory Rare Books near the Pioneer Bar. Old Harbor Books sells topographical maps of SE Alaska. **transport:** The ferry terminal is 11 km N of town. Fortunately, Island Taxi runs a shuttle service ($2.50 OW) which meets all ferries. Ferry service to Sitka is not daily so check your timetable. The airport (SIT) is on Japonski Island, 3 km from town by road.

PLACES NEAR SITKA

Admiralty Island National Monument: Admiralty has the largest concentration of brown bears and bald eagles in North America. A couple times a week the ferry between Sitka and Juneau stops at the Tlingit Indian village of Angoon, the only settlement on the island and one of the most traditional in Southeast. Please show some sensitivity in your dealings with the native people of Angoon if you visit. The Cross Admiralty Canoe Route begins at Angoon and traverses the island via a series of inlets, 7 lakes, rivers, and portages. There are 5 Forest Service cabins for rent along the route at $10 for the whole cabin, but these must be reserved as much as 180 days in advance (Forest Service, Box 2097, Juneau, AK 99803). Fierce tidal currents are experienced in the inlet behind Angoon. For anyone with a canoe or kayak, Admiralty is a natural. *Discover Southeast Alaska with Pack and Paddle* (see "Booklist") has a full description of this trip and details of the West Chichagof Coastal Canoe Run. Alaska Discovery (Box 10, Angoon, AK 99820) keeps canoes for rent at Angoon at $25 a day. These are mostly meant for use on Mitchell Bay, where wildlife is abundant. Ask for Dick Powers at Angoon; advance reservations are required in midsummer (3-4 days is enough to see the best).

Tenakee Springs: The ferry between Sitka and Juneau calls at this small village on Chichagof Island once a week. The hot springs (donation) next to the ferry wharf are the main attraction, although there are hiking trails along the shoreline E and W from the settlement. There are no cars or roads at Tenakee. Supplies are available from a small store.

Hoonah: The Tlingit Indian village of Hoonah gets ferry service on the Sitka-Juneau run several times a week. Hoonah is near Glacier Bay, and whales are sometimes seen offshore. A local museum (open Mon. to Fri. $2) an old cannery, and some hiking trails are the things to do and see. Backcountry camping is a favorite activity here.

The mountain goat is found along the coast from SE Alaska to Washington State and in the Rocky Mountains. It lives in small groups on steep slopes between the treeline and the snowline. The species is distinctive for its long white fur and beard, black horns and hoofs.

Foster A. Carr

JUNEAU

Hugging the mainland facing Gastineau Channel, Juneau is the capital of Alaska and with a population of nearly 20,000 (1980), the third largest city in the state. Juneau perches precariously on a thin strip of landfill at the base of Mt. Roberts, boxed in by the Channel. It offers typically rugged and beautiful Inside Passage scenery and hiking, plus close viewing of the Mendenhall Glacier, and is the gateway to spectacular Glacier Bay National Park. It also provides a variety of good food and services, plus convenient transport. Joe Juneau and Dick Harris found gold here in 1880 and a boom town materialized. There were 2 big mines. The Treadwell Mine, across the channel in Douglas, extracted 3 million ounces of gold from 1881 till a flood closed it in 1917. The Alaska-Juneau Mine, under Mount Roberts, operated until 1944 when it was declared a 'nonessential wartime activity.' The total output of the Juneau goldfield was over 7 million ounces. The A-J Mine's crushing and recovery mill, where the ore arrived through 500 km of tunnels, is on the hillside just S of the city ferry terminal. Much of Juneau is built on tailings from this mine which were dumped into the Gastineau Channel. Franklin St. was originally built on pilings along the shore. Juneau has been capital since 1906, when it was shifted from Sitka to be closer to the wealth and on the direct route to the Klondike. Today, half the residents work for the government. Their jobs and the future of the

city are now in doubt as a campaign is underway to move the capital to Willow, 100 km N of Anchorage, closer to the present centers of economic power. If the move ever materializes, Juneau could well become a ghost town as there is little else the populace has to fall back on. Meanwhile it's a friendly, appealing place where people say hello to you on the street.

SIGHTS OF JUNEAU

downtown: The Alaska State Museum (open Mon. to Fri. 0900-2100, Sat. 1300-2100, Sun 1000-2100, free) has a comprehensive collection of artifacts from Alaska's 4 native groups: Aleut, Eskimo, Athapaskan, and Tlingit. Upstairs are exhibits relating to the Russian period and other aspects of Alaskan history. The highlight of the museum is a full-size bald eagle nest in the circular stairwell. Set aside a couple hours for this excellent museum. Enter the modernistic State Office Building (SOB) from Willoughby Ave. and take the elevator up to the 8th floor where there's a 1928 Kimball organ, a totem pole, the Alaska State Library, and a panoramic view from the balcony. Friday at noon you'll enjoy the added bonus of an organ recital. Just up from Calhoun Ave. from the SOB is the large white Governor's Mansion (no visitors), built in 1913 in the New England colonial style on a hilltop overlooking the lower town. Back on 4th St. is the marble Alaska State Capital (1929). Free tours are available daily, or take the elevator up to the 2nd floor and wander around on your own. You may sit in on the legislature when they are in session (Jan. to May). St. Nicholas Russian Orthodox Church (1894) at 5th and Gold charges $1 admission (or peak in the windows for free). There's a good relief map of Alaska on the wall of the City Planning Office, Rm. 217, Municipal Building, opposite Merchants Wharf. Across the street, Marine Park, with its lively mix of people and picturesque views, is a good place to relax after your tour.

Douglas: Until the flood of 1917, Douglas had a population of 15,000 and was bigger than Juneau. Today it is a bedroom suburb of the capital. Take the hourly Capital Transit bus (25 cents) to the end of the line in Douglas. Continue along the road S past a gate and the DO NOT ENTER sign to explore the remains of the Treadwell gold mine. Keep R on the main trail to reach the Treadwell Glory Hole, once the entrance to a network of shafts under Gastineau Channel but now full of water and wrecked cars—a monument to the throwaway society. Return to the fork in the trail and continue down to the shore where there are more abandoned buildings and good views.

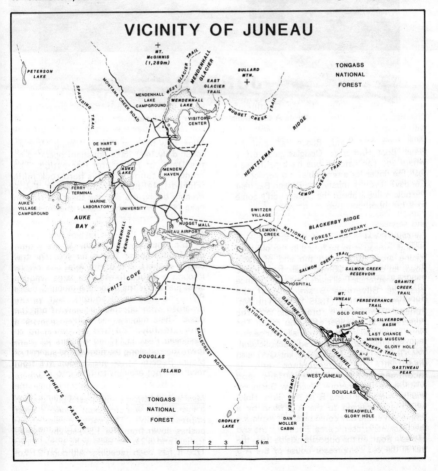

VICINITY OF JUNEAU

the face of Mendenhall Glacier near Juneau

Walk back past Sandy Beach Park and the Small Boat Harbor to Douglas post office where you can catch a bus back to Juneau (ask the driver for a timetable—no service on Sunday). If you're thirsty, the Billiken Bar near the post office is about the closest you'll come to a neighborhood pub in Juneau.

up Gold Creek: Some of the finest hiking around Juneau is to be found in the old gold mining areas up beyond the end of Basin Road, an enjoyable 25-min. walk from town. The Perseverance Trail leads past Last Chance Basin to Silverbow Basin, site of the Perseverance Mine (1885-1895). The Mt. Juneau Trail which branches off the Perserverance Trail just after you round The Horn, is very steep and potentially dangerous (only suitable for experienced backpackers). The Granite Creek Trail (2-1/2 km OW) also leads off the Perseverance and is recommended for its waterfalls and wildflowers. Just before Silverbow Basin yet another side trail leads R to the Glory Hole, which is connected to the A-J Mine by a tunnel. An entire day could be spent exploring this fascinating, scenic area. Back near the end of Basin Road on the opposite hillside from the trail is the old compressor house of the A-J

Mine, now the Last Chance Mining Museum (open daily 1400-1800, donation) operated by the Dept. of Parks and Recreation. The numerous tunnels of this hard rock mine (closed 1944) honeycomb the area. Every evening during the summer there's a salmon bake ($14) by the river below the museum.

Mount Roberts: If you're the type who likes to climb a mountain for the view at every turn, the Mount Roberts Trail is for you. The trail begins at the E end of 6th Ave. and climbs through a spruce forest to a large wooden cross just above the timberline (about 2 hours RT). The hike is strenuous, but you're rewarded with spectacular views from the cross. There may be snow above this point until late July. The trail continues up to Gastineau Peak (1,117 m) 4 hours RT from town, then on along the ridge to the summit of Mount Roberts (1,164 m) 5 hours RT from town. Do not attempt to hike into fog.

Mendenhall Glacier: Southeast's only drive-in glacier, this is without doubt Juneau's most impressive sight. This moving river of ice pushes down from the 1,500-sq-km Juneau Icefield and is 2½ km wide at its snout. Since 1750 it has been receding. Although 21 km

NW of town, the Forest Service Visitor Center (open daily 0900-1800, free) is easily accessible by city bus (see 'transport' below). There are free films, slide shows, and a large relief map of the area in the Visitor Center, plus a short nature trail nearby. The East Glacier Trail, which begins near the Center and provides good views of the glacier, eventually runs into the Nugget Creek Trail which goes back to the parking lot for a 90-min. loop or may be followed further up the creek. Vegetation along the East Glacier Trail consists of young growth since the glacier's recent retreat, while trees along the Nugget Creek Trail are much older. The West Glacier Trail begins from the Mendenhall Lake Campground and requires about 3 hours RT. For the really ambitious there's a route up Mt. McGinnis (1,289 m) from the end of the West Glacier Trail, an additional 6 hours RT. You have to do at least one of these trails if you want to come away with anything more than a shallow, touristic impression. Parks and Recreation offers organized hikes in the Juneau area on Wed. and Saturday. Look in the *Juneau Empire* or call tel.586-3300, ext. 226, for details.

PRACTICALITIES

stay: The Juneau Youth Hostel (open 1 June to 1 Sept. only) in the basement of Northern Light United Church, 11th and A sts., is $2 for members, $4 for non-members. The hostel is closed from 0800-1900, and hostelers must do a housekeeping chore. There are no showers at the hostel, but these are available at the swimming pool nearby which is open daily,

Tlingit whale crest headdress

$2.50 an hour (or 75 cents during 'penny saver' hours). Emergency accommodation is provided by the Cooperative Christian Mission for $2 a night. You must register at The Glory Hole near the City Ferry Terminal at 2015 sharp daily, then take the 2037 bus out to the shelter. Free meals are served. There is an active bed-and-breakfast association in Juneau with 12 host homes taking guests. Rates begin at $30 s, $35 d; call tel. 586-2959 for details. So long as the price doesn't bother you, this is a good way to meet some local people as well as find a place to stay.

hotels: The 'cheapest' hotels in Juneau are the Summit Hotel, 455 S. Franklin; the Alaskan Hotel, 167 S. Franklin; and the Bergmann Hotel, 434 3rd Avenue. All charge over $30 for a single room without bath, a double being just slightly more. This is quite a ripoff; the Summit and Bergmann are so old and decrepit you'd have second thoughts about staying in them anywhere else in the U.S. for a third the price. If you're willing to spend this kind of money, the Alaskan is undoubtedly the best of the 3, but it's often full. There are no weekly rates in summer. Cashen Quarters, 303 Gold St., has small housekeeping units at $35 s, $40 d.

camping: The City of Juneau provides no camping facilities. There are 2 Forest Service campgrounds, both $3 a site. The Auke Village Campground is 3 km W of the Auke Bay Ferry Terminal. The Mendenhall Lake Campground, on the W shore of the lake, is more convenient. Take any Valley bus to Montana Creek and Loop Road, then walk one km. The most likely camping place near town is up Basin Road. Why Parks and Recreation doesn't establish an official backpackers campground in this area isn't clear. People also camp on Mount Roberts.

food: The large number of office workers living in Juneau means many good places to eat out. The cheapest is the cafeteria in room 241 of the Federal Building (open Mon. to Fri. 0700-1530). A Kentucky Fried Chicken is nearby. If you're looking for class, try Fiddlehead Restaurant—very popular with the locals. The French onion soup ($3) is recommended. There's a liquor store opposite which sells groceries and is open every day. Bullwinkle's Pizza Parlor behind the SOB has pizza and beer, free popcorn, and a daily special posted on a board on the wall. Patties,

JUNEAU

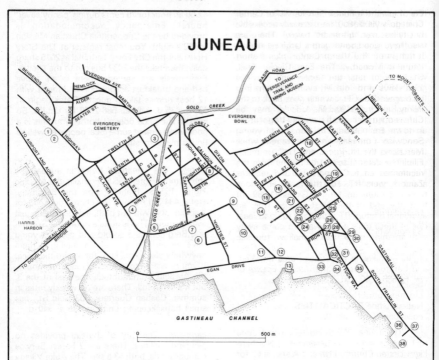

JUNEAU

1. swimming pool
2. ferry office
3. youth hostel
4. Federal Building/post office
5. Kentucky Fried Chicken
6. Alaska State Museum
7. Fiddlehead Restaurant
8. Governor's mansion
9. totem poles
10. Bullwinkle's Pizza Parlor
11. Convention Center
12. Cape Fox Sheffield Hotel
13. Glacier Bay Tours
14. State Office Building
15. public library
16. Alaska State Capitol
17. Russian Church
18. SEACC
19. Bergmann Hotel
20. Cashen Quarters
21. tourist office
22. Patties Etc./Pequeno Mexico
23. Purity Bakery
24. Flag of All Nations
25. Baranof Hotel
26. Baranof Book Shop
27. Brown Bear Cafe
28. Hearthside Books
29. Red Dog Saloon
30. Alaskan Hotel
31. f-stop Photo Finishing
32. Municipal Building
33. Merchant's Wharf
34. Marine Park
35. New Orpheum Theater
36. The Glory Hole/Alaska Discovery
37. Summit Hotel
38. City Ferry Terminal

Etc., near the tourist office log cabin, serves Chicago-style deep dish pizza which is good but takes over half an hour to prepare. They also have good sandwiches ($3.50 a half) at lunchtime. A little pricey, but popular. Pequeno Mexico, downstairs at 224 Seward St., has cheap luncheon specials from 1100-1500 and real Mexican atmosphere; recommended. Get cut-rate day-old bread at Purity Bakery, 2nd and Main. The Brown Bear Cafe is open 24 hours a day. The best burgers in town are prepared at the Great Alaskan Sandwich Company and Burger Factory in Merchants Wharf. Prices are reasonable. The Filipino restaurant beside the Summit Hotel is recommended for dinner. The owner, Mike Zamora, welcomes tourists.

entertainment: Nightlife in staid, old Juneau is a fizzle after the meals, but try the Red Dog Saloon which is touristy but still fun. Good movies are shown at the New Orpheum Theater ($4), which also has coffee house service in the afternoon and evening. *shopping:* The Salvation Army Thrift Store beside the City Ferry Terminal sells warm clothes, paperbacks, etc. The Flag of All Nations shop, 2nd and Main, has a unique collection of old collectables, well worth a look for the off-beat souvenir hunter.

services and information: If you want some film developed in a hurry, f-Stop Photo Finishing in the Emporium at 171 Shattuck Way opposite Marine Park does a professional job, and quickly. The Baranof Book Shop sells

topographical maps of SE Alaska. The tourist office (open Mon. to Fri. 0830-1700) is in the log cabin at 3rd and Seward. There's also a branch in the kiosk in Marine Park (open daily) The Forest Service Information Office in the Federal Building provides maps of hiking trails and related brochures. There's also a small exhibit of native handicrafts on the 3rd floor. The Southeast Alaska Conservation Council (SEACC), Rm. 328, 6th and Harris, has material on environmental issues.

TRANSPORT

by air: Juneau airport (JNU) is 13 km NW of downtown Juneau. To get a bus into town, turn L as you come out of the terminal and walk 2 blocks ahead to Shop 'n Kart, where city buses (50 cents) run into town hourly, Mon. to Sat. (first bus at 0710, last bus at 2340). Look for the timetable taped to the window of the supermarket. If you have to wait long for the next bus, there's a good little delicatessen just up from Shop 'n Kart. Juneau airport closes from 2200-0500, so forget trying to sleep there. Alaska Airlines flies Juneau-Cordova for $108—a convenient connection west.

by ferry: There are 2 ferry terminals in Juneau; the City Terminal is right in town, while the Auke Bay Terminal is 23 km northwest. All ferries arriving from Sitka land at Auke Bay, otherwise it varies. Check your timetable carefully. A minibus ($5) meets the ferries at

The New England-style Governors Mansion stands out on the hillside over Juneau.

Auke Bay. Get on fast if you want a ride as it quickly fills up. Otherwise, you can try hitching. Or walk 3 km S to De Hart's Store (at the junction with Loop Rd.) where city buses (50 cents) run into town hourly from 0650-2336 Mon. to Saturday. If you're arriving in the middle of the night and need a place to crash, walk 500 m beyond this junction till you see a good bus stop shelter on the right.

local buses: All Juneau city buses, except those going to Douglas, follow the Mendenhall Loop Road to within 2 km of the Mendenhall Glacier Visitor Center. The service is hourly Mon. to Sat. (50 cents) but can be confusing because some buses go around the Loop Rd. clockwise, others counterclockwise. On the way back flag down any city bus, whichever direction it is going, as they all eventually run into town.

long-distance buses: Alaska Sightseeing Tours in the Cape Fox Sheffield Hotel can reserve seats on Alaska-Yukon Motorcoaches from Haines to Anchorage ($135) or Skagway to Anchorage ($145). They'll carry your bicycle for $10. There are 2 buses a week out of Haines, one weekly out of Skagway. If you know you'll be using these services, book them in Juneau to avoid arriving in Haines or

Skagway to find a full bus. No stopovers or drop-offs in Canada are permitted.

Alaska Discovery: Southeast's oldest and best-known expedition guiding company runs canoe, kayak, and backpack trips departing Juneau, Gustavus, Wrangell, and Yakutat. These tend to be expensive, averaging $100 pp a day, but are highly recommended if you have the money. Write Alaska Discovery Box 26, Gustavus, AK 99826, USA, for a brochure. They also offer a 14-day University of Alaska-accredited course on the 'Natural History of Glacier Bay' in which remote, ice-filled inlets become the classroom ($420 pp, plus $75 UAJ enrollment fee). Book this one well ahead. Most exciting for the budget traveler are their canoe and kayak rentals which are available at Juneau, Angoon, and Bartlett Cove (Glacier Bay). In Juneau you can rent a canoe or kayak for $25 a day and take it to Tracy Arm Fjord free of charge on the *Riviera* excursion boat, paying only $75 pp RT personal transportaion. The Alaska Discovery office is in the shed at the back of 418 S. Franklin St. (open 1200-1800). Boats are in high demand during July and Aug., but reservations can be made c/o the Gustavus address above. Waterproof rubber boots, rain pants, and rain jackets are essential for kayakers at all times.

Tlingit wood carving

totem poles: These largest of wooden sculptures were carved in cedar by the Tlingit, Haida, Tsimshian, Kwatkiutl, and Bella Bella peoples of the Pacific Northwest. The animals, birds, and marine mammals on the poles were totems which symbolized a clan and, in combination, conveyed a message. The poles proclaimed a chief's clan status or commemorated a person or event. Totem poles were never associated with religion, yet early missionaries destroyed many and, as recently as 1922, the Canadian government outlawed the art in an attempt to make the natives more submissive.

GLACIER BAY NATIONAL PARK

A glacier is one of the most astonishing, overwhelming and awe-inspiring sights in all of nature. Imagine *sixteen* glaciers pouring out of the mountains and calving into inlets, and you get some idea of what awaits you at Glacier Bay National Park. Engulfed by the rugged Saint Elias Mountains, these massive rivers of ice amount to the largest concentration of tidewater glaciers on earth. Since Capt. George Vancouver sailed along Icy Bay in the 18th C., these glaciers have receded rapidly, leaving deep fjords and a bulldozed landscape. Today the vegetation varies from a 200-year-old spruce/hemlock forest at Bartlett Cove, to freshly exposed areas near the glaciers where tenacious plant life is just again taking hold. Wildlife is abundant, and large seal and bird rookeries can be seen from the excursion boats. Orcas and those humpback whales which haven't been driven off by luxury cruise ships are often encountered (boat traffic in the bay is now regulated to avoid harassment of marine mammals). Bear are also numerous in the park. There are 2 basic centers for visitors to Glacier Bay: Gustavus (outside the park) and Bartlett Cove (in the park). A 16-km road connects the two. *note:* Be aware that there is no cheap way to get to Glacier Bay or to get around the park once you're there. If you linger a while on a camping or kayaking trip the per-day average cost drops, but expect to spend a couple hundred dollars for a quick visit.

getting there: There are no roads or ferry services to Glacier Bay; this forces you to fly. You have the choice of taking a fast, comfortable Alaska Airlines jet, or a low, slow float plane or small aircraft. While the views may be better from the small plane, paradoxically the jets are cheaper. Sample fares are $42 OW/$68 RT from Juneau to Gustavus on Alaska Airlines, as against $50 OW/$85 RT for the same trip in a Glacier Bay Airways small aircraft. The transfer bus from Gustavus airport (GST) to Bartlett Cove costs $12 RT. Glacier Bay Airways also flies from Juneau direct to Bartlett Cove, but the price is $58 OW. Check these fluctuating prices carefully if you decide to go.

tours: If you want to buy a tour from Juneau to Glacier Bay, there are 3 alternatives. The most expensive is the overnight trip on the MV *Glacier Bay Explorer* which will run $247 for a cruise up the West Arm of Glacier Bay to Tarr Inlet, a standard berth on the boat, RT jet travel from Juneau to Gustavus, and transfers from Gustavus to Bartlett Cove. Meals on board are $20 pp extra. Book with Alaska Exploration Holidays in the Baranof Hotel, Juneau. The MV *Thunder Bay* offers an 8-hour cruise up the East Arm of Glacier Bay into Muir Inlet. A Park Service naturalist will be on board to explain what you're seeing. The *Thunder Bay* leaves from the dock near the lodge at

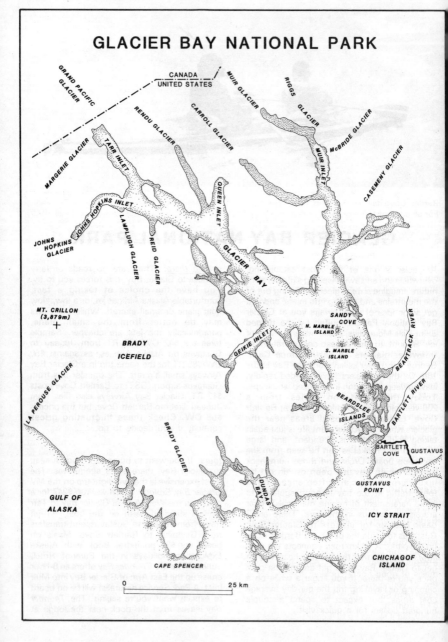

GLACIER BAY NATIONAL PARK

Grand Pacific Glacier pours down into Tarr Inlet from Canada.

Bartlett Cove daily ($79 pp, no meal included). For an additional fee of $16 this boat will drop off and pick up kayakers anywhere along the way. Add airfare and transfers to this and you have your cost. Perhaps the best tour to Glacier Bay is offered on the MV *Glacier Seal.* This is the only excurion boat which cruises both arms of Glacier Bay, and Capt. Howard Robinson will add zany commentary if he's in the mood. The cheapest way to do it is the 'campers special' ($155) which includes a RT small-plane flight from Juneau to Gustavus, plus 2 days of cruising on the *Glacier Seal.* Campers are dropped off at Reid Glacier in the evening and picked up the next morning. Meals are not included, but are available at a reasonable price. The same trip including meals and a berth on board is $265. If you want to camp longer at the glacier, you can arrange to be picked up on a later trip. Canoes and kayaks are carried free on the *Glacier Seal;* folding kayaks pay one seat on the plane. Book this trip through Glacier Bay Yacht Tours which has an office in Juneau on the waterfront opposite the Cape Fox Sheffield Hotel, or write Box 424, Juneau, AK 99802.

stay: During the summer Glacier Bay is jammed with flashy tourists, so don't expect any bargains. Rates at Glacier Bay Lodge (at Bartlett Cove), for example, begin at $60 s, $76 d, plus $2 pp for 'baggage handling.' Gustavus Inn (at Gustavus) is homey, but at $70 pp in a double room with shared bath it's not much of a deal. Rates at Gustavus Inn do include 3 meals of good home cooking. If there are a few of you, consider renting a housekeeping cabin from Salmon River Rentals (at Gustavus, 3 km from the airport). The charge for a cabin is $40, but it sleeps up to 4 adults. Bicycles are

for rent at $5 a day. Write Box 121, Gustavus, AK 99826 for reservations, or call tel. (907) 697-3291. They will pick you up at the airport at no charge, if notified.

camping and hiking: Camping is allowed without a permit anywhere in the park. There's a free campground at Bartlett Cove complete with bear-proof food cache, firewood, and pit toilets. The campground is only 400 m from the lodge and always has space. Park rangers give talks and slide presentations at Glacier Bay Lodge and everyone is free to attend. There are some enjoyable walks in the area. A Forest Trail loops between the lodge and the campground. Beach hiking is good at low tide (consult a tide table to know when to turn back). The Bartlett River Trail (6 km RT) leads from near the Ranger Station to the river mouth with opportunities to observe wildlife. Note that none of these trails go anywhere near the tidewater glaciers for which the park is famous (the closest is 65 km from Bartlett Cove). You have to take an excursion boat to get to them.

services: Although there is a small grocery store at Gustavus, it is better to bring all your own food with you. Topographical maps of the area are sold at the Ranger Station at Bartlett Cove. Alaska Discovery at Bartlett Cove rents kayaks at $25 a day. Write Box 26, Gustavus, AK 99826, for reservations (necessary in summer). Kayaking opportunities at Glacier Bay are fully described in *Discover Southeast Alaska with Pack and Paddle* by Margaret Piggott, available at Juneau bookstores and through Moon Publications, Box 1696, Chico, CA 95927.

Alaskan brown bear

HAINES

As you travel N to Haines (pop. 993 in 1980) out of Juneau on the Lynn Canal (the longest and deepest fjord in North America), the Inside Passage gets narrower and you sense that this long, unique waterway, and your passage on it, is coming to an end. To the E waterfalls tumble off the mountainsides very close to the ferry, while on the W glaciers lumber down from the icefields of the Chilkat Range. The long glacier which you see 40 min. before Haines that almost reaches tidewater is Davidson Glacier. Rainbow Glacier, also on the L, hangs from a cliff just beyond. Both originate from the same icefield which forms part of Glacier Bay National Park. Haines is located on a narrow peninsula between Chilkoot and Chilkat inlets. Long a stronghold of the powerful Chilkat Indians, a Protestant mission was first established here in 1881. During the Klondike gold rush, an adventurer named Jack Dalton developed a toll road from Haines to the Yukon along an old Indian trade route. It cost miners $150 pp to use the Dalton Trail. In 1942 and 1943 the U.S. Army built the 250-km Haines Highway from Haines to Haines Junction as an emergency evacuation route from Alaska in case of a Japanese invasion. Today this paved highway is the most direct route to Fairbanks and Anchorage. For cyclists it is much easier than the Klondike Highway out of Skagway. *fauna:* On the Chilkat River flats 29 km W of Haines, 3,000 bald eagles converge from all over Southeast from Oct. to Dec. to feed on a late salmon run.

sights of Haines: The Sheldon Museum (open daily 1300-1600, $1), near the foot of Main St., has a good collection of local relics and old photographs. Just S of this is Fort Wm. H. Seward (Port Chilkoot) which was built from 1903 to 1905 to maintain order among miners on the nearby goldfields. Until WW II it was the only U.S. Army post in Alaska. The fort closed in 1947 and the large frame buildings were sold to veterans. Today the complex is still very well preserved and contains a hotel and craft shops, as well as private residences. A Tlingit tribal house has been erected in the middle of the former parade ground in which salmon bakes ($15) are held during the summer. In a hall to one side, Indian dances and gold rush comedies are performed for tourists ($4).

Mount Riley Trail: A good day hike from Haines begins off Mud Bay Rd., About one km beyond the point where Small Tract Road rejoins it. Look for the sign MOUNT RILEY PARKING opposite the trailhead. You can also get on the trail by following FAA Road from behind Fort Wm. H. Seward. It's just over 3 km through the forest to the summit of Mount Riley (536 m), but you'll need 1 ½ hours to hike it. From Mount Riley you get a panoramic 360-degree view of the Lynn Canal, Davidson and Rainbow glaciers, the Chilkat River, Taiya Inlet, and 360 degrees of snowcapped peaks. From the summit, return down the trail that

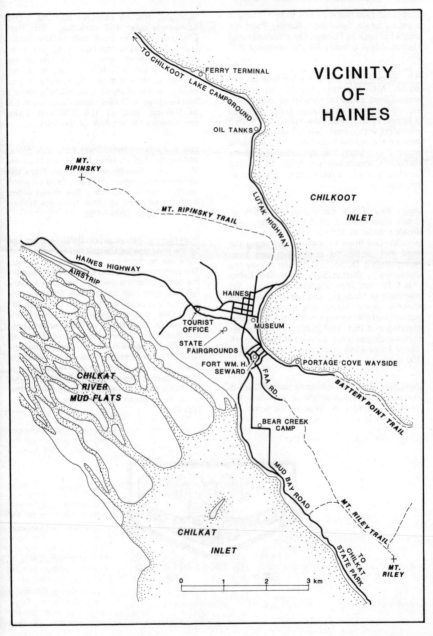

VICINITY
OF
HAINES

TO CHILKOOT LAKE CAMPGROUND

FERRY TERMINAL

OIL TANKS

LUTAK HIGHWAY

CHILKOOT
INLET

MT.
RIPINSKY

MT. RIPINSKY TRAIL

HAINES HIGHWAY

AIRSTRIP

HAINES

TOURIST
OFFICE

MUSEUM

STATE
FAIRGROUNDS

FORT WM. H. SEWARD

PORTAGE COVE WAYSIDE

CHILKAT
RIVER
MUD FLATS

FAA RD

BATTERY POINT TRAIL

BEAR CREEK
CAMP

MUD BAY ROAD

MT. RILEY TRAIL

TO CHILKAT
STATE PARK

CHILKAT
INLET

MT.
RILEY

0   1   2   3 km

comes out near Battery Point (6 km). There is a pebbly beach here. From Battery Point it's only 4 km back to Portage Cove Wayside and Haines. Allow 5 hours for the complete RT.

Mt. Ripinski Trail: The full-day hike up and down Mt. Ripinski (1,088 m) offers unparalleled views of mountains and inland waterways, but it's strenuous. Don't go in bad weather. From Haines take Young Rd. N till it intersects with a jeep road following a buried pipeline around the mountain. The trail begins about 2 km along this dirt road and climbs through a spruce/hemlock forest to muskeg and finally alpine at 600 meters. It's 6 km to the top.

stay: Bear Creek camp (tel. 766-2259) on Small Tract Road, 2 km SE of Haines, rents small cabins at $25 (each holds up to 4 people). Get there by walking out along the road that passes the post office and keep going straight. Do not turn R when you see the signboard to Chilkat State Park. The Camp may offer dormitory accommodations to YH members at $5.25 pp, but call to make sure there's space. Meals are available upon request and the manager is friendly. The Hotel Halsingland (tel. 766-2000), in the former commanding officers' quarters at Fort Wm. H. Seward, has a few 'economy rooms' at $25 s, $30 d.

camping: The best campsite near Haines is Portage Cove Wayside (free), only one km beyond Fort. Wm. H. Seward. No water, no facilities, and no vehicles allowed. The location is quiet and attractive. The Port Chilkoot Camper Park behind the Hotel Halsingland has campsites at $3 per tent. There are showers and a laundromat on the premises. If the NO VACANCY sign is up, ask anyway as there's always tent space. If you have a vehicle or don't mind hitching there's free camping at Chilkat State Park, 10 km SE of Haines, and at the Chilkoot Lake campground, 10 km NW of the ferry.

eats and information: Good ice cream, pizza, and sandwiches are served at Annie's Place on Main Street. Nearby at Sourdough Pizza the pies have an excellent crust and there's a good health food shop adjoining. The tourist office is at the entrance to town from the Haines Highway (open 0900-1900).

from Haines: Haines airport (HNS) is 6 km out on the road toward Canada but be aware that there are no flights to Anchorage or Valdez. The ferry terminal is also 6 km from Haines (in the other direction) and has free coin lockers (you get your coin back). Look for the white Travelot van which will take you into town for $3.50 OW. *buses:* Yukon Stage Lines has a minibus to Whitehorse (US$45) every Tues. and Saturday. There are connections to Tok (US$77), Fairbanks (US$100), and Anchorage (US$127). The terminal in Haines is the Alaska Sport Shop on Main Street. Alaska-Yukon Motorcoaches leave Haines for Anchorage (US$135) twice a week. Their office is in the Hotel Halsingland. Bicycles are carried for US$10.

Chilkat blanket

SKAGWAY

Skagway (pop. 768 in 1980) occupies a narrow plain by the Skagway River at the head of Lynn Canal. During the Klondike gold rush it was the gateway to both the Chilkoot and the White Pass trails, a funnel through which thousands of frenzied fortune seekers passed. Today the plank boardwalks, frame frontier storefronts, and unpaved streets remain to tell the story. The National Park Service is actively engaged in restoring many of the original buildings; a section of town has been declared a National Historical Park. Skagway continues to draw tourists and backpackers from all over the world to walk the trail that led to gold.

SIGHTS OF SKAGWAY

downtown: Begin your visit at the National Historical Park Visitor Center, housed in the old White Pass and Yukon Route Railroad depot (1900). There are free movies, slide shows and talks, as well as maps and displays. Walking tours of the historic district, led by park rangers, are offered daily in the summer and are highly recommended. If you plan to hike the Chilkoot Trail, the rangers will be able to advise you on trail conditions and give you a free map/brochure. Many of the old buildings along Broadway are part of the historical park. For many years the Visitor Center was in the Arctic Brotherhood Hall, the facade of which is made up of 20,000 pieces of driftwood. The Trail of '98 Museum ($2), above city hall in the old stone college building, has many relics of Skagway in the gold rush era.

nearby: The Gold Rush Cemetery is right beside the railroad tracks beyond the railway yards, 4 km NE of town. The largest monument is that of Frank Reid, who 'gave his life for the Honor of Skagway,' while the notorious 'Soapy' Smith only rates a wooden plank. At some time every visitor to Skagway will hear the story of how Soapy Smith, a gambler who ran Skagway with the help of a gang of con men, was shot dead by city surveyor Reid in a gunfight on 8 July 1898 after one of Smith's men stole a miner's gold. Reid died soon after from wounds. While you're there, be sure to follow the short trail above the cemetery to Lower Reid Falls

hiking: A network of well-marked hiking trails on the slopes just E of Skagway offer excellent day hikes and a place to warm up for the Chilkoot Trail. Cross the small footbridge and railroad tracks beyond the end of 3rd and 4th Avenues, then follow the pipeline up the hill. Lower Dewey Lake is an easy 20-min. climb from town. There is a trail right around the lake, with a branch at the S end off to Sturgill's Landing (5 km) on Taiya Inlet. Upper Dewey Lake (944 m) and the Devil's Punchbowl (1,082 m) are a steep 5-km climb from the N end of the lower lake. Icy Lake is a relatively level 3 km NE from the lower lake, but the trail to Upper Reid Falls is steep and hard to follow. There are a number of clearings with picnic tables around the lower lake where camping is possible, as well as at the other lakes and at Sturgill's Landing.

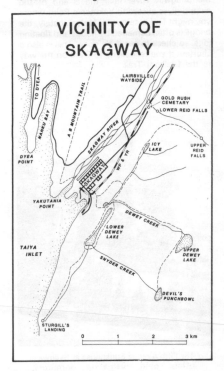

VICINITY OF SKAGWAY

PRACTICALITIES

stay: The Fifth Ave. Bunkhouse provides gold rush style dormitory accommodations in 6 small double cubicles with curtains for doors at $10 pp, showers $1 extra. Curious tourists stand in the doorway, peeping and snapping instamatics. The Skagway Inn (1897), once a rooming house for prostitutes but now a homey little hotel with 14 rooms, charges $30 s, $35 d, $40 t (shared bath). The Golden North Hotel (1891) has 33 rooms complete with antique furniture, $35 s, $40 d (shared bath).

camping: Hanousek Park Campground, Broadway and 14th, 1½ km from the ferry terminal, charges $4 per tent (no showers). Camp free at Liarsville Wayside, but it's 4 km out of Skagway on the road to Whitehorse. People also camp on the trail up to Lower Dewey Lake. A footbridge across the mouth of the Skagway River near the S end of the airstrip gives access to Yakutania Point where you might find a campsite. Unfortunately, the bridge is often damaged by floods and floating logs, so check to see if it's open. This is also a shortcut if you're walking to Dyea on the way to the Chilkoot Trail.

The Fifth Avenue Bunkhouse at Skagway offers gold rush-style dormitory accommodations at a reasonable price.

eats and entertainment: The Sweet Tooth Saloon serves good breakfasts. Moe's Frontier Bar is where the locals hang out. The Sports Emporium sells freeze-dried food, the grub to take with you on the Chilkoot Trail.

FROM SKAGWAY

by boat: In summer, the Alaska Marine Highway offers service daily from Skagway to Haines ($8) and Juneau ($22), 6 days a week to Prince Rupert (US$90), and weekly to Seattle ($155). Reservations are not necessary for foot passengers. The terminal is within spitting distance of town.

by bus: Alaska-Yukon Motorcoaches in the Golden North Hotel has a weekly bus to Whitehorse (US$29) and Anchorage (US$145). Bicycles are carried for $10 extra. Yukon Stage Lines runs a van to Whitehorse (US$32) every morning at 0900, also leaving from the Golden North Hotel.

the White Pass and Yukon Route [WP & YR]: One of the great engineering accomplishments of the 19th C., the historic railway from Skagway to Whitehorse remains a unique vestige of the Klondike gold rush. Contractor Michael J. Heney built his narrow-gauge railroad over the Continental Divide in just 2 years (1898-1900) using only pack horses, black powder, and muscle. From sea level at Skagway, the line rises to White Pass (884 m) in just 34 km with grades up to 4 percent. At Whitehorse, gold seekers and cargo transferred to sternwheel riverboats for the 735-km journey to Dawson City. In 1908 it cost $100 RT to go from Skagway to Dawson, train and riverboat included. Otherwise, you could take a steamer Seattle-Skagway, train Skagway-Whitehorse, riverboat Whitehorse-Dawson City-Nome, and steamer Nome-Seattle (the "circle route"), all for $200, although the meal at Bennett was $1 extra. During WW II the railway was taken over by the U.S. Army which used it to supply construction units building the Canol Pipeline and Alaska Highway. On one amazing day, 34 trains ran along the single line of track! Today the WP & YR, the longest operating narrow-guage railroad in North America, is a vital outlet for lead-zinc concentrate ores from mines in the Yukon.

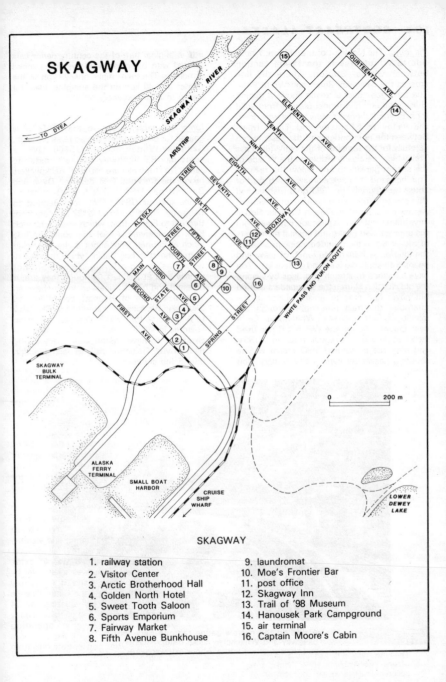

SKAGWAY

SKAGWAY

1. railway station
2. Visitor Center
3. Arctic Brotherhood Hall
4. Golden North Hotel
5. Sweet Tooth Saloon
6. Sports Emporium
7. Fairway Market
8. Fifth Avenue Bunkhouse
9. laundromat
10. Moe's Frontier Bar
11. post office
12. Skagway Inn
13. Trail of '98 Museum
14. Hanousek Park Campground
15. air terminal
16. Captain Moore's Cabin

the route: The highlight of the 177-km, 7-hour ride to Whitehorse is the 11-km section between Glacier Station, where the line crosses the Skagway River, and White Pass. The train goes over a trestle above a gaping chasm and enters a tunnel blasted from solid rock. Beyond, there is a view all the way down the valley to Skagway and Taiya Inlet. Between the next bridge and the pass, watch carefully for the remains of the old White Pass Trail which are clearly visible on the W side of the stream parallel to and below the railway. The thousands of pack animals which died of abuse here during the 1898 gold rush earned this stretch the name Dead Horse Gulch. Across the summit you are in Canada. Notice how dramatically the landscape changes from the snowcapped peaks and coastal rainforests of SE Alaska to the rounded alpine hillsides of the interior. A bunkhouse lunch of stew and beans with apple pie is served at Bennett. You have a chance to stretch your legs by visiting the old wooden church the stampeders started but never had time to finish. Later in the afternoon the train runs right through the middle of Carcross (see 'Whitehorse' for a description). Though the WP & YR has used diesel engines on it's regular runs since 1964, you may see a restored 1947 steam engine shunting passenger cars in the station. You

ride in original turn-of-the-century parlor cars refitted with big glass windows and padded armchairs. The trains make only 29 kph on the grades and 40 kph on the straights, ideal for taking in all the scenery.

fares: Inevitably, to survive, the WP & YR is geared for package tourism, so fares are high. Skagway-Whitehorse is US$60 OW; a same-day RT Skagway-Bennett costs the same. No stopovers are allowed. Backpackers hiking the Chilkoot Trail between Dyea and Bennett pay US$49 OW from Bennett to Whitehorse or US$42 OW from Bennett to Skagway. There is also a US$22 OW fare from Bennett to Fraser, from which you could hitch back to Skagway. All of the above include lunch at Bennett. Ask about a cheaper ticket from Bennett to Log Cabin, which the railway was considering offering. Tickets are not usually sold at Bennett (although they are, if pressed) and hikers are asked to purchase an open ticket out of Bennett before leaving Skagway. Bicycles are carried from Skagway to Whitehorse for US$10. You pass Canadian customs in Whitehorse and U.S. customs in Skagway, so have identification ready as the train arrives. Trains run daily in each direction during the summer.

A ride on the narrow gauge railroad between Skagway and Whitehorse packs history, scenery, and transportation into a 7-hour extravaganza.

THE CHILKOOT TRAIL

One of the best reasons for coming to Skagway is a chance to hike the historic Chilkoot Trail, an old Indian route from tidewater at Dyea (pronounced DIE-EE) to the headwaters of the Yukon River. A minimum of 3 days (but preferably 4 or 5) are needed to cover the 53 km to Bennett over the 1,082-m-high Chilkoot Pass. This is no easy Sunday outing: you must be fit and well-prepared. Weather conditions can change quickly on the trail and you should be ready for cold, fog, rain, snow, and wind at all times. The first stretch can be extremely swampy; snowfields linger between Sheep Camp and Happy Camp well into the summer. You will be above the treeline and totally exposed to the weather the 16 km from Sheep Camp to Deep Lake (the hardest stretch). Nonetheless, thousands of people follow the Trail of '98 every summer and make fast friends along the way. For scenery and historical value, the Chilkoot is unsurpassed in Alaska and Western Canada.

history: Gold was discovered in the Klondike in the summer of 1896, but word of the strike didn't reach the outside world until July, 1897. Within 3 months, Skagway and Dyea were thronging with stampeders eager to get over the passes to the goldfields. There were 2 choices. Horses could be taken over the White Pass Trail from Skagway to Bennett, but it was muddier and longer than the Chilkoot, and a stiff toll was collected on it. Most would-be miners opted for the Chilkoot Pass Trail out of Dyea, even though gear had to be backpacked over it. Canadian officials at the pass required that each person entering Yukon bring with him enough food for a year. It took each man an average of 3 months and dozens of trips back and forth from cache to cache to pack his ton of supplies into Canada. By the spring of 1898, 3 aerial tramways were operating on the Chilkoot. The thousands of stampeders stopped at Lindeman and Bennett, built boats and rafts, and waited for the spring break-up which would allow them to sail the 900 km to Dawson City along a series of lakes and rivers. When the ice broke up in May, 1898, some 7,124 boats and rafts sailed from the shores of lakes Lindeman and Bennett. Mounted Police records show 28,000 people traveling from Bennett to Dawson in 1898. Ironically, by the time they got to Dawson, every claim in the Klondike was already staked. By 1900, Dyea and the Chilkoot trail became deserted after the railway opened from Skagway to Whitehorse. Today it is possible to follow the gold rush trail all the way from Seattle to the Klondike in much the same way the stampeders did—ship to Skagway, hike to Bennett, train to Whitehorse, canoe to Dawson City.

Stampeders at The Scales, just below the 375-m incline to Chilkoot Pass, during the winter of 1897 to 1898. Those who could afford to had their ton of supplies hoisted to the summit on aerial tramways. Most, however, carried their goods on their back, up the "Golden Stairs" cut in the snow, often making 5 trips a day from cache to cache.

the route: The Chilkoot Trail begins just before the bridge over the Taiya River at Dyea, 15 km NW of Skagway. There is no bus to Dyea, although the manager of the the Fifth Ave. Bunkhouse has a small van in which he will carry groups to the trailhead for $30 per trip. Little remains to be seen at Dyea except for the Slide Cemetery where 60 men and women killed in the Palm Sunday avalanche of 1898 are buried. The first 21 km of the trail are a gradual climb through the rain forest, followed by a very steep ascent to the pass. At Canyon City, 12 km from the trailhead, a short side trail and a suspension bridge across the Taiya River give access to the remains of one of the villages which sprang up during the rush. The hardest part of the trip is the 30-degree incline from The Scales to the summit. This section was known as the 'Golden Stairs,' for the steps carved in the ice and snow. Photos of men going up here in single file are still the best known images of the gold rush. There is a U.S. park ranger at Sheep Camp and a Canadian park warden at Lindeman City. They recommend that you hike N from Dyea rather than S from Bennett as this is the historic route and, also, a descent down the 'Golden Stairs' can be dangerous. At Bennett you reach the railway which can take you to Whitehorse or Skagway (see 'Skagway' for a complete description). To avoid paying the prices charged by the railroad, some people walk out to the Klondike Highway at Log Cabin and hitch. The cutoff trail begins near Bare Loon Lake Campground, a couple km beyond Lindeman City. Look for a red sign with an arrow reading BENNETT on the L; the old blocked-off trail on the R cuts over to the railway line which you follow to the highway. The WP & YR doesn't like you to do this and there are NO TRESPASSING signs beside the tracks, so beware of trains. The railway was considering offering a cheap ticket from Bennett to Log Cabin (no lunch at Bennett) to discourage people from walking along their tracks. Ask about this in the railway station at Skagway.

flora and fauna: The vegetation changes from coastal rainforest up the Taiya Valley to alpine tundra as you approach the pass and rise above the 900 m level. On the drier Canadian side you'll find an open boreal forest of alpine fir and lodgepole pine. Although bears are seen along the trail occasionally, there has never been an attack on a hiker. Help keep it this way by storing food and garbage properly (see 'Introduction—Coexisting with the bears' for tips).

practicalities: Camping along the trail is permitted only at designated areas where outhouses are provided. There is a free campground near the trailhead, also a ranger station which could supply a map/brochure if you don't already have one. Campfires are permitted only at Canyon City and Sheep Camp. There are shelters with wood stoves at Canyon City, Sheep Camp, and Lindeman, but these are for drying out only (not

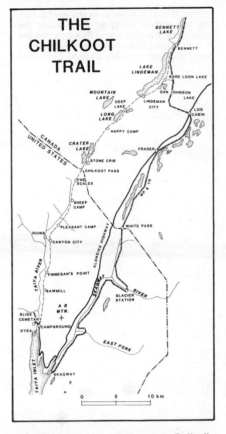

bald eagle

overnighting). You must camp. Boil all drinking water or use purification pills. Everything along the trail dating from the gold rush (even a rusty old tin can) is protected by law, and there are severe penalties for those who damage or remove them. Everyone entering Canada must clear Canadian customs. If you come in along the Chilkoot Trail and do not speak to an official at either Whitehorse or Fraser, you should report at the first opportunity to either the RCMP in Carcross or the Immigration Office (open Mon. to Fri.) in the Federal Building in Whitehorse. This applies mostly to those who walk out to the Klondike Highway at Log Cabin and hitch into Canada. If you take the train from Bennett, you will clear customs with the tourists.

others: If you are in Skagway and want to hike the trail without going on into Canada, the cheapest and easiest way to do it is to take the Yukon Stage Lines minibus from Skagway to Log Cabin (daily at 0900, US$8.50 OW), then hike down to Dyea. Or you could hike to Bennett and take the train (US$42) back to Skagway. This is better, though more expensive.

the north star: Polaris, the north star, lies almost directly above true north. The further one travels N the higher the north star will appear in the sky until at the North Pole it is directly overhead. It is easy to locate the north star by finding first the Big Dipper (part of Ursa Major, the Great Bear). An imaginary line drawn between the 2 stars at the front of the bowl of the Dipper points directly to the north star.

YUKON

INTRODUCTION

Yukon Territory covers 482,515 sq km of NW Canada, yet only 25,000 people live here, over 60½ of them in the capital, Whitehorse. Some 6,000 are native Indians, mostly Athapaskan. The name Yukon comes from "yuckoo," an Indian word for "clear water." The dry, empty, open countryside makes a lasting impression on anyone who has experienced it. Yet Yukon also has the mightiest mountain range in Canada, great herds of caribou, and beautiful wildflowers which paint the landscape bright pink in the summertime.

history: From the most ancient archeological finds in the Americas unearthed at Old Crow, to evidence of fur traders, gold miners, and military engineers, Yukon boasts a kaleidoscopic, colorful history. In 1848, Robert Campbell of the Hudson Bay Company established a trading post at Fort Selkirk on the Yukon River. Tlingit Indians from Southeast Alaska burned his post in 1852, but trading continued at Fort Yukon until 1869. In 1870 Canada purchased Rupert's Land from the Company, of which Yukon was a part. The government didn't show much interest in the

area until 1887 to 1888 when George Dawson was sent N at the head of the Canadian Yukon Exploration Expedition. By this time, mining had already replaced fur trading as the main focus of interest and hundreds of prospectors were searching for the big strike everyone could feel was about to occur. On 17 Aug. 1896 a sourdough named George Carmack and 2 Indian companions, Skookum Jim and Tagish Charlie, found gold in the Klondike Valley on a tip from fellow prospector Robert Henderson. This sparked the last great gold rush of the 19th C. and changed Yukon forever. In 1898 it was separated from Canada's Northwest Territories and Dawson City was made the capital.

the Alaska Highway: After 1900, mining went into a slow decline and nobody paid much attention to the territory until early 1942 when a threatened Japanese invasion prompted President Roosevelt to order construction of a military road NW through Canada to Alaska. By November, an incredible 8 months later, the opening ceremony of the pioneer road

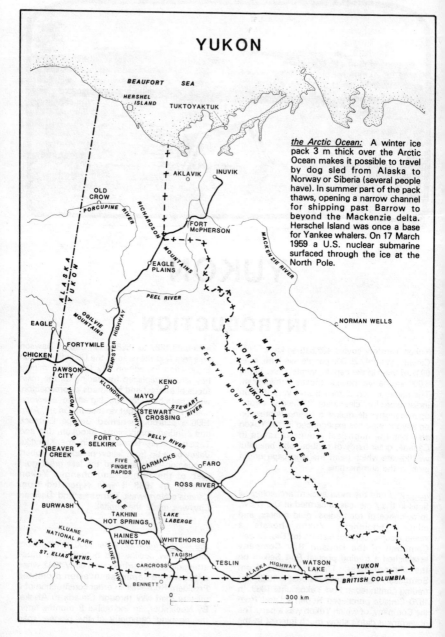

YUKON

the Arctic Ocean: A winter ice pack 3 m thick over the Arctic Ocean makes it possible to travel by dog sled from Alaska to Norway or Siberia (several people have). In summer part of the pack thaws, opening a narrow channel for shipping past Barrow to beyond the Mackenzie delta. Herschel Island was once a base for Yankee whalers. On 17 March 1959 a U.S. nuclear submarine surfaced through the ice at the North Pole.

took place at Soldiers's Summit beside Kluane Lake. Upgrading work continued on the road and by the following year all 2,437 km from Dawson Creek, B.C., to Fairbanks had been gravel surfaced. Some 25,000 men labored on the road for 20 months, building 130 bridges. The total cost to the U.S. Government was $140 million—a fortune in those days. The Alaska Highway had an impact on Yukon equivalent to that of the Klondike gold rush. Whitehorse replaced Dawson City as the capital in 1953. But although the highway is the vital link that Roosevelt foresaw and a highly scenic route in its own right, to discover the Yukon which Robert Service expressed so well, you must take to the rivers and trails where the real country is waiting.

warning: Beware of arriving in Canada without enough Canadian currency to tide you over until you can get to a bank. There are no exchange facilities at the borders and business people give the worst possible rate of exchange to anyone paying in U.S. dollars. On the brighter side, the value of the Canadian dollar is considerably lower than U.S., so you get a nice bonus every time you change your money. Large American and European banks will sell you Canadian dollars at the current rate, or you could buy some Canadian dollar travelers cheques. Canadian immigration officials may ask to see your money to guarantee that you will not compete for nonexistent jobs or social benefits. See "money" in the main "Introduction" for further information.

WHITEHORSE

With 16,500 inhabitants, Whitehorse is the largest city in Northern Canada. To the east, the bare, rounded hulk of Grey Mountain (1,494 m) fills the horizon. The Yukon River, fifth largest in North America, paces powerfully past the city on its 3,200-km journey northward and westward to the Bering Sea. Whitehorse began as a tent city on the banks of the Yukon River at the end of the Whitehorse Rapids, just downstream from Miles Canyon. In 1900, the WP & YR narrow-gauge railroad reached Whitehorse, finally connecting tidewater at Skagway to the mighty Yukon. Here passengers and freight transferred to riverboats for the trip down the Yukon River to Dawson City. In winter, horse sleighs were used. The town mushroomed 'overnight' between 1942 and 1943 after work had begun on the Alaska Highway. The town sits at the 1,475th km of the road, with 460 km to go till the Alaska border just beyond Beaver Creek. Today, what impresses the visitor is the easy-going vitality of the place, a friendly oasis in the heart of an unforgiving land. Don't come looking for another of those quaint, turn-of-the-century towns you saw in Southeast Alaska, because Whitehorse is brash and modern, pulsing with reckless frontier energy.

SIGHTS OF WHITEHORSE

downtown: The MacBride Museum, 1st Ave. and Steele (open daily 0900-2100, $2), has a large and varied collection, including the old government telegraph office, engine no. 51 (1881) from the WP & YR, Sam McGee's cabin, and a display of stuffed Yukon wildlife. At a long table are hundreds of gold rush photographs in large albums, which you're welcome to sit and ponder. Notice the 1,175 kg copper nugget on the corner of the property, just outside the museum fence. The Old Log Church (1900) and rectory, at 3rd Ave. and Elliott, have been restored and opened as

a religious museum ($1.50). Nearby, have a look (from the street) at the log 'skyscrapers.' Just a couple blocks away the big, modern Territorial Administration Building (1976) is definitely worth exploring. The officials inside have built themselves the plushest office block N of Edmonton. Ask at the information desk for a free tour (Mon. to Fri. 1400-1700, Sat., Sun. 1000-1800). The colorful tapestries and acrylic resin murals in the building interpret the land, history, and people of Yukon. Downstairs there's a good public cafeteria. The adjoining public library and Yukon Archives often have exhibits of old maps and photographs. Use these facilities to the maximum. Without doubt, the most interesting man-made sight in Whitehorse, located beside the Yukon River, is the riverboat SS _Klondike II,_ built in 1937—the largest and last of its kind to steam between Whitehorse and Dawson City. The _Klondike II_ was retired in 1955, but has been beautifully restored by Parks Canada (open daily 0900-1700, free). Don't miss it.

to Miles Canyon: An excellent all-day hike from Whitehorse will take you right around Schwatka Lake, with a number of historical and scenic attractions along the way. Take a lunch. Begin by crossing the bridge beside the _Klondike II._ A nature trail leads through the woods on the E bank of the Yukon River, towards the hydro dam (1959) which created Schwatka Lake. The once-feared Whitehorse Rapids, where many gold rush stampeders drowned, have been tamed by this dam. A fish ladder beside the dam is designed to allow salmon to get around this man-made obstacle to their spawning grounds up river. Above the dam is a high hill which the more energetic may want to climb for the view. Go down the other side (or around along the shore) and out onto Chadburn Lake road. Follow this road S till you see some paths along the lake or river; follow one of these for a more enjoyable walk.

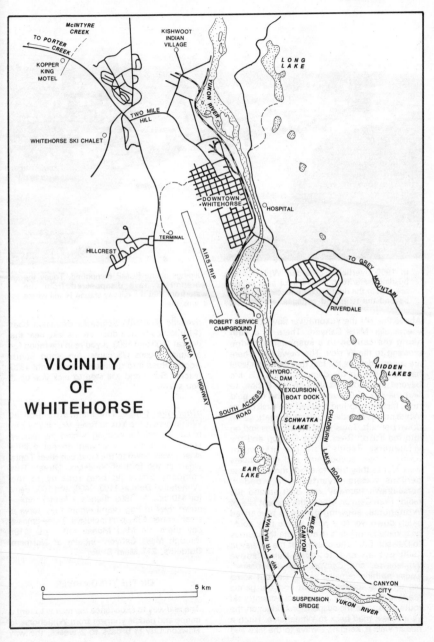

VICINITY
OF
WHITEHORSE

McINTYRE CREEK

TO PORTER CREEK

KOPPER KING MOTEL

KISHWOOT INDIAN VILLAGE

LONG LAKE

YUKON RIVER

TWO MILE HILL

WHITEHORSE SKI CHALET

DOWNTOWN WHITEHORSE

HOSPITAL

TERMINAL

HILLCREST

AIRSTRIP

TO GREY MOUNTAIN

RIVERDALE

ROBERT SERVICE CAMPGROUND

HIDDEN LAKES

HYDRO DAM

EXCURSION BOAT DOCK

SCHWATKA LAKE

CHADBURN LAKE ROAD

ALASKA HIGHWAY

SOUTH ACCESS ROAD

EAR LAKE

WP & YR RAILWAY

MILES CANYON

CANYON CITY

SUSPENSION BRIDGE

YUKON RIVER

0   5 km

In 1900 riverboats crowded Whitehorse's bustling waterfront. Slipways for boat building are seen in the right foreground; directly above, beyond the tents and cottages, are the large buildings of the RCMP compound. Today the warehouses have disappeared from the waterfront, but the railway station is still where it was then.

Above the lake the Yukon River flows through spectacular Miles Canyon. There is a path along the canyon to a suspension bridge crossing to the W side. The views along here are superb, despite the fact that the water level has risen due to the dam. Continue 1½ km beyond the bridge, staying on the E side, to find the site of Canyon city. During the gold rush, miners who had crossed the Chilkoot or White passes boarded boats at Bennett, sailed down Bennett, Tagish and Marsh lakes and on into the Yukon River. Miles Canyon and the Whitehorse Rapids were the first major obstacles they encountered and many boats were lost as they tried to shoot through these perilous waters. Eventually, a wooden, horse-drawn tramway was built around the rapids from Canyon City to the present site of Whitehorse, allowing goods to be carried safely downriver to a point where they could be reloaded into boats to complete the journey to Dawson City. The opening of the railway in 1900 put an end to river travel above Whitehorse, and Canyon City disappeared. Today nothing remains at the site but some old tin cans scattered about and the gentle grade of the tramway, now a cross-country ski route. Return to the suspension bridge; on the W side is a road back to Whitehorse. Hitch a ride or walk it, keeping always to the lake and

riverside. The MV *Schwatka* excursion boat ($10) leaves from a dock on the lake near the dam at 1400 and 1900, if you're in the mood for a cruise. Buses (75 cents) run along South Access Road into town every hour until 1820 (except Sun.) and will stop to pick you up if you wave.

other river trips: The main attraction at Whitehorse is the Yukon River, which you can of course visit for nothing behind the railway station anytime. If you want to get a little closer, walk down to the Goldrush River Tours wharf at the foot of Strickland Street. This company offers jet boat runs up to the Whitehorse Dam at 1100, 1400, and 1600 daily for $10 pp. At 1800 there's a launch cruise down river to Egg Island where they serve a steak dinner, $35 pp all inclusive. Three times a day there are Mad Moose raft trips ($19) through Miles Canyon; inquire at Northern Outdoors, 211 Main Street.

ON THE YUKON RIVER

The *real* way to experience the river is to rent a canoe and paddle yourself from Whitehorse to Dawson City in 5 days to 2 weeks, the way many gold rush stampeders did it. This is quite feasible and easily arranged; there are several companies in Whitehorse in the business of supplying everything required for such a trip at a reasonable price. For example, Goldrush River Tours at the foot of Strickland St. rents 4.9-m canoes with 2 life preservers and 3 paddles for $239. This price is for the whole rental (not pp) for up to 14 days, and the equipment may be dropped off with company agents in Carmacks or Dawson City at no extra cost. A larger 5.2-m canoe suitable for 3 people is $30 more. If you don't wish to paddle all the way to Dawson City (735 km), they charge only $126 as far as Carmacks (320 km) or $59 to Lake Laberge (one day). Write Goldrush River Tours, Box 4835, Whitehorse, YT Y1A 4N6, Canada (tel. 403-667-7496) for a brochure. Canoes are also available in Whitehorse from Yukon Canoe Rental, 6159 6th Ave. (tel. 667-7773), and Listers Motor Sports (tel. 667-7491). When checking around, remember to ask about drop-off charges (if any), life preservers, etc. You could also buy a canoe for about $600 at the Hudson Bay Company and paddle yourself right into Alaska, terminating at Eagle, Circle, or the Haul Road. Or bring an inflatable raft with you on the bus.

the route: For nearly half a century the river was the main highway to the Klondike, so wrecks of old riverboats, abandoned Indian villages, and trappers' cabins are seen all along the way. Sometimes you'll see evidence of the former government telegraph line or the old stage route from Whitehorse to Dawson City. Fort Selkirk, at the junction of the Pelly and Yukon rivers, has been partially restored by the Canadian government. There's good camping and fishing up most of the creeks flowing into the river. Wildlife is best seen at dusk. The Yukon flows at 16 kph, so it doesn't take much effort to head downstream at a reasonable clip. The trip is not dangerous, but keep close to shore while traversing unpredictable Lake Laberge. The Five Finger Rapids are not especially hazardous, and a channel has been blasted through the Rink Rapids. Try to keep your weight down; a heavily loaded canoe is easily tipped over. Also, tie what gear you do take to the canoe—just in case. And don't forget to take enough libation (but please do not litter). Detailed maps and river guides are sold at the Yukon Gallery in the Sheffield Hotel, Whitehorse. Don't delay too long to do this trip as a proposed hydro dam at Eagle's Nest Bluff near Carmacks could soon flood much of the river, ruining this premier recreational opportunity.

VICINITY OF WHITEHORSE

Takhini Hot Springs: These excellent hot springs, 27 km from Whitehorse off the road to Dawson City, feature a 36 degree C. mineral water pool which you may use for $2.50 per day, if you care to sit in them and warm yourself for that long. Camping is $5. Call tel. 403-633-2706 or ask at the tourist office in Whitehorse about transportation. A taxi costs $33 OW!

Carcross: This small town (pop. 200), 72 km S of Whitehorse on the narrows between Bennett and Tagish lakes, was originally a hunting camp. The Indians called it Caribou

The Caribou Hotel is still a focal point in downtown Carcross.

Crossing for the countless ruminants which once passed through; later the name was shortened to Carcross. Human activities in the area have reduced the number of caribou from half a million in the 1920s to about 5,000 today. The last spike of the WP & YR Railroad was driven in Carcross and the town hasn't changed much since then. The railway station remains the center of the community. _sights:_ Trains enter Carcross over the original swing bridge, built to allow sternwheel riverboats to pass. Tagish Charlie, one of the 3 men who discovered gold in the Klondike in 1896, drowned when he fell off this bridge in 1905. On the R as the train pulls into the station is the _Tutshi_ (pronounced TOO-SHY), a steamer which once carried passengers and cargo down Tagish Lake towards Atlin. The tiny locomotive, Duchess, which connected with the _Tutshi_ and pulled a train over the 3 km separating Tagish and Atlin lakes, stands nearby. To the L is Matthew Watson General Store and the Caribou Hotel ($25 s, $35 d),

built in 1911. A parrot and a myna bird converse at you as you sit in the hotel's cafe. In the old Carcross Cemetery, 1½ km SE of town, notables such as Skookum Jim, Tagish Charlie, and Kate Carmack rest. Just outside the gate is the grave of Polly, the original Caribou Hotel parrot, which died in 1972 at the age of 150. _from Carcross:_ The Atlin Express minibus connects Carcross to Whitehorse ($6.75) mornings on Mon., Wed., and Fri., and to Atlin afternoons of the same days. If you get off the train at Carcross, they will not honor your ticket on to Whitehorse the next day, forcing you to take the bus or hitch.

Atlin: The village of Atlin, 175 km SE of Whitehorse, sits on the E shore of scenic, 795-sq-km Atlin Lake. A minor gold rush in 1898 brought a flood of hopefuls and the Atlin Historical Museum keeps photographs from that period. The old Court House (1900) is nearby. Also in town is the lake boat SS _Tarahne_ which once connected Atlin to Scotia Bay, on the W side of Atlin Lake, where supplies from Carcross arrived. The cold mineral springs in town are also worth a look. The pioneer cemetery is 3 km east. Ten km E is Discovery, site of the original 1898 strike on Pine Creek. A number of abandoned buildings remain. Mining continues in the area on a small scale. _from Atlin:_ The Atlin Express minibus leaves the Atlin Inn for Whitehorse ($15) Mon., Wed., and Fri. at 0630, returning the same afternoon (see "from Whitehorse" below). The service is via Carcross.

Liard Hot Springs: A good place to break the long bus ride down the Alaska Highway is Liard River Hotsprings Provincial Park, midway between Whitehorse and Dawson Creek, B.C. In summer Greyhound buses pass here 6 days a week in each direction and a free stopover is allowed if you tell the driver when he takes your ticket. Use of the hot spring pool is free, but the water is very hot (40 degrees C). There are actually 3 springs here, but only the first one you come to is open due to pesky bears near the other two. There's an official campground ($6) only 700 m from the first pool. Satisfactory meals are served at Liard River Lodge, just 1 km from the campground. People travel 781 km up the Alaska Highway from Dawson Creek just to enjoy these mineral hot springs.

Signboards near the Watson Lake Hotel, a rest stop on the bus ride from Whitehorse to Dawson Creek, B.C.

PRACTICALITIES

stay: The Fourth Avenue Residence, 4051 4th Ave. (tel 667-4471), provides college-dormitory style accommodations at $23 s, $17 pp d, $13 pp t. There are low monthly rates, but no weeklies during the summer. Coin-operated washing machines are available. The Chilkoot Motel, opposite Qwanlin Mall (tel. 668-4910), has pleasant rooms with cooking facilities at $28 s, $40 d, or $150 weekly. The cheapest hotel in town is the Fort Yukon, 2163 2nd Ave. (tel. 667-2595); spartan rooms with shared bath are $22 s, $26 d. If you don't mind commuting, the Kopper King Motel 5 km out on the Alaska Highway (tel. 668-2347) has rooms at $24 s, $28 d, or $75 weekly. The bar at the Kopper King is the most popular in Whitehorse; there's also a grocery store and fast-food outlet. Get there every 30 min. on the Porter Creek bus, but no service after 1845 or on Sunday. Also on the Alaska Highway at Porter Creek are the Casa Loma Motel (tel. 633-2266) and the Trails North Truck Stop (tel. 633-2327). Both have daily and weekly rates similar to those at the Kopper King, but are not as good (Trails North is not recommended).

camping: The Robert Service Campground ($5 per site) is 2 km S of town by the river off the South Access Road. This campground is for tenters only and hopefully facilities will improve. If the Robert Service is full or you just don't want to pay the fee, continue walking S past the dam and along the lakeshore. There are plenty of good places to pitch a tent in the woods just above the lake, but for privacy, keep your tent out of sight of roads, trails, houses, etc. Other unofficial campsites are along the top of the bluff above the town up

towards the airport (walk straight up Cook St. from Qwanlin Mall), along the McIntyre Creek Trail opposite the Kopper King (see above), and at Long Lake.

eats and entertainment: About the cheapest place in town to eat is the coffee shop on the 2nd floor in Hougen's Department Store (open Mon. to Saturday). Try their sourdough pancake breakfast ($3) or spaghetti dinner ($3). Mr. Mike's, 4114 4th Ave., has steak and salad, plus hamburgers at reasonable prices. The No Pop Sandwich Shop behind the post office has luncheon specials, expresso coffee, and Sunday brunch—good food, great atmosphere. Bars in Yukon stay open 7 days a week and the drinking age is nineteen. The locals hang out in the hotel bars at the Capital and the 98, but be aware that the 98 is rough. For more sedate drinking, try the happy hour (Mon. to Thurs. 1600-1900) at the T & M Hotel.

shopping: An outstanding array of items made by the Indians and Eskimos of Canada's Northwest Territories are available for sale at Northern Images, 4th Ave. and Jarvis. This large store is owned by a Native coop and all of the articles are hand made. Even if you're not buying, Northern Images is well worth a visit and is better than most museums. Get to know your endangered species! Remember that clothing or souvenirs made from animals which are considered endangered species (including lynx, wolf, grizzly bear, or otter) or from marine mammals (whales, porpoises, seals, sea lions, walruses, or polar bears) are prohibited from entry into the United States. People who appreciate wildlife don't buy these articles anyway. For handicrafts made by Yukon Indians, visit Yukon Native Products, 105 Main Street.

services and information: If you haven't been immunized for diptheria, tetanus, or polio during the last 10 years, get these shots free at the Whitehorse Health Center (Mon. to Fri. 0800-0830). This service is available to everyone. If you're camping and want a shower, go to Lions Public Swimming Pool ($2) beside the Fourth Ave. Residence. Take soap, shampoo, and a towel. The tourist office, 302 Steele St. (open daily 0800-2000) can answer questions and has plenty of useful brochures. Ask about free guided hikes in the

DOWNTOWN WHITEHORSE

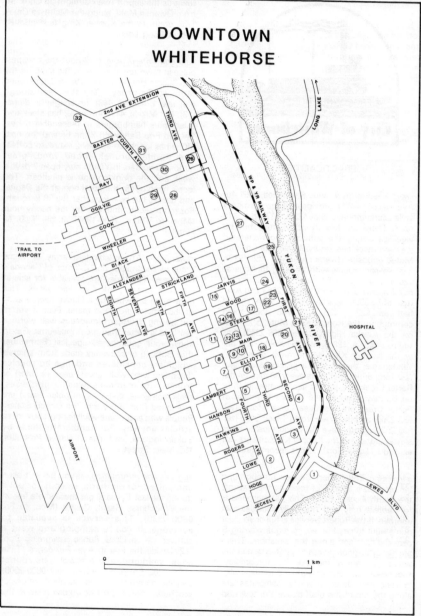

Whitehorse area which are often arranged by the Yukon Conservation Society; these are highly recommended. Offer to contribute something to the gas if they drive you out to a trail. The Yukon Gallery in the Sheffield Hotel sells excellent topographical maps of the territory. They also have special guidebooks for river runners.

FROM WHITEHORSE

by air: Whitehorse Airport (YXY) is 5 km SW of town. An Airport bus ($3) meets all CP Air flights. Walk to town in 20 min. by following the footpath along the fence around the NW end of the runway and over to the bluff directly above the city. *by rail:* The WP & YR train to Skagway leaves daily at 0945. The CDN$78 fare includes lunch. For a complete description of this railroad, see under "Skagway."

by bus: Coachways, a subsidiary of Greyhound, has daily buses to Dawson Creek, B.C., with connections to all points in the U.S. and Canada. The fare is $99 to anywhere in Canada as far as Montreal, $132 to points in the Maritimes. You may take up to 60 days to complete your journey and unlimited stopovers are allowed. In summer there is a Coachways bus to Fairbanks every other day—CDN$69.50 for the 15-hour trip. Coachways will carry your bicycle provided you dismantle it and put it in a carton. Greyhound's Ameripass is valid from anywhere in Canada or the U.S. right up as far as Beaver Creek, Yukon, but not into Alaska. You buy another ticket (US$40) at the border. Norline Coaches has a service to Dawson City ($57.50—Ameripass not valid) 3 times a week. The driver will stop at the Five Finger Rapids viewpoint just beyond Carmacks if enough of you ask him. Yukon Stage Lines has a minibus service to Skagway (CDN$39, daily), Haines (CDN$53, 3 times a week), and Anchorage (CDN$134, weekly). This company allows no stopovers. All of the above leave from the bus station at 3211a 3rd Ave., behind the Hudson Bay Company. There are no coin lockers. The Atlin Express minibus departs the Taku Hotel on Mon. Wed., and Fri. at 1145 for Carcross ($6.75) and Atlin ($15).

local buses: Whitehorse Transit buses (75 cents) run Mon. to Fri. from 0630-1900, with reduced service on Sat. and no buses on Sunday. Ask the driver for a schedule. A Day Pass is available from drivers at $2. All routes begin and end beside the Hudson Bay Company opposite Qwanlin Mall. *hitching:* To hitch W take the Porter Creek bus and ask the driver to drop you as far out as he goes on the Alaska Highway. To hitch E take the Hillcrest bus to the corner of Alaska Highway and South Access Road.

WHITEHORSE

1. SS *Klondike II*
2. Fourth Avenue Residence/swimming pool
3. Kentucky Fried Chicken
4. Territorial Administration Building
5. liquor store
6. Old Log Church
7. R.C.M.P.
8. T & M Hotel
9. Taku Hotel
10. Hougen's Department Store
11. Mr. Mike's Restaurant
12. post office
13. Federal Building
14. No Pop Sandwich Shop
15. Northern Images
16. tourist office
17. Yukon Gallery
18. Whitehorse Health Center
19. log skyscraper
20. Capital Hotel/Yukon Native Products
21. railway station
22. city hall
23. MacBride Museum
24. 98 Hotel
25. Goldrush Rentals Ltd.
26. bus station
27. Fort Yukon Motel
28. Qwanlin Mall
29. Chilkoot Motel
30. Hudson Bay Company/city bus stop
31. laundromat
32. Indian Cemetery

DAWSON CITY

Dawson City squats on a flat floodplain among eroded mountains at the confluence of the Yukon and Klondike rivers. Only 300 km below the Arctic Circle, it gets 21 hours of daylight during summer solstice, 21 June. In 1898 Dawson was the end of the gold rush trail, the great destination thousands of men and women struggled across cold mountains and down raging rivers to reach. The Klondike goldfields cover an area of 2,000 sq km SE of the city. Over millenia, rich placer streaks accumulated on the unglaciated bedrock. The Canadian government permitted non-citizens to stake mining claims in the Klondike (the U.S. government didn't) so hopefuls poured in from all over North America. By the time they got there, however, every claim worth working within 150 km of Dawson had already been staked by prospectors who happened to be in the area in 1896; most of the newcomers wound up working for wages. For a few short years Dawson City boomed. In 1899, it had 30,000 inhabitants and was the largest Canadian city W of Winnipeg; today 838 people live there. Lousetown, the red light district, was just S across the Klondike River. In 1899, news reached Dawson of a new strike at Nome, Alaska, and within weeks thousands boarded riverboats for the Bering Sea. By 1902 most of the individual claims around Dawson had been bought up by large corporations which continued to dredge the creeks until 1966. Today a second gold rush is underway, sparked by the soaring gold prices. Millions of dollars in mining equipment has been brought in and 58,420 fine ounces were recovered in

1980 (1,077,550 fine ounces were taken out in 1900). Several hundred placer mines are operating and sluicing is underway on all the old gold rush creeks. Visitors should be aware that unauthorized gold panning or meddling with active mining operations is illegal and risky. You are permitted to wander anywhere you like, but miners deal quickly with anyone who looks like a claim jumper, so be careful. Dawson City and the surrounding area offer many opportunities for adventure, as authentic and valid today as ever. If you come all the way from Seattle the *real* way (ship, foot, train, and paddle), you'll share the thrill the stampeders felt on arriving, and forge a living link with the past which will stay with you long into the future.

SIGHTS OF DAWSON CITY

downtown: The riverboat SS *Keno* (1922) sits beached and restored on Front St. in Dawson City; open daily 1000-1300/1400-1800 for free tours. The *Keno* once plied the Stewart River, bringing lead/silver/zinc ore concentrates from the mining area around Mayo down to the confluence with the Yukon where larger riverboats, such as the *Klondike II*, picked them up for transport to Whitehorse and the railhead. The exterior of the Canadian Imperial Bank of Commerce, near the *Keno,* hasn't changed much since 1900 when it was built. The poet Robert Service worked as a teller here from 1908 to 1909. Upstairs there's a

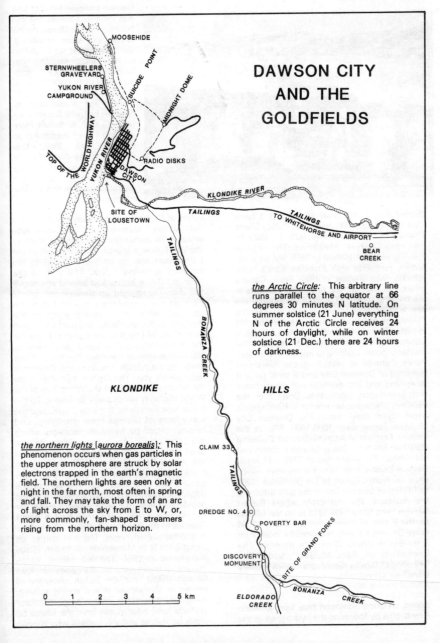

DAWSON CITY AND THE GOLDFIELDS

MOOSEHIDE

STERNWHEELERS GRAVEYARD
YUKON RIVER CAMPGROUND

SUICIDE POINT

MIDNIGHT DOME

TOP OF THE WORLD HIGHWAY

YUKON RIVER

RADIO DISKS

DAWSON CITY

SITE OF LOUSETOWN

KLONDIKE RIVER

TAILINGS

TAILINGS
TO WHITEHORSE AND AIRPORT→

BEAR CREEK

TAILINGS

BONANZA CREEK

KLONDIKE

HILLS

CLAIM 33

TAILINGS

DREDGE NO. 4

POVERTY BAR

DISCOVERY MONUMENT

SITE OF GRAND FORKS

BONANZA CREEK

ELDORADO CREEK

the Arctic Circle: This arbitrary line runs parallel to the equator at 66 degrees 30 minutes N latitude. On summer solstice (21 June) everything N of the Arctic Circle receives 24 hours of daylight, while on winter solstice (21 Dec.) there are 24 hours of darkness.

the northern lights [aurora borealis]: This phenomenon occurs when gas particles in the upper atmosphere are struck by solar electrons trapped in the earth's magnetic field. The northern lights are seen only at night in the far north, most often in spring and fall. They may take the form of an arc of light across the sky from E to W, or, more commonly, fan-shaped streamers rising from the northern horizon.

0   1   2   3   4   5 km

Dawson's original red light area was the alley between 2nd and 3rd from King to Queen. As the city became more established, the prostitutes were shifted across the Klondike to Lousetown where they continued to do a brisk business until the respectable ladies of Dawson led a campaign to close the brothels. Surreptitious bordelos such as Ruby's Place on 2nd Ave. continued to operate until 1957. One wonders if the Parks Canada restoration program includes any plans for the reestablishment of this historic activity...

display in the old assay room of the bank (open daily 1000-1500, free). The Palace Grand Theater on King St. was built in 1899 by "Arizona Charley" Meadows. The original building was demolished in 1959, but an exact replica, complete with Klondike Kate's room upstairs, was erected in 1962. Parks Canada offers free slide shows, talks, and concerts in the building (open 1000-1800) throughout the day, with a special activity at 1430. At 2000 the "Gaslight Follies" ($8) is performed for tourists. The old post office finished in 1900, just across the street from the theater, was the first large public building to appear in Dawson. Parks Canada is restoring the historical buildings of Dawson City and a stroll up and down 2nd and 3rd avenues will reveal many with explanatory signboards. Don't miss the excellent photographic exhibit in Harrington's Store (open daily, free). The Dawson City Museum (open daily 1000-1800, $2), in the former Territorial Administration Building (1901) on 5th Ave., has gold rush artifacts and old photos. The slide show at 1330 is $1 extra. Several locomotives from the railways which once ran from Dawson to the goldfields (1906 to 1914) may be seen free in the park adjoining the museum. The log cabin where Robert Service lived from 1909-1912 is on the hillside on the E side of town. Visit at 1000 or 1600 when Service's poetry is recited by local actor Tom Byrne (free). Service's poems "The Cremation of Sam McGee" and "The Shooting of Dan McGrew" are known to every Canadian schoolchild.

hiking: A good afternoon hike from Dawson City begins by following the hydro lines at the

E end of Queen St. directly up the slope to a point where it levels off, and you see 2 large white radio transmitters through the trees to the left. Follow a branch cable through to the transmitters and go up the dirt road to the smaller, uppermost disk. The trail to the Midnight Dome begins just behind and above this disk. Go straight up through the woods passing the abandoned Yukon Ditch, an aqueduct which once carried water to the dredges on the goldfields, and past an unused loop of the old road to the summit. From the top of the Dome (885 m) you'll get a complete 360-degree view of the area. The Yukon River stretches out in both directions and Dawson is right below you. The Ogilvie Mountains line the horizon to the NE; to the W the Top of the World Highway winds away to Alaska. To the S you look directly up Bonanza Creek, past the wavy lines of tailings from dredging, and hillsides pitted by hydraulic monitors which still bring paydirt down for sluicing. After a good look, follow the ridge down W towards the Yukon River. This trail affords an even more spectacular view of Dawson City. After passing the clear area near the end of the ridge, the path winds down through a young deciduous forest to a point where it meets the Moosehide Trail. Take this trail a short distance to the R to Suicide Point, where there is another superb view. The trail carries on about 2 km N to Moosehide, an Indian village abandoned in 1957. The log cabins, cache houses, schoolhouse, St. Barnabas Anglican Church (1908), and the Indian cemetery all remain at Moosehide. If you decide to visit, remember that this is private property. Many artifacts have been stolen from the village by previous visitors and any Indians who happen to be around won't be very excited when they see tourists arriving. Turn back with grace if asked to. Chances are, however, that you won't meet anyone. On the way back to Dawson you'll cross Moosehide Slide which hangs over the NE side of the city. Look up above you to see some remains from the old aqueduct (see above). Watch for blueberries, cranberries, and raspberries all along the way. _note:_ Don't bother asking about these trails at the Klondike Visitors Association. They have no information on hiking and will only try to convince you not to go.

to the goldfields: A trip up Bonanza Creek to the Discovery Claim, 16 km SE of Dawson City, where George Carmack and his Indian companions found gold in 1896, is highly recommended. A monument marks the spot. Just 1 km beyond the monument is the confluence of Bonanza and Eldorado creeks, site of the gold rush town of Grand Forks.

Nothing remains at "the Forks" as the area has since been dredged. The Klondike Visitors Association owns a claim at Grand Forks where you may pan for gold as much as you like free of charge (bring your own pan). On the way up from Dawson you will have passed 2 commercial panning operations, Claim 33 and Poverty Bar, where you pay $5 a pan and are guaranteed gold because the pans are spiked. Still, it's good fun. If you wish to pan elsewhere in the Klondike, ask permission of the claim holder first. Although present-day miners own the mineral rights, they do not own the land itself. You're within your rights to wander where you please, but keep clear of any active mining operations. Although the endless heaps of gravel tailings are the dominant impression on a trip up Bonanza Creek, the highlight is Dredge No. 4, the largest wooden-hulled gold dredge in North America. Built in 1912, this massive piece of machinery scooped paydirt from the creek beds right up until 1966. The dredge is 2 km

Miners operating rockers at King Solomon's Hill up Bonanza Creek in 1898. Gravel was shoveled into the wooden boxes which were rocked back and forth manually using handles on the sides. Larger particles were screened out on top while gold, which is twice as heavy as lead, would collect in the bottom after the other material had been removed. Water was dipped out of pipe-fed troughs beside the rockers and poured over the gravel to help wash the gold down. The stampeders arrived to find every claim within 150 km of Dawson already staked; many turned to working for wages.

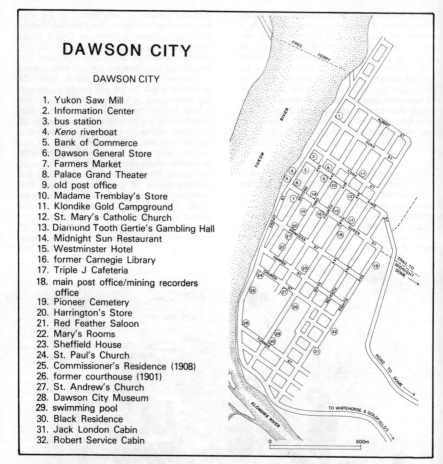

DAWSON CITY

DAWSON CITY

1. Yukon Saw Mill
2. Information Center
3. bus station
4. *Keno* riverboat
5. Bank of Commerce
6. Dawson General Store
7. Farmers Market
8. Palace Grand Theater
9. old post office
10. Madame Tremblay's Store
11. Klondike Gold Campground
12. St. Mary's Catholic Church
13. Diamond Tooth Gertie's Gambling Hall
14. Midnight Sun Restaurant
15. Westminster Hotel
16. former Carnegie Library
17. Triple J Cafeteria
18. main post office/mining recorders office
19. Pioneer Cemetery
20. Harrington's Store
21. Red Feather Saloon
22. Mary's Rooms
23. Sheffield House
24. St. Paul's Church
25. Commissioner's Residence (1908)
26. former courthouse (1901)
27. St. Andrew's Church
28. Dawson City Museum
29. swimming pool
30. Black Residence
31. Jack London Cabin
32. Robert Service Cabin

below the Discovery Monument on the road from Dawson and has been opened to the public by Parks Canada (free). *getting there:* Gold City Tours at the Sheffield House runs a 3-hour tour to Dredge No. 4 and the Discovery Monument at 0900 and 1300, $12 pp. Panning for gold at Poverty Bar is $5 extra.

PRACTICALITES

stay: The only hotel in Dawson City with any character left is the Westminster Hotel, $25 s, $40 d (bath down the hall). Don't let the

appearance of the Westminster scare you; the rooms on the 3rd floor are clean and quiet. Mary's Rooms is homey but expensive at $35 s, $45 d (shared bath). The rest of Dawson's hotels have Disneyland exteriors, Howard Johnson interiors, and charge the earth. The high prices are partially due to the short tourist season (June to Aug.); the other 9 months the facilites are unused.

camping: The Yukon River Campground on the W bank of the river is $5 a site, although often no one bothers to collect. Camp free anywhere on this side of the river, either on the

Only wooden braces prevent Straits' Auction House from joining many other vanished gold rush buildings at Dawson City.

river bank itself or down beyond the campground. A free car ferry crosses the Yukon every hour 24 hours a day—a pleasant trip even if you're not camping. Walk down past the campground to the sternwheelers' graveyard where 3 big riverboats disintegrate where they were beached many years ago. The Klondike Gold Campground ($6 per tent) is just a few blocks from downtown Dawson City. This is perfect if you want to camp on an ugly gravel parking lot surrounded by motor homes. There's a laundromat on the premises which is open to the public. There are lots of places to camp free on the hillside above Dawson, but this is officially prohibited so keep out of sight.

food and entertainment: There's nowhere cheap to eat in Dawson City, so groceries from the Dawson General Store are highly recommended (or better still, bring them with you from Whitehorse). The Midnight Sun Restaurant serves good dinners, but be prepared to pay double what the same thing would cost you anywhere else. If you want coffee in the morning, the cafeteria in the Triple J Motel opens at 0700. Diamond Tooth Gertie's Gambling Hall offers the only legal gambling in Canada, plus cancan girls and lots of local color. Of course it's a bit touristy, but at $2 admission to see the show and try your luck it's excellent value (until you lose at the tables). There's blackjack, poker, and roulette ($25 limit)—the real thing, no play money or pretending. Doors open at 2000 every night

except Sunday; shows are at 2100, 2300, and 0100. All proceeds go to the Klondike Visitors Association. For something a little more earthy, try the 2 bars in the Westminster Hotel.

services and information: Change your money before coming to Dawson City (if possible) as the one bank gives a poor rate of exchange. There is a large information center at King and Front streets. Topographical maps are sold in the Mining Recorders Office adjoining the main post office. They also sell an excellent blueprint map of the Klondike Placer Area showing all the goldfields for only $1—a bargain.

from Dawson City: Norline Coaches has a bus to Whitehorse ($57.50) 3 times a week during the summer. The same company runs a minibus from Dawson to Tok, Alaska (CDN$55), also 3 times a week. Ask about connections in Tok as you sometimes have to wait a day for the bus to Fairbanks. It is cheaper to buy a combination ticket to Fairbanks than one to Tok and another to Fairbanks. You could hitch to Whitehorse, but mostly senior citizens in motor homes travel along the Top of the World Highway to Alaska, and they never stop. It's better to go up and ask for rides while vehicles are still lined up waiting for the ferry across the river. Check the notice board in the tourist office for people offering rides in exchange for gas or driving, or put up a destination notice of your own.

ABOVE THE ARCTIC CIRCLE

Inuvik: The only highway in Canada to cross the Arctic Circle is the Dempster Highway, opened in 1979. This highway and a proposed lateral pipeline now threaten the Porcupine caribou herd (120,000 animals), by cutting across its range. This herd is one of the last of its kind in the world. The first stretch of highway, which crosses the Ogilvie Mountains, is spectacular. The Dempster terminates 775 km NE of Dawson City at Inuvik, Northwest Territories (pop. 3,000), the largest Canadian community above the Arctic Circle. Inuvik was founded on the E side of the 60-km wide MacKenzie River delta in 1955. Its original Eskimo population relocated from Aklavik on the W side of the delta, which was thought to be sinking. Today an even mix of Eskimos, native Indians, and whites live in this modern town where the sun never sets from 24 May to 24 July. A church in town was built to look like a big igloo; otherwise there is little to see or do. Camp at the Happy Valley Campground ($5), right in the center of town. *getting there:* There is no bus service to Inuvik and a flight from Dawson City costs $200 OW. The highway is the only real attraction to make you come up here, so put up a notice in the tourist office in Dawson City offering to share the gas and driving with a motorist and hope for the best. A more adventuresome way of doing it would be to paddle yourself several thousand km down the MacKenzie River from Fort Providence, N.W.T., to the Dempster Highway. There is scheduled bus service from Edmonton to Fort Providence (Ameripass valid). Allow a whole summer to pull this one off.

Jacob's ladder

KLUANE NATIONAL PARK

The lofty ice-capped mountains of SW Yukon, overflowing with glaciers and flanked by lower ranges rich in wildlife, have now been set aside as Kluane National Park. Although the Alaska and Haines highways which run along the fringe of the park make it easily accessible, Kluane is a wilderness as yet hardly touched by the hand of man. There are many opportunites here for uncrowded backcountry experiences; once you leave the highways you will see few other people. No highways run into the park itself, so to experience the true magnificence of this wilderness you must embark on an overnight hike. Signposts identify the trailheads and all of the trails offer splendid mountain scenery and a chance to see wildlife. The fishing is also good and a $4 license lets you fish in any national park in Canada for the rest of the year (a territorial licence is not required). *note:* In the planning stages is a bizarre scheme to transport tourists along the Slims River in a Disneyland-style shuttle to a chairlift up Vulcan Mountain. Business interests have recognized the money-making potential of the park.

the land: The St. Elias Range, running from Alaska through Yukon to British Columbia in a NW/SE direction parallel to the Alaska/Haines highways, is the highest mountain range in North America and the second highest coastal range in the world (the Andes are higher). Mount Logan (5,950 m), totally inside the park, is the highest peak in Canada. The 2,500-m-high front ranges you see from the

highways are impressive enough, but only through gaps can you glimpse the fantastic Icefield Ranges lying directly behind. The many 5,000-m-high peaks of this range are surrounded by a gigantic icefield plateau from 2,500 to 3,000 m high, the largest non-polar icefield in the world. Radiating out from the icefield like spokes on a wheel are valley glaciers up to 6 km wide and 60 km long, some very active. During the late 1960s, Steele Glacier advanced 11 km in only 4 months. Kaskawulsh Glacier is unusual in that it drains into both the Yukon River and the Pacific Ocean. Such is the importance of the area that together with Wrangell-Saint Elias National Park in Alaska, Kluane has been declared a World Heritage Site by UNESCO.

flora and fauna: Although more than half of Kluane is ice, rock, and snow, the remainder includes a wide variety of climates and habitats, drier to the N and damper to the south; the wetter the area, the denser the vegetation. Some 4,000 Dall sheep, one of the largest populations of them on earth, reside on the high open hillsides NW of Kaskawulsh Glacier and elsewhere in the park. Many can be seen from the highway in the vicinity of Sheep Mountain. Kluane also has significant numbers of moose, caribou, mountain goats, and grizzly bears. Kokanee, a dwarfed, land-locked variety of freshwater sockeye salmon, are found in Sockeye Lake (fishing prohibited).

SIGHTS OF KLUANE PARK

from the highway: The Kluane National Park Visitor Center at Haines Junction is open daily 0900-2000 in the summer. There are interesting displays, including a relief map of the park and an excellent free sight-and-sound slide show beginning hourly from 0930-1930 (see it at least twice!). Buy a topographical map here if you're planning on doing any hiking. *tours:* Flightseeing over the park is available in small planes based at Burwash Lodge near the N end of Kluane Lake. The one-hour flight ($47.50 pp, 4 passenger minimum) affords a spectacular view of Mount Logan plus several glaciers, and is highly recommended if you happen to be there on a clear day.

hiking: Everyone setting out on an overnight hike into the park must register in advance, either at the Visitor Center in Haines Junction or Sheep Mountain, or by phone (tel. 634-2251 or 634-2345). There is no charge for this and no one will be refused permission, but the park wardens want to know who is in the park and where. When you complete your trip, please have the courtesy to call the park office again to let them know (it is, in fact, mandatory to do so). Phones are readily available at most trailheads. This system is for your own protection and, if you forget to sign out, an unnecessary search may be mounted to determine if you are in trouble. A free permit must also be obtained if you wish to make a campfire.

"SURE HOPE THE CAMPERS
DON'T GET A WHIFF OF THIS..."

Cottonwood Trail: A minimum of 4 days is required to complete this 85-km loop trail from Kathleen Lake to Dezadeash Lodge on the Haines Highway (or vice versa). There is some climbing involved, several creeks to wade across, and portions of the trail can be difficult to follow. The dividends are a great variety of plants and wildlife: many ptarmigan can be seen in the alpine areas, and watch for Dall sheep on the steep slopes. This is also prime grizzly habitat. You'll see many signs of old copper and placer gold mining sites along the way. Try to avoid camping above the treeline in the alpine areas as the tundra is very fragile. There are primitive campsites at Goat Creek and at the point where Dalton Creek crosses Mush Lake Road. *the route:* From the Kathleen Lake Campground you follow an old mining road along the S shores of Kathleen and Louise lakes. Goat and Victoria creeks must be forded. Beyond Victoria Creek the road continues through the spruce forest, passing the ruins of the Johobo mine where copper was extracted in the 1960s. From the mine continue along a cut trail through the forest, across some meadows, up a creek bed, then across a long stretch of alpine tundra to Dalton Creek and the Mush Lake Road, which leads back out to Dezadeash Lodge. The great cheeseburgers with fries ($4) served at the lodge (pronounced DEZ-DEE-ASH) reward you at the end of the trail.

Auriol Trail: This 19-km loop trail begins 6 km S of Haines Junction and can be done in a day. There are excellent views from several points and a great variety of plant and animal life. About 1 km up the trail take the fork to the R which climbs steeply to the treeline; the L-hand side is more gradual, and safer for the descent. The creek, which is located halfway up both sides of the trail, is narrow and easy to cross. There is a primitive campground near the top on the L-hand side of the loop.

Alsek Pass Trail (Dezadeash-Alsek River Valley): This 24-km trail begins near Mackintosh Lodge, 10 km W of Haines Junction, and is relatively flat and easy to follow. The first 21 km take you on an abandoned mining road which ends at a washout; the last 3 km lead to Sugden Creek. As recently as 125 years ago this area was submerged under a lake which formed when Lowell Glacier pushed up against the W side of Goatherd Mountain, blocking the Alsek River. The lake, which once extended up the

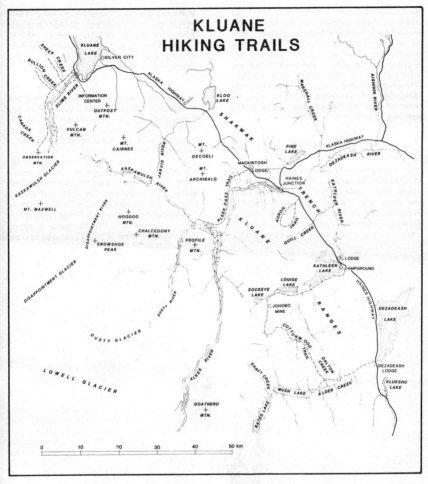

KLUANE
HIKING TRAILS

Dezadeash River well beyond Haines Junction and rose as much as 81 m above present river levels, drained when the glacier receded. Today the old beach line is clearly visible as a sandy strip complete with driftwood, high along the hillsides in the Dezadeash, Alsek, and Kaskawulsh river valleys. Another thing to look for are the rare plants on the old sand dunes at the junction of the Dezadeash and Kaskawulsh rivers.

Slims River Trail: This is perhaps the best short (24 km OW) hike in Kluane Park because it offers old mining relics, excellent wildlife viewing, and a spectacular view of Kaskawulsh Glacier at the base of the St. Elias Mountains. The trail begins near the Sheep Mountain information trailer and leads up the W side of the Slims River. The first 9 km are on an old mining road. After the road ends you have to find your way along between the hillside and the riverbed. There are 3 major creeks to cross. The trail ends at Observation Mountain, which should be climbed for the "classic" view of the Kaskawulsh. There are several sidetrails off to the right. The first leads up to Sheep Creek Canyon (6.5 km OW) where abundant wildlife may be found. The second runs in to the historic Bullion Creek placer gold-mining area (9.5 km OW). There is also a route up the E side of the Slims, and this is often easier due to fewer creek crossings. Information on the trails and various attractions in the area, plus backcountry camping and campfire permits, can be obtained from the Parks Canada trailer at the trailhead.

PRACTICALITES

stay: The Kathleen Lake Campground ($3) has 41 sites with firewood, well water, and flush toilets. The waters of the lake are very clear and deep, and the fishing is good. Food is available at Kathleen Lake Lodge nearby. Brewster's Service, near the crossroads at Haines Junction, has rooms with bath for $24.

At Haines Junction camp by the river, down behind the Vehicle Weigh Station and just before the bridge on the road to Haines. *money:* There is no bank at Haines Junction, although a banking agency opens Tues. to Fri. afternoons in the Territorial Building.

from Haines Junction: Coachways has a bus to Whitehorse and Fairbanks every other day during the summer. They will try to drop you off at Mackinosh Lodge, 10 km W of Haines Junction, so if you want to go to the Visitor Center ask the driver when you board to let you out at the Blue Mountain Motor Inn (tel. 634-2646) in Haines Junction itself. If you're trying to catch the bus in Haines Junction, call Mackintosh Lodge (tel. 634-2301) and ask for instructions. Beware of buses leaving early, as they sometimes willl Yukon Stage Lines offers service to Haines (CDN$38) twice a week. Hitching is a matter of being prepared to wait.

Dall ewe

above, clockwise: giant fireweed (National Park Service photo by Robert Belous); flora in Aniakchak Crater, AK (National Park Service photo by Ben Guild); Muir Glacier, Glacier Bay, AK (National Park Service); Olympic National Park, WA (National Park Service); Portage Glacier, AK (Foster A. Carr)

above, clockwise: caribou (Anchorage Convention and Visitors Bureau); Stellar sea lions on Chiswell I., Kenai Fjords, AK (National Park Service photo by M. Woodbridge Williams); willow ptarmigan (Anchorage Convention and Visitors Bureau); Vancouver geese (U.S. Fish and Wildlife Service photo by Gerry Atwell); bald eagle (U.S. Forest Service)

above, clockwise: Eskimo woman, Kotzebue Sound area, AK (National Park Service photo by Robert Belous); Totem Bight Park near Ketchikan, AK (Division of Tourism); Eskimo woman making berry baskets of birch bark at Kobuk, AK (National Park Service photo by Robert Belous); Tlingit totem at Ketchikan, AK (National Park Service photo by Robert Belous)

above: Mt. Rainier in winter from White Pass, WA (National Park Service); below: the Alaska Highway and Wrangell Mountains, AK (Foster A. Carr)

ALASKA AND THE INTERIOR

INTRODUCTION

The name Alaska is derived from the Aleut word *alyeska,* which means The Great Land. In fact, Alaska's 1,517,740 sq km stretch across 4 time zones and constitute a fifth of the total area of the United States. Alaska is the largest in size (over twice the size of Texas) and smallest in population (two-thirds the population of Delaware) of the 50 states. Its 50,000 km of coastline is 50 percent again as long as that of the rest of the country combined. Alaska has 3 million lakes bigger than 8 hectares; 17 of the 20 highest mountains in the U.S. are Alaskan. Truly, this is a Great Land. But Alaska is not only big, it is also varied. Travel 1,000 km in several directions from Anchorage, an urban metropolis, and you might be in a waterlogged Southeastern rainforest, a frozen Eskimo village on the edge of the Arctic Ocean, or a treeless, windswept Aleutian Island, yet you will still be in Alaska. Barrow is bathed in 3 months of continuous sunlight in the summer, and socked in by 3 months of continuous darkness in the winter. Ketchikan receives up

to 4 m of yearly precipitation, while sections of the Brooks Range get less than 10 centimeters. In June the total biomass of mosquitos outweighs that of caribou. Alaska boasts the largest brown bears and tiniest shrews in the world. Record-breaking salmon, halibut, and king crab abound. But Alaska is also a land of misconceptions. Ask people what their image of Alaska is and you usually hear, "frozen wasteland, igloos on the tundra, polar bears." Even though Alaska's roughly 4,000 glaciers make up half the glaciers in the world (the Malaspina Glacier is larger than Switzerland), it is erroneous to think of Alaska as topped by an icecap. Actually, permanent glaciers cover no more than 3 percent of the state. Another popular misconception is that the greatest icefields are in the far north. In fact, very dry conditions on the Brooks Range have prevented the formation of large glaciers in that area and the Tanana/Yukon valley was *never* glaciated, not even during the pleistocene. The great concentration of glaciers is in the S, to the N and E of the Gulf of Alaska. Here, heavy snowfall on the lofty Coastal Mountains feeds these massive, moving tongues of ice.

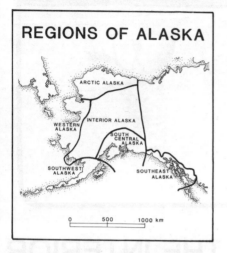

REGIONS OF ALASKA

ARCTIC ALASKA

INTERIOR ALASKA

WESTERN ALASKA

SOUTH CENTRAL ALASKA

SOUTHWEST ALASKA

SOUTHEAST ALASKA

0   500   1000 km

the regions of Alaska: Alaska can be divided into 6 natural regions. We have seen how *Southeast Alaska* is a lush rainforest of western hemlock, cedar, and Sitka spruce, backed by rugged coastal mountains and bathed in unending rainfall. *Southcentral Alaska* is also coastal, but with more moderate rainfall, and sparser forests of less commercial value. The mountains of Southcentral, on the other hand, are high and broad with a great basin and inlet between the Chugach and Alaska ranges. Trees disappear entirely beyond Kodiak Island in *Southwest Alaska.* The Alaska Peninsula and Aleutian Islands form a barren, mountainous 2,500-km chain of stepping stones pointed at the heart of Asia. Between the crests of the Alaska and Brooks ranges is *Interior Alaska,* a great lowland plateau sloping gently towards the Bering Sea. Interior, with low rainfall and extreme temperatures, is also a region of great rivers: the Porcupine, Yukon, Tanana, Koyukuk, and Kuskokwim. The woodlands feature white spruce, birch, and aspen. *Western Alaska* encompasses the lake-filled delta areas of the Kuskokwim and Yukon rivers and the low, rounded hills of the Seward Peninsula. *Arctic Alaska,* which includes the Brooks Range and North Slope, is underlain by continuous permafrost. No trees grow on the North Slope.

history: Alaskan history has been a continuous cycle of boom and bust. The story of the first boom predates written history, but it is generally agreed that primitve Mongolians from eastern Asia migrated across the Bering land bridge in pursuit of great herds of prehistoric animals. Climatic changes, which saw the disappearance of the woolly mammoth, giant beaver, yak, ground sloth, camel, and mastodon, probably account for the bust side of the cycle. Vitus Bering, a Dane in the employ of Russia, is credited as the European discoverer. His arrival in 1741 touched off a ruthless quest for the fur of the sea otter and fur seal which ended only when the animals approached extinction and the hunt became unprofitable. Resulting hard times prompted Russia to sell Alaska to the United States in 1867. The price was $7,200,000, less than 5 cents a hectare. The gold rushes of the late 19th C. vindicated this purchase and led to the opening of the interior and the establishment of many of the towns which exist today, though the mining boom lasted only a decade and the bust dragged on until WW II. Most of the present transportation facilities date from a defense boom in the early 1940s. Alaska became a U.S. territory in 1912 and the 49th state in 1959, but the momentous event which shook Alaska out of its postwar lethargy was the discovery of oil at Prudhoe Bay on the Arctic Ocean in 1968. The state is riding high on the oil boom today.

the economy: The Alaskan economy is based on fishing, forestry, tourism, government spending, mining, and oil. Fishing fleets crowd the towns along the S coast and canneries are numerous. The largest annual catches of salmon, halibut, and king crab in the U.S. are taken from here and, under careful management and conservation, the fisheries are flourishing as never before. Timber is important in Southeast Alaska, and there are pulp mills at Ketchikan and Sitka. Tourism is concentrated in the Anchorage/Denali Park and Juneau/Glacier Bay areas. The federal government is the largest employer in the state with its sprawling military bases at Fairbanks and Anchorage and its abundance of government workers who administer federal lands. The development of agriculture has been limited by the short growing season and by drought, but grain farming around Delta Junction and dairying in the Matanuska Valley have done well. Most food, however, is imported from the Lower 48. Small-scale

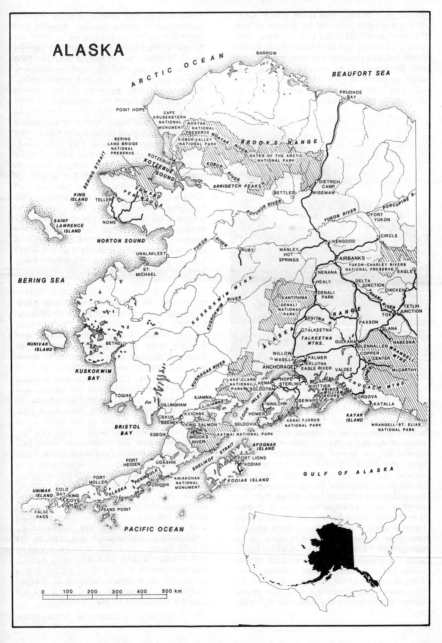

placer gold mining still takes place. Coal mining has more potential for growth as half the reserves of coal in the U.S. are here, with mining underway just N of Denali Park. Today the oil industry provides the state government with 89 percent of its income; Prudhoe Bay alone accounts for 17.7 percent of the total U.S. production. Twenty-five percent of U.S. oil reserves are in Alaska.

The Trans-Alaska Oil Pipeline cuts across open tundra north of the Brooks Range.

land and development: The 1968 oil strike has led to the carving up of Alaska. Prior to 1958, most of Alaska's 151.75 million ha. were owned by the federal government. In that year, the Alaska Statehood Act granted almost 42 million ha. to the state for development purposes. These areas were still being selected when oil first gushed from the North Slope and caused the policy to change dramatically. Native Eskimo and Indian groups became vocal, claiming the oil fields and the land over which the oil would have to be transported. Environmental groups filed suit to stop the proposed pipeline and oil tanker route. The oil industry lobbied in Washington. Then Secretary of the Interior Udall took the courageous step of halting the transfer of any further federal land to the state until the native

claims were settled. After 3 centuries of brutal exploitation of native peoples, America had decided to soothe its conscience. In 1971, the Alaska Native Claims Settlement Act granted nearly 18 million ha. of federal land and $900 million to 12 regional corporations presently owned by Alaska's Eskimos and Indians. Business interests, eager to get on with oil development, backed the legislation. In 1991 public trading in the stock of these corporations will begin and it is envisioned they will quickly pass out of native hands. The big-money boys knew what they were doing. Environmentalists were thrown a choice bone in the form of the 1980 Alaska National Interest Lands Conservation Act which set aside some 42 million ha. for new national parks, wildlife sanctuaries, and preserves. This far-sighted move will protect many unique and fragile environments from pressures for development, which are certain to become fierce in the future. Anyone interested in learning more about these controversial matters should refer to the "Booklist" of this book, or talk to any Alaskan.

the people: In 1867, there were only 1,000 Caucasians out of a total of 30,000 inhabitants. By 1959, the population was 211,000, with 171,000 whites. Today, native Indians and Eskimos make up about 17 percent of all Alaskans: approximately 55 percent of these are Eskimos, 35 percent Indians, and 10 percent Aleuts. The Indians are divided between the Athapaskans of the interior, and the Tlingits, Haidas, and Tsimshians of Southeast Alaska. Currently, there are a total of some 400,000 people in the state, most living in the S near the Pacific Ocean. Very few live in places over 300 m elevation. Nearly half the population lives in Anchorage alone. Right up until 1940 Juneau was the largest city in the state, but wartime spending pushed Anchorage ahead. After the war the huge air force and army bases remained and Anchorage also became the business center of Alaska. The city continues to grow by leaps and bounds. Alaskans are passionately individualistic. A sourdough in a cabin on the Brooks Range is as much, or more, a part of the Alaskan scene as a secretary typing nameless reports in the back of a government office. For an excellent overview of Alaskan individuals and lifestyles, see *Coming into the Country* mentioned in the "Booklist."

INTERIOR ALASKA

Interior Alaska is a great tilted plateau between the crests of the Alaska and Brooks ranges. The mighty Yukon and Tanana rivers are the main features of this region, but the mountains are almost always in view. Interior Alaska is basically one medium-sized city, Fairbanks, and a number of bush villages, the most interesting of which are along the rivers rather than beside the highways. Much of the region is difficult to visit unless you have a vehicle, but there are great adventures awaiting on the many wild and scenic rivers, in the wildlife refuges, and in spectacular Denali National Park.

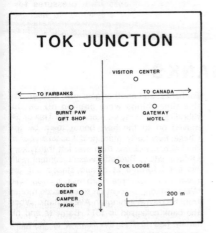

TOK JUNCTION

VISITOR CENTER
○

← TO FAIRBANKS   TO CANADA →

○   ○
BURNT PAW   GATEWAY
GIFT SHOP   MOTEL

○
TOK LODGE

○
GOLDEN
BEAR
CAMPER   0   200 m
PARK

Tok Junction: Tok Junction sits at the intersection of the Alaska Highway and the Tok Cut-off (an extension of the Glenn Highway). This is where you leave the Alaska Highway if you're headed to Anchorage (525 km). Otherwise, you're only 330 km from Fairbanks, 640 km out of Whitehorse. The Taylor Highway from Eagle (and Dawson City) joins the Alaska Highway at Tetlin Junction, just 20 km east. Tok Junction is a major supply center for the western interior and the main gateway for travelers arriving from Canada. It has commercial campgrounds, grocery stores, fast-food outlets, and native Indian handicrafts. Stop at the Visitor Center (open daily 0700-2200) near the crossroads on the Alaska Highway for brochures and free coffee; have a look at their mini-museum. The sled dogs at Burnt Paw Gift Shop, also near the junction, put on a free mushing show nightly except Sun. at 1930. Otherwise, there is nothing to detain you at Tok.

stay: The Gateway Motel at Tok has rooms for $25 s or d (shared bath). The most convenient campground is Golden Bear Camper Park ($7.50 for 2 people, showers included), just a few minutes walk from everything. Movies are shown free at the Golden Bear nightly. The Sourdough Campground (2 km S) and the Tundra Lodge Campground (2 km W) both charge about $6 per tent.

from Tok: Alaska-Yukon Motorcoaches has 3 buses a week from Tok to Anchorage ($59), 2 a week to Haines ($79). Their terminal in Tok is the Burnt Paw Gift Shop. Coachways has buses every other day to Fairbanks ($25) and Whitehorse (US$44). Norline Coaches has a minibus to Dawson City (US$45) 3 times a week. Coachways and Norline both stop at Tok Lodge. None of these services makes any effort to connect, so check the schedules ahead of time or be prepared to wait a day or 2 for an onward service. Hitchhikers tend to pile up in Tok and long waits are common. You'll have plenty of company by the side of the road if you get out at Tok!

Eskimo bird mask

FAIRBANKS

Fairbanks (pop. 22,645 in 1980), the northernmost city of its size on the continent, sits near the geographical center of Alaska. The Chena River, a tributary of the Tanana, winds through the city (elevation 133 m). Fairbanks gets 22 hours of sunlight on 21 June, but only 4 hours on 21 December. All the symbols of American civilization are here, from Colonel Sanders to a motel jungle. Yet just a few blocks from downtown, little log cabins line the streets. Fairbanks is funky. The University Museum and Alaskaland are well worth seeing, and it's fun just to wander around town and meet the people. A day or 2 here is recommended, and the good transportation and camping facilities make this easy to arrange.

history: Captain E.T. Barnette set up a trading post in 1901 on the site of present-day Fairbanks. Actually, he didn't have much choice in the matter. After a heated argument, the captain of the riverboat on which Barnette was a passenger refused to proceed any further up the shallow Chena River and dropped Barnette and his goods unceremoniously on the shore. This proved to be a fortuitous fiasco for Barnette because a year later a prospector named Felix Pedro found gold on Pedro Creek, just 26 km NE of

Fairbanks, and another gold rush was on. By this time things were cooling off on the Klondike and many veterans of the Trail of '98 moved on to the new boom town by the Chena. Eventually, more gold was taken out of the Fairbanks claims than ever left the Yukon. Unfortunately, Barnette wasn't content with his good fortune at having staked out the townsite of rich little Fairbanks. In true Wild West fashion, he went on to embezzle money from his own Washington-Alaska Bank. When the bank collapsed in 1911, Barnette and his family had to flee the town they founded, never to return again. Fairbanks, over the years, suffered fire and flood, but steadily grew to be the communications center of the interior. By 1913 there was a road from Fairbanks to Valdez on the coast. In 1923 the Alaska Railroad arrived to connect the city to Seward and Anchorage. When the Alaska Highway was pushed through to Fairbanks from Canada in 1942, the city's survival was assured. With the construction of the Trans-Alaska Pipeline in 1974-77, Fairbanks boomed again. The pipeline passes within 16 km of downtown. The 944-km North Slope Haul Road was built from Fairbanks to the oilfields at Prudhoe Bay. The road is presently open to the public only as far as Dietrich Camp (455 km), but there is pressure from business interests to open it all the way. North Slope Eskimos, who fear the effect the increased traffic could have on wildlife, are opposing this. If and when work begins on the Alaska Highway Natural Gas Pipeline, Fairbanks will experience a new boom.

SIGHTS OF FAIRBANKS

downtown: Start your visit at the tourist office (open daily 0830-1730) on 1st Ave., in a log cabin by the Chena River. They provide free brochures and offer an excellent, free walking tour of the city daily at 1000 and 1500. Ask to see the booklet *Ghosts of the Gold Rush* ($1.50). Visit the Immaculate Conception Church (1904), just across the river from the tourist office, for its beautiful stained-glass windows. Further N along Illinois St. are the old wooden coal bunkers erected in the 1930s to supply fuel to steam locomotives. They are still in use; you just park your truck under a chute and pull the rope.

hiking: Creamer's Nature Path is a 3-km loop trail which gives you a chance to see native animals and migratory birds, plus most of the kinds of vegetation common to Interior Alaska. All 8 types of trees native to the region are found here. The Nature Path, of exceptional interest to naturalists, is well-maintained, but bring insect repellant as the mosquitos are thick and persistent. The trail begins along the E side of the road beside the Alaska Department of Fish and Game, 1300 College Road (bus no. 1). Pick up a free trail guide booklet at the Fish and Game office (Mon. to Fri. 0800-1630) or from the box at the trailhead. The office also has a series of free leaflets on Alaskan wildlife.

to the university: The University of Alaska/Fairbanks, 6 km W of downtown, is the main educational facility in Alaska. Get there on bus no. 1 (COLLEGE ROAD) or bus no. 11 (AIRPORT WAY). Both cost $1 (no service on Sunday), and leave from the corner of 7th and Noble. The bus will drop you at the Campus

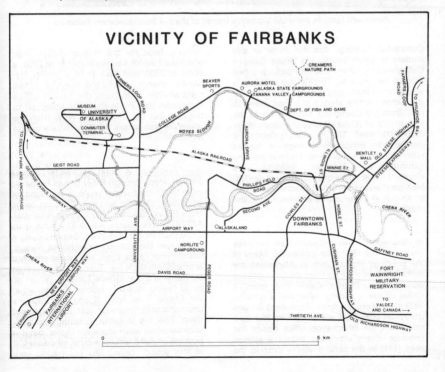

VICINITY OF FAIRBANKS

Alaskaland features many old log cabins moved to the site from downtown Fairbanks

Commuter Terminal. Ask the driver or any student to direct you to the Wood Campus Center nearby, where you can pick up a free map of the grounds. There's also a cafeteria (cheap breakfasts) and pub (good lunches) in the Center. A free shuttle bus runs every 15 min. from the Commuter Terminal up to the University of Alaska Museum (open daily 0900-1700, free). The museum collection is divided into geographical areas—a feature which is especially convenient for visitors. The exhibits of Alaskan wildlife are excellent—don't miss them. On a clear day Mt. McKinley, across the broad Tanana Valley, can be seen in all its awesome eminence from the museum.

to Alaskaland: This enjoyable park occupies the site of the 1967 state centennial. Many of the buildings and exhibits at Alaskaland are authentic, brought here from various locations around town. There's a gold rush town, a native village, a mining valley and a genuine 1933 sternwheel riverboat. Alaskaland is open daily from 1100-2100, admission free. Pick up a map from the information office beside the entrance. Every afternoon there's a salmon bake ($11) in the park. If you're there in the

evening, head for the Pioneer Saloon (free admission) which has live music from 2100, a show at 2200, and beer at $6 a pitcher (for Alaska, cheap). Alaskaland provides a free tram shuttle train from the tourist office downtown (ask inside about the schedule) to the site. Bus no. 11 (Airport Way) from the university also passes the door (hourly except Sunday).

river running: A quiet backwater, Noyes Slough, loops through the N side of Fairbanks from the Chena River. If you're in the mood for adventure, consider renting a Coleman canoe from Beaver Sports, 2400 College Road (tel. 479-2494). The charge will be $15 a day, plus $1.50 each for life preservers. Beaver Sports is just across the highway from Noyes Slough; launch your canoe there and you're off on a scenic 20-km circle trip. Take a lunch, and start by heading E for Graehl Landing, so as to avoid having to battle against the current in the Chena River later. If you run into any obstructions in the slough, just portage around them. This trip is easier in spring and early summer when water levels are higher, but it is possible anytime (except winter, of course). If all this sounds tame, why not paddle your canoe down the Chena River to the Tanana, then on to the town of Nenana (12 hours). Check at the Alaska Railroad station about the possibility of bringing canoe and yourself back to Fairbanks on the train.

Nenana: Several times a week the local train from Fairbanks to Anchorage (but not the daily express) stops at Nenana (pop. 470 in 1980), at the junction of the Nenana and Tanana rivers. Freight is barged from here all summer to villages along the Tanana and Yukon rivers. Each spring the town holds a lottery to see who can predict the exact minute the ice will go out on the Tanana. As the ice breaks up, a line from a wooden tripod stops an official clock. Payoffs of over $100,000 are common in the Nenana Ice Classic, but only Alaska residents may participate. Before the road from Nenana to Denali National Park (118 km) was completed, access to the Park was difficult. When the George Parks Highway opened in 1972, Park attendance soared and the Park Service was forced to close the internal park road to private vehicles and institute the free shuttle buses (see "Denali National Park" below).

PRACTICALITIES

stay: The Fairbanks Hotel, 517 3rd Ave., has rooms at $25 s, $31 d (shared bath). The Tamarac Inn, 252 Minnie St. (tel. 456-6406), an easy walk from the bus or train stations, has rooms with shared bath at $28 s, $32 d, weeklies available. The Aurora Motel (tel. 456-7361) on College Road near the Fairgrounds charges $27 s or d (private bath). Take bus no. 1 to get there. Fairbanks has an active bed-and-breakfast program which locates you in a private home ($30 s, $35 d). Representatives often meet the trains and buses, or you could call tel. 452-4967. For a longer stay try Harvey's Rooms, 750 8th Ave. (tel. 456-6327). The price is $16 pp daily, $75 pp weekly for a bed in a double room; cooking facilities and a TV room are provided. Look in the classified section of the _Daily News-Miner_ for cheap rooms for rent. If you're broke, Fairbanks Rescue Mission (tel. 452-6608) next to Foodland offers free accommodations. Check in at 1830 and be up by 0600 for the Christian service and breakfast. The Salvation Army Shelter, 117 1st Ave. (tel. 452-5005), is similar but tends to fill up. Because these facilities are provided for locals, use them only

if you have to. Freeloading might close a place that could be used by someone in true need.

camping: Fairbanks offers 2 convenient commercial campgrounds. The Norlite Campground on Peger Road near Alaskaland charges tenters without a vehicle $5 s, $8.50 d, $9.50 t. The campground has its own laundromat, showers (25 cents), and a store, but no campfires are permitted and the place is full of RV drivers. Norlite is very convenient to Alaskaland, so pick it if you're into sightseeing and socializing. Get there on bus no. 11; the last bus out leaves at 2100 Mon. to Saturday. The Tanana Valley Campground on College Road beside the Fairgrounds charges $6 for a site (up to 4 people—2 tents). Showers are free and campfires are allowed. This one is closer to canoeing and hiking possibilities, and is in a more natural setting. Bus no. 1 runs to the campground Mon. to Sat. until 2130. Unfortunately, the bus from Whitehorse often arrives too late for you to catch a city bus out to either of these campgrounds. If you're not ready for an invigorating walk after the long bus ride, look for others with whom to share a taxi and campsite.

eats and entertainment: The cafeteria on the 3rd floor of the Federal Building serves cheap

Foster A. Carr

The willow ptarmigan is the state bird of Alaska. Early sourdoughs weren't sure how to spell or pronounce the name, so they called them chickens. There are now 13 streams in Alaska named Chicken Creek, plus a Chicken Cove, Chicken Island, Chicken Mountain, and Chicken Ridge.

breakfasts and lunches Mon. to Friday. The Pastime Cafe, 1st at Cushman, has good pancake combinations for breakfast and is open 24 hours a day. The locals eat here. Terry's Cafe on Illinois St. has friendly, efficient service and reasonable prices. Have breakfast here before catching the train to Denali. The Sonshine Inn, 419 2nd Ave. is no fast-food stand; the meals are homemade and healthy, if a little pricey. This is also a great place to sit and talk over a pot of herb tea. For some local color check out the bars along 2nd Ave. from Cushman to Lacey.

information and services: The tourist office in the log cabin by the river is very helpful. At the Arctic Wildlands Information Center, 201 1st Ave. (open Mon. to Fri. 0800-1700), you can get detailed directions on how to reach the most remote wilderness areas of Alaska's new national parks, or just pick up a map of Denali. Topographical maps of all of Alaska are available for a price in Room 126 in the Federal Building, 101 12th Ave. (open Mon. to Fri. 0900-1630). Visit also the Northern Alaska Environmental Center, 218 Driveway, across the river near the railway station. If you'd like some film developed quickly, try the Photo Factory, 226 Illinois Street.

FROM FAIRBANKS

airport: Fairbanks International Airport (FAI) is 6 km SW of downtown Fairbanks. There is no city bus service; transfers are provided by an airport limousine (tel. 456-8414) at $4 pp. There is a tourist information counter at the airport.

by train: The Alaska Railroad offers smooth, comfortable service daily at 1000 to Denali Park and Anchorage. Reservations are not usually required on this standard gauge, government-owned line, but they are accepted. You may sit anywhere you please on the train. The $63.25 OW fare to Anchorage allows you to stop over at Denali Park. Bicycles are carried for $2 extra. A ride on the Alaska Railroad is a capital way to see this part of Alaska.

by bus: Coachways, a subsidiary of Greyhound, has buses to Whitehorse (US$69.50) every other day. Bus fares in Canada are cheaper than in the U.S., so you'll probably save money by buying a ticket only as far as Beaver Creek, Yukon (US$39.50), then getting another there. Have enough Canadian money with you to do this or lose on the exchange. The maximum fare as far as Vancouver or Montreal is CDN$99. For some unknown reason, Greyhound's Ameripass is not valid on Greyhound buses in Alaska; you start or stop using them in Beaver Creek. The Greyhound station at 208 Wendell Ave. in Fairbanks sells these passes. Alaska-Yukon Motorcoaches (office in the Golden Nugget Motel, 9th Ave. and Noble) has buses twice a week to Valdez ($64), daily to Anchorage ($64) via Denali Park. Book your seat the day before.

hitching: If you want to hitch towards Delta Junction (for Valdez or Canada) consider taking bus no. 50 (NORTH POLE) to the corner of Laurance Road and Richardson Highway ($2). This would avoid a lot of local traffic, but the bus only runs every couple of hours, so check the times beforehand (no service on Sunday). To hitch S to Denali Park or Anchorage, take bus no. 1 or 11 to the university, then walk west 2 km to George Parks Highway.

FAIRBANKS

1. coal bunkers
2. Terry's Cafe
3. The Photo Factory
4. railway station
5. Immaculate Conception Church
6. tourist office
7. Pastime Cafe
8. Sonshine Inn
9. Fairbanks Hotel
10. post office
11. Harvey's Rooms
12. Foodland
13. Fairbanks Rescue Mission
14. Federal Building
15. Golden Nugget Motel
16. Salvation Army Shelter
17. Arctic Wildlands Information Center
18. Greyhound (Coachways)
19. Burger King
20. Tamarac Inn
21. Kentucky Fried Chicken

DOWNTOWN FAIRBANKS

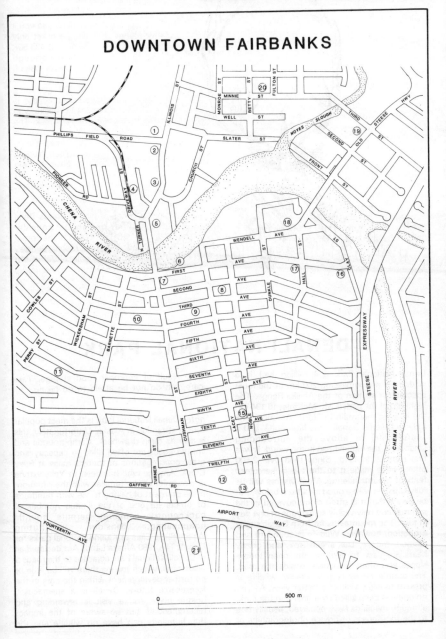

0 — 500 m

Foster A Carr

DENALI NATIONAL PARK

Denali National Park (2.4 million ha.) is a wilderness encompassing 200 km of the most spectacular section of the Alaska Range. The highlight of the park is Mt. McKinley (6,194 m), the highest mountain in North America. The Indians called it Denali, "the high one," and it soars 4,800 m above the surrounding landscape, the highest rise in the world. It was first climbed in 1913. Since then over 2,500 others have made it to the top in herculean feats of mountaineering. Most visitors will be fully satisfied with a good look from below, but be aware that it is often cloud covered in the summer and only visible an average of one day in four. The mountain is far from Denali's only attraction, however. Wildlife is abundant and caribou, moose, Dall sheep, fox, and grizzly bears are easy to spot on the open tundra slopes and often seen right beside the road. The shuttle buses stop whenever wildlife is present to allow visitors a better view. As yet, no one has been killed by a grizzly in the park, although maulings have occurred, usually due to the foolishness of novice photographers or

as a result of improper food storage. Take care, but do not be afraid to go hiking.

note: Denali National Park is the most popular tourist attraction in Alaska. Unfortunately, this is also its main drawback. Campgrounds and shuttle buses are often filled to capacity and great congregations of tourists mass at Riley Creek. Anyone who has been to Yellowstone or Yosemite will be familiar with the situation. If the prospect of having to vie with hundreds of others for one of the limited number of backcountry camping permits sounds unappealing, consider substituting Wrangell-St. Elias or Kluane national parks for Denali. The 1980 Alaska Lands Act declared all of Denali National Park adjacent to the roads a wilderness, which means there will be little or no further development within the park in the foreseeable future. Denali is a spectacular, unique place and a visit is rewarding and recommended, but be aware of the impact that humanity can have on wildlife and the pressure that both you and the environment will suffer from overcrowding.

SIGHTS OF DENALI NATIONAL PARK

along the road: Free shuttle buses run along a 135-km dirt road from Riley Creek to Wonder Lake (see "transport" below). The scenery is magnificent, with memorable views of the angular, ice-topped mountains along the way. Mount McKinley is not visible from the Park entrance at Riley Creek; you'll first see it as you approach Savage River. McKinley will again disappear behind jagged lower peaks as the road descends into the broad, glacial Sanctuary and Teklanika river valleys. Watch for moose, caribou, fox, and waterfowl along this stretch. Once across the Teklanika, you'll enter a narrow canyon between Igloo and Cathedral mountains. Dall sheep are frequently spotted on these slopes. The road then climbs Sable Pass (1,189 m), the second highest elevation on the route. This area is prime grizzly habitat. Keep your eyes peeled for these light brown kings of the tundra. The first rest stop is at Polychrome Pass, one of the most spectacular spots on the road. On your way back, if it's not too late, get off the bus here and go for a short hike up over the tundra above the road. The Toklat River is the last you cross, on a rickety, one-lane bridge, before climbing over Thoroughfare Pass (1,204 m). This is wolf and caribou country.

Eielson to Wonder Lake: On a clear day there's a splendid view of Mt. McKinley from Eielson Visitor Center (open daily 0900-2000). Many of the free shuttle buses terminate at this center, 106 km from Riley Creek. If you want to continue on, put your name on the waiting list for a later service to Wonder Lake. Have a look at the informative display at Eielson and ask about ranger-led activities which often begin here. Several rough trails lead down to the river from the Visitor Center. It is possible to cross the wide, braided channel and hike over Muldrow Glacier, which is covered by a thick layer of glacial till. A whole day would be necessary for this. Even more impressive is the view of Mt. McKinley from Wonder Lake, where the north face of the mountain rises majestically above the intervening plains and stands alone, with the whole Alaska Range stretching out on each side. If the clouds are cooperating, be sure to go on to Wonder Lake to see it.

hiking: There are no designated trails in the park except those in the vicinity of the hotel. Rather than create trails, the Park Service encourages visitors to get off the shuttle buses

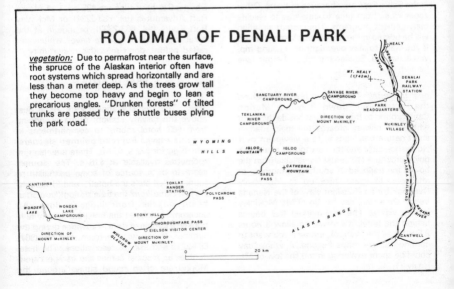

ROADMAP OF DENALI PARK

vegetation: Due to permafrost near the surface, the spruce of the Alaskan interior often have root systems which spread horizontally and are less than a meter deep. As the trees grow tall they become top heavy and begin to lean at precarious angles. "Drunken forests" of tilted trunks are passed by the shuttle buses plying the park road.

Polychrome Pass

wherever they please and explore the area freely. This is the main attraction of hiking in Denali Park; you often feel like no one's been there before you. The wide, open tundra and long-range vistas make it easy to pick a direction and go. Also, it is extremely difficult to get "lost" in the park—just remember whether you're N or S of the road. Topographical maps of the area are sold at the Riley Creek Visitor Center to assist hikers. One place where open-area hiking is not allowed is in the Sable Pass area because of bears. Other zones close from time to time due to wildlife management programs. The current situation will be posted in the Riley Creek Visitor Center. If you want to stay overnight on a hiking trip, you'll need a Backcountry Use Permit (see below).

near the hotel: There are a few trails behind the hotel and down beyond Morino Campground to the river. Just beside the point where the railway crosses the main road, a short nature trail leads in to a viewpoint over Horseshoe Lake and the new tourist chalets. A guide brochure (10 cents) is available from the box at the trailhead. If you have a morning or afternoon to spare, hike up to Mt. Healy Overlook for an excellent view of the Nenana Valley. On a clear day the tip of Mt. McKinley is also visible. The well-marked trail begins behind the hotel; it's steep, so allow 3 hours RT as far as the overlook, longer if you want to continue up the ridge beyond. A whole day could be spent exploring in the shadow of Mt. Healy (1,742 m).

river trips: Two companies run whitewater rafting trips down the Nenana River from McKinley Village to Healy. The trips leave daily at 0900 and 1430, taking 4 hours to cover the 35 km down the valley and through Nenana Canyon. Try to go on a day when the water is high, although it's an exciting experience anytime. The cost is $40 pp including transportation to and from Denali railway station. Rubber boots and raincoats are usually included in the price, but check. Shorter 2½-hour trips are $25 pp. Call Alaska Raft Adventures (tel. 683-2234) or McKinley Raft Tours (tel. 683-2392), or inquire at the hotel tour desk. If you've never whitewater rafted before, don't miss this opportunity.

PRACTICALITIES

stay: The Denali National Park Hotel, just above the railway station, offers everything from $63 hotel rooms to compartments in surplus Alaska Railroad pullman sleepers, which go for $22 s, $27 d. There are also tiny roomettes available at $16 s. The sleepers seem to be a source of some confusion to tourists: "where's the hotel?" and "I thought we just *came from* the train station!" are often heard on the front luggage dock. All accommodations at the hotel are usually fully booked a couple of days in advance during the summer. If you want a room, call tel. (907) 683-2215 and ask for reservations. The hotel doubles as a social center and campers from Morino are often found sitting around the lobby or using the hotel washrooms. If you don't have a tent or would rather be inside, the Denali Park Youth Hostel has accommodations for 60 people in 3-tier bunks housed in 3 reconverted troop-train cars near the railway station. A sleeping bag is required and baggage must be removed from the hostel during the day. Reservations are not accepted and the hostel closes from 0900-1930. The overnight charge is only $1 pp and there's almost always space.

campgrounds: There are 7 official campgrounds in Denali National Park: Morino, Riley Creek, Savage River, Sanctuary, Teklanika, Igloo, and Wonder Lake. The location of each is indicated on the map. All but Morino require a permit available from the Riley Creek Visitor Center at a cost of $4-6 per site. Permits are issued on a first-come first-served basis and in summer all but Morino may be full by 1000. The Morino campground (free) has been set aside by the Park Service for the use of backpackers who arrive on public transport too late to get into the other campgrounds. No permit is required; you just go there and put up your tent (no vehicles allowed). Rangers at the Visitor Center may tell you that Morino is for overnight use only, but there's always lots of space and no one will bother you if you stay an extra day or so. Once you're registered at one of the other 6 campgrounds or are at Morino, you may book campsites for the rest of your continuous stay, but no advance reservations by mail or telephone are accepted. You are limited to 14 nights in the park during a single year. Unfortunately, the Wonder Lake campground, which would be an ideal way to break the long bus ride into the park, has only 20 sites and is hard to get into. Beware of swarms of mosquitos at Wonder Lake in June and July. Campsites at Riley Creek and Savage River usually open up in the morning before 1000. Campground permits are issued from 0530 on, backcountry permits from 0800. Campers at Morino can get water at the railway station or hotel (both nearby), while at Sanctuary and Igloo there is only river water (boil or chemically purify). You must take your own water supply to Wonder Lake.

backcountry camping: Rather than staying at one of the campgrounds, consider backcountry camping as an alternative. A Backcountry Use Permit (free) must be obtained at the Riley Creek Visitor Center for

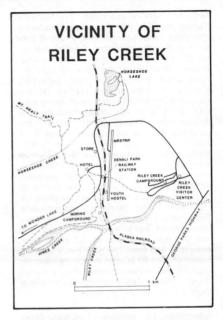

VICINITY OF RILEY CREEK

all overnight camping outside the campgrounds. The park is divided into 31 zones and each zone has a limit as to the number of people who will be able to camp in that area each night. The idea is to spread people out to reduce the impact. Backcountry campers choose their own campsite wherever they like within the zone they have been assigned. Tents must be kept one km from and out of sight of the road. Campfires are not allowed. If this is what you came for, go to the Visitor Center as soon as you arrive at Denali and see what's available. If all the zones are already full, you may have to spend a night at Morino or another campground waiting for something to open up. The rangers will outline the situation for you. This is an excellent way to get closer to nature and enjoy the freedom the wilderness offers, but heed all warnings about encounters with wildlife, safe hiking techniques, and minimum impact ethics. As always, National Park Service publications and employees are your best guides in this regard.

eats and entertainment: There's a dining room, snack bar, and saloon in the hotel. You won't escape from the dining room for under $5 for lunch or $10 for dinner (plus tip), but the food and service are good. Try Nancy's Tundra Mud Pie ($3) for a mouth-watering chocolate treat. A burger with a side of fries will run $4 at the snack bar. A better deal are the 80 cent ice cream cones. There's a small grocery store just down the road from the hotel where you can buy beer, cigarettes, deodorant, chips, and magazines—all the necessities of backcountry travel. Bring your own food with you from Fairbanks or Anchorage. Freeze-dried foods are recommended for backcountry camping. A free shuttle bus runs hourly from the hotel to the McKinley Chalets, just outside the Park on the road to Fairbanks. The bar at the Chalets is a hot spot. There's a whole range of organized activities for people staying in the vicinity of the railway station. Lists of these are posted in the Visitor Center, hotel, and campgrounds. They include campfire programs, discovery hikes, nature walks, slide shows, talks, and sled dog demonstrations. All are informative, enjoyable, and free. The park has a working kennel of over 40 huskies which are used for maintenance and winter patrol. They put on 3 demos a day at Park Headquarters for which there are special shuttle buses.

information and services: The Riley Creek Visitor Center has information on every aspect of the park. Get a copy of *Denali Alpenglow*, a free paper full of useful information. Check out the programs in the audio-visual center at the back of the hotel beyond the gift shop. There

are some coin lockers in the railway station, but the building is only open from 0800-2000, so it's better to use the ones in front of the hotel. If they're all full, chain your pack to something here or in the hotel lobby. Behind the grocery store is a public shower house (75 cents); bring your own soap, shampoo, and towel.

transport: Denali is one of the easiest national parks in the U.S. to visit without a car. Free yellow shuttle buses run 20 times a day from Riley Creek Visitor Center to Eielson Visitor Center (106 km) and Wonder Lake (135 km). The trip to Eielson takes 7½ hours RT, to Wonder Lake 10 hours RT, so get an early start. The first bus leaves Riley Creek at 0600, but you have to be there by 0530 to get on. The morning buses fill up fast. You may get off and on the buses wherever you like along the route. Take your own food and water with you, as none is available in the park. There's also a "wildlife tour" from the hotel. These Blue Bird buses go as far as Stony Hill and cost $27 pp (guided tour and box lunch included). *from Denali:* The Alaska Railroad has daily service to Anchorage (374 km, 6 hours) and Fairbanks (196 km, 3½ hours)—a lovely trip through untouched countryside. This train ride is one of the main pleasures of a visit to Alaska. Stopovers at Denali are free for those holding through Fairbanks-Anchorage tickets.

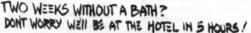

TWO WEEKS WITHOUT A BATH?
DON'T WORRY WE'll BE AT THE HOTEL IN 5 HOURS!

SOUTHCENTRAL ALASKA

ANCHORAGE

The city of Anchorage (pop. 173,017 in 1980), lies in a wide bowl bounded by Cook Inlet and the scenic Chugach Range. Across the inlet, the junction of the Alaska and Aleutian ranges may be seen. Captain Cook enjoyed the view as he sailed up this inlet in 1778 in search of a Northwest Passage from Pacific to Atlantic. Anchorage was founded in 1915 as a base camp for the construction of the Alaska Railroad. Much of the equipment used in that project was brought from Panama, where the U.S. federal government had just finished building a transcontinental canal. The military moved in during WW II and they still occupy a huge reserve along the N side of the city. Alaska's boomers push skyscrapers up downtown; other developments mushroom E and S into the foothills. Nearly half the population of the state lives here. This is Suburbia, U.S.A.—a chance to indulge in all the Big Macs and pizza you've been missing out in the wilderness. It's also the Los Angeles of Alaska, so don't feel badly about giving it short shrift.

downtown: Start your walking tour above the waterfront at the far W end of town. From Resolution Park, 3rd and L, you'll get a magnificent view of Cook Inlet. The long, low mountain you see to the NW is Susitna, the "Sleeping Lady." The SW end of the Alaska Range is to the L of Susitna, the tip of Mt. McKinley to the R, but you'll only see these on a clear day. A statue of Capt. Cook surveys the scene. Just one block E of this on K St. is the impressive "Last Blue Whale" sculpture. Further up K St., just before 5th Ave., is another monument commemorating Cook's voyages. Return to 4th Ave. and proceed E past the tourist office and an attractive park. Go N on E St. to 2nd Ave., for a good view of the railway station (1942), the port, Knik Arm, and the Chugach Mountains. The old steam locomotive (1907) in front of the station, brought from Panama, was used until 1952. The Anchorage Museum, 121 W. 7th Ave. (open Mon. to Sat. 0900-1800, Tues. and Thurs. till 2100, Sun. 1300-1700, admission free), combines exhibits relating to the history of Alaska with contemporary art. Free films are shown in the auditorium daily at 1500. _others:_ Earthquake Park, at the W end of Northern Lights Blvd. just N of the airport (bus no. 93), has an exhibit which vividly describes the devastating earthquake which struck Alaska in 1964, killing 115. The area just below the viewpoint sank to its present level at that time.

Visitors on the weekly tour of Elmendorf Air Force Base near Anchorage are taken into a hangar where the latest aircraft, such as this F-15, are kept.

There's a fine panorama of the Anchorage skyline from here and (if you're lucky) a view of Mt. McKinley.

military bases: Since WW II Anchorage has thrived on military spending, as a visit to the largest of the installations, Elmendorf Air Force Base just NE of downtown, will illustrate. The weekly free tour of the base is highly recommended, but you must call tel. 752-2318 a few days ahead to make a reservation. The highlight of the tour is a visit to a hangar to see an F-15 and talk to the pilot. The size and sophistication of this giant fighter-bomber base is mind-boggling; the way tourists are allowed to wander around and take pictures will startle visitors from abroad. All in all, Elmendorf is Anchorage's most impressive sight. Even if you can't get on the tour, the Wildlife Museum (open Mon. to Fri. 0745-1145/1245-1645, Sat. 1000-1500, admission free) on base is worth visiting for the exhibits and large relief map of Alaska. Get to Elmendorf on bus no. 14 from the BAC. If you wish, you may also visit Fort Richardson, Alaska's biggest army base, which also has a Wildlife Museum. Get there on bus no. 75.

ACCOMMODATIONS

youth hostel: If you're only going to be in town a night or two, the best place to stay is Anchorage Youth Hostel, corner of Minnesota Dr. and 32nd Ave.—4 km SW of downtown (tel. 276-3635). The YH can accommodate 52 people in dormitory bunkbeds. Members pay $6.25, non-members $8.25, and a housekeeping chore is mandatory. The hostel is open year-round, but closes daily from 0900-1700 and there is a 2300 curfew. You may leave your pack in the dormitory during the day; there's also a left-luggage service (50 cents a day) if you want to leave something while you're traveling. Cooking facilites are available. Get there Mon. to Sat. until 2130 on bus no. 6, which runs between the BAC, 6th and G, and Anchorage International Airport. Bus no. 31 goes to Minnesota Dr. and Northern Lights Blvd., 2 blocks from the hostel. *nearby:* The Anchorage YH is in suburban dragstrip territory where the locals go cruisin' in their "sleds" (big old cars). Fast food joints, bottle shops, shopping centers, drive-in banks, and adult book stores abound—all the symbols of American society. If by chance you can't get into the YH or would like a little privacy, check out Palm Motel, 3307½ Spenard Rd. (tel. 279-8023), which has rooms for $26 s or d (private bath). In the same area is the Fireweed Hotel, 604 W. 26th Ave. (tel. 277-2911). This one has rooms with a fridge, but shared bath, at $18 s, $26 d; a community kitchen and TV room are provided. It's more pleasant than the cheapies downtown and would be okay for couples, though it could get noisy.

downtown: The Palace Hotel, 4th and Barrow (tel. 277-6313), has rooms for $17 s, $22 d (shared facilities). The Alaska Hotel, 4th and C (tel. 279-4243), is not recommended. Push your way in the door through the mob of seedy derelicts outside. The Armed Services YMCA, 609 F St., has a 34-bed dormitory ($8.50 pp) for men. Anchorage Rescue Mission, in the church at 7th and F, provides free dormitory accommodations (sign in at 1600). There is a 3-night maximum stay and baggage must be removed during the day. Meals are free to those who do KP duty and attend the church service. Also try the Salvation Army, 8th and C Street. If these fail to please, the Dow Mar Sands Motel, 321 E. 5th Ave. (tel. 277-8212), is plush with color TV, kitchenette, and private bath in every unit, but the charge is $38 s, $43 d. The Ram's Head, 330 E St. (tel. 277-6311) next to the Hilton, is in the same price range as the Dow Mar, but not as chintzy.

others: If you'd rather stay in a local home than a hotel, Bed and Breakfast International (tel. 274-2561 during business hours, tel. 279-2228 evenings and weekends before 2100) can arrange it on request. Charges begin at $25 s, $30 d, and go up. Stay With a Friend (tel. 274-6445) has a similar B & B program for seniors over 50 years of age (3-night minimum stay). *longer stays:* Visiting students can stay in the dormitory at Alaska Pacific University, when there's space. The charge is $15 a night

or $42 a week in 3-bed rooms. Call tel. 276-8181, ext. 218, for details. Get there by taking bus nos. 3, 45, or 93 to Providence Hospital. Roberts Rooms, 310 W. 8th Ave. (tel. 276-9547), has single rooms (men only) at $20 nightly, $90 weekly. The bath and cooking facilities are shared with other tenants. Doubles are $120 weekly. Fifth Ave. Room and Board, 435 E. 5th Ave. (tel. 274-5253), provides food and a bed for $85 a week. They're often full, so call first. For similar places, check the "For Rent, Rooms" classified column in the *The Anchorage Times* or the *Daily News.* Also look in the yellow pages of the telephone book under "boarding houses" and "rooming houses."

camping: Lions Camper Park (tel. 333-1495) in Russian Jack Springs Park off Boniface Parkway has tent space at $4 a site. Showers are free, but there's a 7-night maximum stay in this city-operated park. Bus no. 8 stops at 6th and Boniface Parkway, only a block from Lions Camper Park, while bus no. 12 stops at Debarr Ave. and Boniface Parkway (just a little further). Centennial Park Campground (tel. 333-9711) is bigger than Lions Camper Park, but farther from town. The entrance is off Boundary Ave.; take bus no. 3 or 75 to Muldoon and Boundary avenues, then walk 10 min. to the office. This park is also city owned, so the charges and facilities are the same as at Lions.

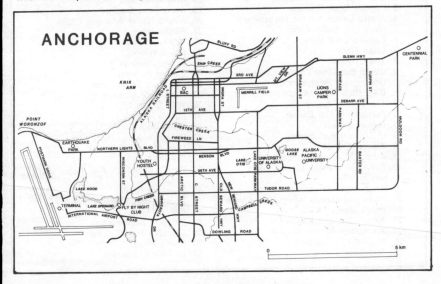

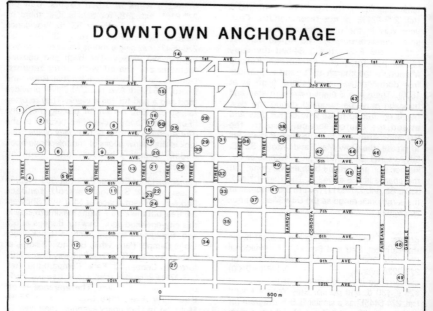

DOWNTOWN ANCHORAGE

ANCHORAGE

1. Resolution Park
2. Last Blue Whale sculpture
3. Captain Cook Fountain
4. Alaska Center for the Environment
5. Municipal Health Clinic
6. Captain Cook Hotel
7. Legal Pizza
8. The Cauldron
9. Valdez Bus Lines/Captain Cook Travel
10. Oomingmak Producers Co-operative
11. BAC (Bus Accommodation Center)
12. The Bread Factory
13. Performing Arts Center
14. railway station
15. U.S. Geological Survey
16. Alaska Airlines
17. Alaska Yukon Motorcoaches
18. Grayline/Columbia Glacier Tours
19. tourist office
20. Anchorage Convention Center
21. Parks and Forests Information Center
22. public library
23. Armed Services YMCA
24. Anchorage Rescue Mission
25. McDonald's Restaurant
26. The Book Cache
27. steam locomotive
28. downtown post ofice
29. Army Navy Surplus
30. Alaska Native Arts and Crafts
31. Alaska Hotel
32. Monkey Wharf
33. police station
34. Roberts Rooms
35. Federal Building
36. Peninsula Stage Lines
37. Anchorage Museum
38. Wild Cherry Club
39. Palace Hotel
40. Open Door Clinic
41. Salvation Army Thrift Store
42. Dow Mar Sands Hotel
43. Crawford Park
44. Bean's Cafe/Fifth Ave. Room and Board
45. Sheraton Hotel
46. Great Alaskan Bush Company
47. Kitty's Playgirl Club
48. Safeway Supermarket
49. Church's Fried Chicken
50. Ram's Head
51. La Mex Restaurant

FOOD

downtown: There are several excellent places to eat in downtown Anchorage. One is The Cauldron, 328 G St. (open Mon. to Sat. 1100-2300). They serve good homemade soups, salads, and sandwiches; in the evening there's folk music. Legal Pizza, nearby at 330 H St., has pizza by the slice and a good salad bar. Also recommended is The Bread Factory, 835 I St. (open daily 0700-1600 — breakfast until 1100 weekdays, all day on weekends). Go there for good natural food, including crepes, omelettes, and Mexican specialties. Another Mexican place, La Mex, 6th and I St., is more expensive, but serves gigantic portions and you get unlimited tostadas and salsa; try a Margarita grande ($3.50). Monday to Fri., one of the best places downtown for breakfast (0700-1000) or lunch (1100-1330) is the cafeteria in the Federal Building — plush, modern surroundings and reasonable prices. Bean's Cafe, 425 ½ E. 5th Ave. (enter from the alley), serves free breakfast (0800-0900) and lunch (1200-1300). This is charity, so only go if you're broke.

near the YH: There are 2 good eating places at the corner of Minnesota and Spenard. The Center Cafe (open daily 0700-2200) in the bowling alley on the SE corner, serves a good breakfast for $1.75 (coffee 50 cents extra). Skippers, on the NE corner, has an all-you-can-eat salad bar for $2.75. Thee Bakery (open daily), in the plaza just N of the hostel, has great cakes and pastries. Shakeys Pizza Parlor, Benson Blvd. and Minnesota, is good for pizza and beer. Monday to Fri. 1100-1330 there's an eat-your-fill luncheon buffet for $4. You don't have to go far to get a Big Mac or a Whopper, but if you're staying at the hostel and want a *real* burger do yourself a favor and go to Shenanigan's, 501 W. Fireweed. Their ½ pound burgers are charbroiled and served on black pumpernickel bread ($3.40 with bleu cheese). They also do deli platters and soups. Sometimes there's live music in the evening (call tel. 272-3663 and ask).

ENTERTAINMENT AND SHOPPING

bars downtown: The Monkey Wharf, 529 C St., features live monkeys and rock music

There's always action in front of the garish bars along 4th Ave. in downtown Anchorage.

(dancing from 2100). Reasonably priced meals are served until 2000 Mon. to Fri., most including soup or salad. Watch for specials posted on the blackboard by the door. The bars along 4th Ave., east from C St., are extremely colorful and extremely rough. Prostitutes, drunken natives, and con men abound. Anchorage offers the best striptease in the North. At The Great Alaskan Bush Company, 531 E. 5th Ave., they strut their stuff at eye level for the price of a beer (no cover charge). Tippers get a table dance. Wild Cherry on 4th Ave. is similar, but doesn't have as much class. If you're staying at the YH and want to indulge, PJ's on Spenard just E of Minnesota is the most convenient. Numerous "escort services" along Spenard W from Minnesota and in the alley behind the Fireweed Hotel offer you know what, but prices begin at $100 an hour. Kitty's Playgirl Club, behind the fast-food place at 4th and Gambell, features male exotic dancers for the ladies. It's open Mon. to Sat. from 1700-0230; $1 cover Mon. to Thurs., $3 cover Fri. and Sat. for females and escorts, $10 cover anytime for unescorted males. It's all good fun.

near the YH: Chilkoot Charlie's, Spenard and W. 25th, is *the* place to go in Anchorage: sawdust on the floor with all the local rock 'n roll groupies. It's not particularly cheap (their slogan is "we cheat the other guy and pass the savings on to you"). Go at happy hour (Mon. to Fri. 1630-1830) when the drinks are 2 for one, or Sun. when there's a free feed at 1800. Monday to Fri. from 1630-1900 it's happy hour at the Northern Lights Inn, 598 W. Northern Lights Boulevard. Well drinks, wine, and domestic beers are 2 for one, sandwiches are free. You have to be neat to get in. Mr. Whitekey's Fly By Night Club, 4811 Spenard Rd. near the airport (open Tues. to Sat.), has a good happy hour from 1600, live music from 2130. The place has great atmosphere and you can dance. Float planes land on the lake right behind the club. Get there on bus no. 7, which runs along Spenard Rd. near the YH; make the last bus back at 2115.

shopping: Drop in to Oomingmak Producers Co-operative, 604 H St., to see the very rare and expensive scarves, stoles, caps, and tunics hand-woven in isolated Eskimo villages from the downy, ash-brown underwool of the Alaskan musk ox. Army-Navy Surplus, 316 W. 4th Ave. sells clothes and camping gear at reasonable prices; pick up all the necessities you didn't think to bring, or lost along the way. For recycled clothes try the Salvation Army Thrift Store, 110 E. 6th Avenue. The Bishop's Attic, 11th and Gambell (Mon. to Sat. 1000-1730—bus no. 2), has a better selection of the same.

SERVICES AND INFORMATION

services: The Municipal Health Clinic, 825 L St. (open Mon. to Fri.), deals with all types of infections (including hepatitis, TB, VD, throat, and minor skin infections) and their services are free. Travel immunizations cost $8.50 for the series. If you need to see a doctor, try the Open Door Clinic, 140 E. 5th Ave. (tel. 279-7561). Charges begin at $17 for a brief consultation, $23 for a limited examination. Avoid the federally subsidized Neighborhood Health Clinic, 1217 E. 10th Ave., where the female clerks are unsympathetic and the charge, unless you submit to a humiliating means test, is $32 for even the briefest consultation. People who have never experienced it tell you to go there. If you have a specific problem (social services, emergency accommodations, etc.), and can't find help elsewhere, call the Resource Line (tel. 277-0222) for some leads.

information: The tourist office at 4th and F (open daily 1000-1800) is a tourist attraction in itself, with its sod roof and log walls. They have the usual maps and brochures: the "Anchorage Walking Tour" leaflet is the best. The Parks and Forests Information Center, 540 W. 5th Ave. (open Mon. to Fri. 0800-1700), can provide maps and trail guides for most parts of Southcentral Alaska, plus all of the National Parks. Ask for a map of the Chugach National Forest and for leaflets on any hiking trails that

might interest you. Free movies are shown at 1200 and 1500. Topographical maps of all of Alaska are available from the U.S. Geological Survey, 508 2nd Ave. (open Mon. to Fri. 0900-1700). The Book Cache, 436 W. 5th Ave., has the best selection of books on Alaska. The Alaska Center for the Environment, 1069 W. 6th Ave., can refer visitors to organizations working on any specific environmental issues which might interest them. The Center has an excellent alternative energy library and sells puffin T-shirts ($8) which make excellent gifts. The Sierra Club, 545 E. 4th Ave., keeps a list of names of people looking for hiking and canoeing companions, and organizes as well weekend outings for visiting members.

TRANSPORT

airport: Anchorage International Airport (ANC) is 8 km SW of downtown. The new international terminal opened in 1982, but most passenger facilities are still located in the old domestic terminal, 500 m east. (All of the

---

VICINITY OF ANCHORAGE YOUTH HOSTEL

1. Anchorage Youth Hostel
2. Thee Bakery
3. Shakeys Pizza Parlor
4. Payless Discount Drugs
5. Pay 'n Pak Hardware
6. bus no. 60 to S edge of town
7. Safeway Supermarket
8. Baskin-Robbins Ice Cream/The Book Cache/Pay 'n Save Drugs
9. First National Bank
10. Burger King
11. Kentucky Fried Chicken
12. Chilkoot Charlie's
13. REI Coop
14. National Bank of Alaska
15. Taco Bell
16. McDonald's Restaurant
17. Fireweed Motel
18. Shenanigan's Burgers
19. Northern Lights Inn
20. Palm Motel
21. Pizza Hut
22. post office
23. PJ's
24. Skippers
25. Center Cafe
26. Thrifty Rent-a-Car

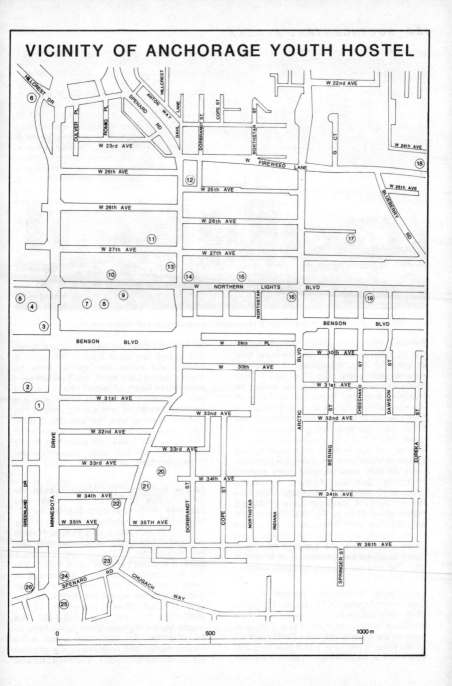

VICINITY OF ANCHORAGE YOUTH HOSTEL

The stunning Chugach Mountains backdrop the city of Anchorage.

following refers to the latter.) "People Mover" bus no. 6 (50 cents) runs from the lower level at gate 33 into downtown Anchorage, approximately every hour Mon. to Fri. from 0600-2200, every 2 hours Sat., no service on Sunday. Bus no. 6 passes in front of Anchorage Youth Hostel. Bus no. 93 also runs from the airport to near the YH (Benson and Minnesota), but does not go downtown. At other times there is a minibus limousine service ($5 pp) leaving from outside the baggage claim area. This service operates every 30 min. until midnight every evening including Sunday. There's a tourist information stand in the baggage claim area (lower level). A National Bank of Alaska branch (open Mon. to Fri. 0900-1700) is near gate 22 (upper level). There are no coin lockers in the airport, but a baggage storage room (open until 0100) in the baggage claim area (lower level) will keep backpacks at $2 each a day. The terminal is open 24 hours a day.

airport trivia: Anchorage styles itself the "air crossroads of the world." Every day 130 flights of 12 major airlines arrive at the airport, which handles 4 million passengers a year. Details of services are given in the main "Introduction" to this book. If you have a little time to spare, take a look at the collection of stuffed Alaskan animals and fish near gate 33 (upper level). The largest sea plane base in the world is situated just across the highway from the airport, around Lake Hood. You'll seldom see a more mixed batch of aircraft than here. The city skyline and Chugach Mountains are visible; instead of just sitting around the terminal wasting time, go over for a walk. *note:* Individuals trying to sell off unwanted air tickets to the Lower 48 advertise in the classifieds of the daily papers under "Transportation" or "Travel."

by train and ferry: The Alaska Railroad has daily service to Denali Park ($44) and Fairbanks ($63), 10 percent discount for RT, bicycles $2 extra, reservations accepted (free seating). There's also a daily train to Portage ($7) and Whittier ($9), which connects with the ferry service to Valdez ($34) 5 times a week. If you don't wish to go to Valdez, you can make a day trip from Anchorage to Whittier for $16 RT, with several hours layover in Whittier before returning to Anchorage. The railway ticket office is open Mon. to Fri. 0630-1300, Sat. and Sun. 0630-1100. The Alaska Marine Highway office (open Mon. to Fri. 0830-1700, Sat. 0830-1200) is also in the railway station and reservations are required for all ferries to Valdez, Cordova, Kodiak

Island, and the Aleutians. Count your change carefully if you buy a ticket here.

by bus: Bus transportation in Alaska is still in a primitive stage of development, with many small companies competing for what little business there is. There is no central bus station in Anchorage (or elsewhere) and schedules change quickly. The information below, which is intended only as a guide, should be rechecked carefully before setting out. Tranportation Services Inc. (tel 279-5592) has a bus to Seward ($13) Mon. to Fri. at 0800, leaving from the Hotel Captain Cook. A ticket as far as Alyeska is $5. They also have a bus to Palmer ($3 OW, $5 RT) Mon. to Fri. at 1725, leaving from the Sheraton Hotel. Reservations are not accepted. Seward Bus Lines (tel. 278-2760) runs an 11-seat minibus to Seward ($15) daily except Sat., leaving from the Hotel Captain Cook; call for reservations. Peninsula Stage Lines (office in the parking lot at 4th and B) has a daily minibus service leaving at 1700 for Cooper Landing ($10), Sterling ($13), Kenai ($15), and Homer ($30). Anchorage-Valdez Bus Lines, 743 W. 5th Ave., has service daily except Mon. to Palmer ($7) and Valdez ($52) in a 10-seat van. Yukon Stage Lines has a weekly minibus service to Whitehorse (US$110—no stopovers permitted), departing Captain Cook Travel, 743 W. 5th Avenue. The overnight stop at Beaver Creek is at your own expense. Alaska-Yukon Motorcoaches, 327 F St., has service twice a week to Haines ($135), weekly to Skagway ($145). The Skagway run takes 3 days due to overnight stops (at your own expense) in Tok Junction and Whitehorse. The route of the daily Alaska-Yukon Motorcoach service to Valdez alternates via Whittier ($82) or Glennallen ($53). Bicycles are carried at $10 extra charge and tickets must be purchased in advance.

local buses: Most of the places you'll want to visit in Anchorage are accessible on "People Mover" city buses. Most leave from the Bus Accommodation Center (BAC), 6th and G streets. Pick up timetables for all routes here, or ask the drivers for them, or buy a small schedule booklet ($1) at The Book Cache. There can sometimes be long intervals between buses, so it pays to check the timetable. The system is being expanded, so check routes as well. The fare is 50 cents and free transfers are issued for stopovers, bus changes, or round trips for up to 3 hours (no service on Sunday).

package tours: For those on a short visit to Alaska, Columbia Glacier Cruises (tel. 276-8866) offers a 2-day RT bus/boat/train tour, Anchorage to Valdez (20 May to 18 Sept. only). The full price is $225, but this can be reduced to $135 by going on a standby, space available basis Sat. or Sunday. Tickets must be purchased in Anchorage through the company office. The tour price includes the bus from Anchorage to Valdez, a

An Alaska-sized cabbage at the Matanuska Experimental Farm near Palmer.

double-occupancy hotel room in Valdez, the *Glacier Queen* to the face of Columbia Glacier and on to Whittier, lunch on the boat, the train to Portage, and a bus to Anchorage. A northbound tour is preferable to taking the boatride the first day. If your time is extremely limited and you're looking for the very best package excursion, this is it.

car rentals: If you can get a group of 4 together, a car rental might be worth considering. Roads on the Kenai Peninsula are good and you can cover a lot of ground in a few days. Rates at the different agencies vary considerably, so call around to find the best deal. Rent-a-Dent, 919 E. 5th Ave. (tel 274-1607), has cars at $14 a day, 14 cents a mile, plus $4.50 insurance and $250 deposit (or credit card). Try also Rent-a-Wreck (tel. 243-8459). Closer to the YH is Thrifty Rent-a-Car, Spenard and Minnesota (tel. 276-2855), whose vehicles run $36 daily (240 km included free), plus $5.50 insurance and $200 deposit (or credit card). *by bicycle:* You can borrow a bicycle free of charge from Earth Cycle (Mon. to Sat. 0900-1600), which operates a stand in front of the old courthouse, 4th and F (leave $5 deposit and identification). The best cycling places are the parkland along Chester Creek, which stretches across the waist of Anchorage just S of downtown, and out to Earthquake Park.

hitching: To hitch N to Denali Park or Tok, take bus no. 76/78 (EAGLE RIVER) to Peter's Creek Trading Post, 35 km N of Anchorage on the Glenn Highway. To hitch S toward the Kenai Peninsula take bus no. 60 to Old Seward Highway and Venus Way, the furthest out the city buses go. Walk 1 km S on Old Seward Highway to New Seward Highway. If you're leaving from the YH, catch bus no. 60 eastbound on Hillcrest Dr. in front of West Anchorage High School (see the map). These buses are a bargain at 50 cents each.

PLACES NEAR ANCHORAGE

Southcentral Alaska is a land of short rivers, long mountain ranges, and wide valleys, extending N from the Gulf of Alaska to the crest of the Alaska Range. A rugged strip 100 km wide swings NE along the gulf, from Cook Inlet to the Yukon border. These are the Kenai and Chugach Mountains. To the N lie the Matanuska and Susitna valleys, with Mt. McKinley visible beyond. Much of the area around Prince William Sound and on the Kenai Peninsula is included in the Chugach National Forest. In many ways, Southcentral is the rich heartland of Alaska, with one big metropolis (Anchorage) and many picturesque small towns, plus some of the finest scenery and best hiking and camping opportunities in the state. Getting around is easy and an efficient ferry system brings the best within reach. Southcentral Alaska offers something for everyone.

Palmer: This small town in the Matanuska Valley, 64 km N of Anchorage, is famous for its New Deal cooperative agricultural settlement

The Athapaskan Indians built miniature spirit houses, such as these at Eklutna, over the graves of their dead. The cross of the Russian Orthodox Church stands before each.

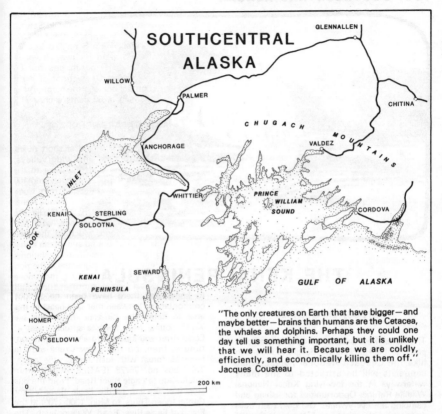

SOUTHCENTRAL ALASKA

"The only creatures on Earth that have bigger—and maybe better—brains than humans are the Cetacea, the whales and dolphins. Perhaps they could one day tell us something important, but it is unlikely that we will hear it. Because we are coldly, efficiently, and economically killing them off."
Jacques Cousteau

scheme sponsored by the federal government in 1935. Although the program did not work out exactly as its planners envisioned, the valley today is an important dairy and vegetable producing area. Plants grow to spectacular sizes during the 20-hour days of the Alaskan summer: 20 kg cabbages are common. Alaska imports most of its food, including fresh produce, from the Lower 48, however. The tourist office, near the old railway station downtown, is worth a visit for information, a 25 cent coffee, and the small historical museum in the basement. *events:* The best time to visit Palmer is during the Alaska State Fair from late Aug. to early Sept. when special trains ($10 RT) run from Anchorage (no railway service at other times). The fairgrounds are 3 km S of downtown; the Transportation Museum (free) adjoining the fairgrounds is open Wed. to Sun. from

1000-1600 during the summer. As might be expected, the fair is mostly an agricultural affair and record-sized vegetables are on display. *stay:* The municipal campground is $3 a site, showers 50 cents. The Hotel Palmer (tel. 745-4111) is $10 s, $15 d (shared bath), or $61 s, $82 d by the week. Both of these are a short walk from the center of town. *tours to Palmer:* The Gray Line offers a 6-hour Matanuska Valley Tour ($22 pp plus $5 for lunch) from Anchorage. In addition to Palmer, the tour visits the Athapaskan Indian burial ground at Eklutna, the University of Alaska Experimental Farm between Palmer and Wasilla, and a typical valley vegetable farm. *from Palmer:* Transportation Services Inc. runs a commuter bus to Anchorage ($3) Mon. to Fri. at 0630, departing from the Frontier Cafe.

THE KENAI PENINSULA

OUTDOOR EXPERIENCES

The Kenai Peninsula is an outdoorsperson's paradise: backpackers will delight to mountain hike the Chugach National Forest, while canoeists will be attracted to the many waterways in the low-lying Kenai National Wildlife Refuge. Opportunities for fishing and camping are everywhere. Old gold rush trails crisscross the area and the remains of one-time mines punctuate both sides of Turnagain Arm. The Kenai is the major recreational playground for urban Anchorage. Since it is easily and quickly accessible from the city, you'll probably have to hike further off the road to find solitude. All in all, the scenery is beautiful and the facilities well-developed. Grab your chance to make a trip into this area.

the Old Iditarod Trail: This 37 km, 3-day hiking trail from Eagle River SE to Crow Pass combines scenery, wildlife, and history with an opportunity to bypass Anchorage. The Old Iditarod Trail was used by miners and dog mushers until 1918 when the railway replaced it. Today hikers are drawn by the spectacular Chugach Mountains, the wildflowers, and the wildlife (bears, sheep, moose, birds). Although you may see a bear on the trip, it's comforting to know that there have been no serious confrontations between man and beast in this area to date. The bio-zone transitions are worth noting: from a white spruce forest at Eagle River you'll pass into alpine vegetation, tundra, then, on the Crow Creek side, a hemlock forest with lush ferns. *the route:* Take bus no. 76/78 (EAGLE RIVER) from Anchorage to Eagle River Road. From the bus stop it's 20m km to the Eagle River Visitor Center (open Thurs. to Mon. 1000-1700) at the E end of Eagle River Road. Walk or hitch. The ranger at the Visitor Center can advise you on trail conditions and supply a map. Camping is allowed along the trail (at least 2 km beyond the Visitor Center), but campfires are prohibited. The recently upgraded gradual climb from the Visitor Center up to Crow Pass passes mostly through Chugach State Park. There are several creeks and rivers to ford along the way, the fiercest being the crossing of the Eagle River itself, midway on the trail. It might be wise to camp in this area and cross in the morning, when the glacial run-off will be lower. Raven Glacier and Crystal Lake are scenic highlights near Crow Pass (1,065 m). From the pass there'a a steep descent down to the S trailhead at Crow Pass Road. Watch for old goldmining ruins in this area. It's 8 km down rough Crow Creek Road to the access road to Alyeksa Ski Resort, then a further 3 km out to the Seward Highway.

Portage Glacier: Portage Glacier sits at the head of Turnagain Arm on the narrow neck of land which joins the Kenai Peninsula to the Alaskan mainland. This heavily promoted attraction is only 85 km SE of Anchorage. Big chunks of blue glacial ice calve off the face of Portage Glacier and float across 5-km-long Portage Lake to the Forest Service Visitor Center. This Visitor Center is 9 km off the Seward Highway. There are 3 Forest Service campgrounds ($4) along the road to the Visitor Center; the first is 5 km off the Seward Highway. Portage railway station (daily service to Whittier—$4 OW) is 2 km back along the Seward Highway towards Anchorage. A short trail leads from the Visitor Center to Byron Glacier. Be aware that there is no way to hike across the mountains to nearby Whittier (see "Whittier" below for a map). The Gray Line has a 6-hour bus tour ($22) from Anchorage which includes a stop at Portage Glacier and lunch (own expense) at Alyeska Ski Resort.

Resurrection Pass Trail: This relatively easy trail blazed by prospectors in the late 1800s runs from near Hope due S to Cooper Landing on the Sterling Highway. The 60 km can be covered in 3 days, with Resurrection Pass (793 m) the highest point. There are 7 Forest Service cabins ($10) along the old prospectors' route, but these must be booked in advance, preferably 180 days ahead. (Write: Anchorage Ranger District, Box 10-469, Anchorage, AK 99511, USA). Camping is allowed anywhere and is a good alternative. Hope, on Turnagain Arm, is an old mining town founded in 1896 that has a local historical museum. The Resurrection Pass Trail is the most popular (and crowded) on the peninsula, but the trailhead on the Hope side is 30 km off the Seward Highway and 5 km from Hope. This can make it inconvenient if you don't have a ride, so consider entering via the Devil's Pass Trail (Forest Service Trail no. 5) which begins at Mile 39 on the Seward Highway. It only takes 5½ hours to cover the 16-km Devil's Pass Trail, so you'd be able to reach Cooper Landing in 2 days easy. The fishing and scenery are great.

Russian Lakes Trail: This trail begins just a little E of the Resurrection Pass trailhead at Cooper Landing. It runs 34 km to Cooper Lake, where it joins the 20-km-long Snug Harbor Road back out to the Sterling Highway. Work is presently underway to extend this trail down the Resurrection River Valley, which would

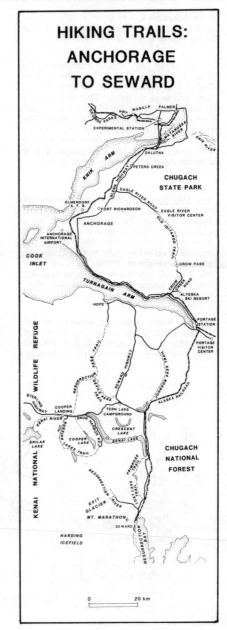

HIKING TRAILS: ANCHORAGE TO SEWARD

make it possible to hike all the way from Hope to Seward, right across the peninsula. Ask about this at any Forest Service office.

Johnson Pass Trail: A good alternative to the Resurrection Pass Trail is the Johnson Pass Trail (Forest Service Trail no. 10) which is fairly level and easy to follow. This is actually a 37-km portion of the Old Iditarod Trail of gold rush fame, once heavily used by miners. The route begins at Mile 64 on the Seward Highway and terminates at the S end of Upper Trail Lake (Mile 33). There are bridges over all streams and drinking water is available. Allow 2 days.

Lost Lake Trail: This trail (Forest Service Trail no. 12) begins near the Bear Creek Fire Station, 8 km N of Seward, and leads 11 km to Lost Lake, which is above treeline. It is possible to continue down the Primrose Trail from the N tip of Lost Lake to Kenai Lake near the Seward Highway. Brown bears are rare in this area, but blackies may be seen in spring. There are opportunities for cross-country hiking here.

rafting: Alaska Campout Adventures (tel. 907-595-1350) offers an exciting 6-hour raft trip ($55, picnic lunch included) through fabulous Kenai Canyon on the blue-green Kenai River. They supply all equipment and their office is conveniently located at Cooper Landing on the Sterling Highway, just 1½ km W of the Resurrection Pass trailhead. Float trips begin at 1100.

canoeing: There are several excellent canoe trips possible in the Kenai National Wildlife Refuge, NE of Soldotna. The Alaska Pioneer Canoers Association (Box 931, Soldotna, AK 99669, USA) keeps canoes at the end of the canoe routes at Pedersens Moose River Resort, Sterling, midway on the road from Anchorage to Homer. Rental canoes cost $55 per canoe for 4 days (paddles and life jackets included), plus $30 to transport yourself and equipment to West Entrance on Canoe Lake. This is the start of the Swan Lake Canoe Route, which delivers you back to Moose River Bridge in 3-4 days. The rivers are gentle and suitable for beginners; the lakes are full of fish. This is an excellent opportunity to see many kinds of wildlife in their natural habitat, while enjoying a leisurely camping and fishing trip. Moose are especially abundant in the refuge. Free camping is available at Isaac Walton State Wayside, just across the Moose River from Pedersens Resort, and the Anchorage-Kenai bus stops at Sterling Chevron nearby. Call tel. 907-262-4003 or 262-4515 for details.

The moose, largest member of the deer family, ranges from Alaska across Canada to Maine, and down the Rocky Mountain chain to Colorado. The horse-sized males are much larger than the females and stand up to 225 cm tall at the shoulder. Males have antlers up to 200 cm wide, which they shed in winter. The moose feeds on the bark, branches, and buds of certain trees, especially willow, and is normally a solitary animal. They have been known to charge humans, especially during the mating season (Oct. to November).

KENAI

The town of Kenai (pop. 4,324 in 1980) sits on a bluff above the mouth of the Kenai River overlooking Cook Inlet. Across the inlet to the SW rise Mts. Redoubt and Iliamna, active volcanoes at the end of the Aleutian Range. The Alaska Range is visible to the northwest. Great white beluga whales enter the mouth of the river on the incoming tides to look for fish. Kenai was founded in 1791 by Russian fur traders, as several old buildings attest. Oil was discovered just offshore in Cook Inlet in 1957 and is today the mainstay of the town's prosperity. Kenai is an 18-km side trip off the Sterling Highway at Soldotna, worthwhile if you have the time and are into history.

The chapel of St. Nicholas at Kenai was erected over the grave Father Nicolai in 1906.

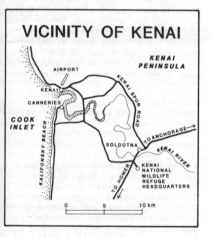

VICINITY OF KENAI

sights: All the sights of Kenai are in one small area, which you can tour on foot in 1 ½ hours. Holy Assumption Russian Orthodox Church was built in 1896. Peek through the windows at the painted altar and brass chandelier. St. Nicholas Memorial Chapel (1906) nearby also reflects the traditional Russian Orthodox architectural style. Across the street from the church is the local Historical Society Museum (open Mon. to Sat. 1000-1700, Sun. 1100-1700, donations accepted). The U.S. Army built Fort Kenay here in 1869: a replica of this vanished fort was erected behind the museum in 1967. From its present condition, the replica seems destined, before long, to follow the fate of its predecessor. From a viewpoint just E of the church, there is a panoramic view over the riverside canneries, with the Kenai Mountains behind and the Aleutian and Alaska ranges strung out from across Cook Inlet.

practicalites: You may camp at Kenai Municipal Park on Forest Dr., just W of town. The cheapest place in town to eat is Time Saver Grocery at the entrance to town (yellow sign), which has a good little deli counter and a picnic table out back. The tourist information office (closed Sun.) is in Moose Meat John's Cabin on the main highway. *from Kenai:* Peninsula Stage Lines (tel. 283-3883) has a bus to Anchorage ($15), leaving the Kenai Sheffield Hotel at 0700 daily.

sea otters

HOMER

Homer (pop. 2,209 in 1980), on Kachemak Bay at the W end of the North American road network, is a pleasant little town with a mild climate. It's affectionately referred to as the "banana belt" of Alaska. The mountains and glaciers of the Kenai Range provide a splendid backdrop for the town. Homer began in 1895 as a coal mining center, an industry which soon failed and was replaced by fishing. The fishing fleet ties up at the end of the Homer Spit, 8 km from the center of town. The Alaska Marine Highway ferry terminal is also at the end of the Spit. A lot of very creative people seem to gravitate to Homer; craft shops and art galleries are numerous.

sights: The Pratt Museum on Bartlett St. (open daily 1000-1700, $1.50 admission) has especially good wildlife and marine exhibits. Films are shown at the museum Thurs. at 1900 (donation). The waterfront below Homer at the foot of Main St. provides some rewarding opportunities for beach walking at low tide. This is a good place to be alone. Go R towards the cliffs, but beware of getting stranded by an incoming tide. There are plenty of exotic little creatures to look at and the setting is superb. The hard black material you find washed up on the beach is coal, which drops from natural deposits in the area.

stay and eat: There are 3 places in a row to note on Pioneer Ave. in downtown Homer. The Heritage Hotel has 11 rooms without bath at $31 s, $36 d. Next door, the Sterling Cafe is very popular with young cannery workers.

Finally, Alice's Champagne Palace is the night spot. The snack bar in front of Family Theater on Pioneer Ave. serves cheap Mexican food and is open for lunch (see previews of the movies as you eat your tacos). The moderately-priced Willow Wind Restaurant, between Homer and Homer Spit, specializes in soup, sandwiches, omelettes, and vegetarian dinners.

camping: The City Campground behind the fairgrounds above Homer charges $3 a site. The individual campsites are unusually private, separated by trees and vegetation, and drinking water is available. If it's raining there's a shelter at the fairgrounds where you may sit. Camp free on Bishop's Beach at the foot of Main Street. Campfires are allowed, but don't leave debris, please.   _services:_   Showers ($2.30—bring a towel) and laundry facilities are available at the Homer Cleaning Center on Main St. between Sterling Highway and Pioneer Avenue. Rent a bicycle at $2 a day from 4 Season Sports on Pioneer Avenue. East End Road is a good place to go cycling.

from Homer: Both Alaska Aeronautical Industries (tel. 235-8250) and Southcentral Air (tel. 235-6171) have frequent flights to Anchorage ($47). Call both and ask about standby fares. Ferry services are described under "Homer Spit" below. There's a minibus service to Anchorage ($30) leaving daily at 1030 from the service station opposite the Heritage Hotel. The easiest way to get out of Homer is to hitch.

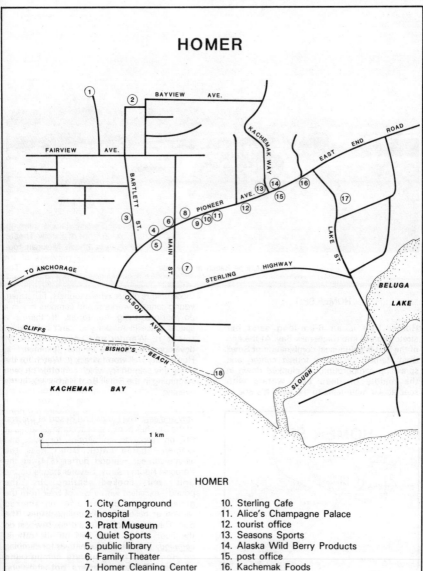

HOMER

HOMER

1. City Campground
2. hospital
3. Pratt Museum
4. Quiet Sports
5. public library
6. Family Theater
7. Homer Cleaning Center
8. Proctor's Grocery
9. Heritage Hotel
10. Sterling Cafe
11. Alice's Champagne Palace
12. tourist office
13. Seasons Sports
14. Alaska Wild Berry Products
15. post office
16. Kachemak Foods
17. Lakeside Mall
18. camping area

Bishops Beach at low tide

HOMER SPIT

Homer Spit is an 8-km-long sand bar stretching out into Kachemak Bay. At the end of the Spit is an unusual combination of Small Boat Harbor, canneries, tourist center, and sprawling campground, all plunked down in the middle of deep blue waters with spectacular mountains to the east. It's one of those unique places where tourists, fishermen, young cannery workers, and campers mix in a do-your-own-thing free-for-all. If there's a special place in Alaska you can't help liking, this is it. Wander and enjoy. Hopefully, development schemes by the "planners" in Homer City Hall won't wreck it. Watch for the many tiny salmon fry which can often be seen swimming in the Small Boat Harbor late in the evening.

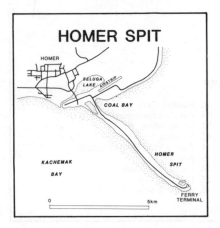

stay and eat: The Lands End Resort at the end of the Spit has bunkhouse accommodations at $12 pp (separate dormitories for men and women—shared bath). Don't miss the all-you-can-eat seafood buffet ($14) in the Porpoise Room nearby. Several stands on the Spit sell cooked shrimp by the pound—excellent with a can of beer from the general store. You can also get smoked salmon or halibut in take-out packages. The Salty Dawg is the place for a drink: sawdust on the floor and a dusty owl on the rafters. _camping:_ There are 2 alternatives for camping on Homer Spit: the private campground charges $7.75, but offers hot showers; camping on the beach is $3. Use of the showers by beach campers is $2.25. Both camping areas are a stone's throw from the ferry wharf.

from Homer Spit: The state ferry MV *Tustumena* (no showers) sails to Seldovia ($9) and Kodiak ($27) twice a week. Once a week the ferry goes all the way to Cordova ($78), with stops in Seward and Valdez. Three times a year there's a service to Dutch Harbor ($136) in the Aleutian Islands. The ferry terminal is near the end of Homer Spit. This ferry is a lot less crowded than those on the Inside Passage in Southeast Alaska. The open-sea journey across the Gulf of Alaska is an experience in itself. A daily 4-hour cruise, leaving at 1300, on the *Danny J* to Gull Island and Halibut Cove costs $30 pp. This boat will obligingly drop campers off in Kachemak Bay State Park, and pick them up again a few days later, at no extra charge.

SELDOVIA

This small town (pop. 479 in 1980), 25 km from Homer across Kachemak Bay, is accessible by state ferry twice a week. The ferry docks right in town. Most of the original boardwalk was swallowed up by the 1964 earthquake, but Seldovia retains its fishing-village charm. Commercial fishing thrives on a small scale. St. Nicholas Russian Orthodox Church (1891) is the only tourist attraction. Hike up to the dam site behind the airport for the view. Camping is allowed at Outside Beach, 1 ½ km from town. There are toilets and showers in the Harbormaster's office.

The arctic tern (*Sterna paradisaea*), a small shore bird which nests along the coast of Alaska in summer, is one of the greatest of all travelers. Every fall it flies S to the coast of Chile and the antarctic ice flows where it spends the winter. Their 17,500 km annual migration route is the longest of any bird. The arctic tern is recognizable by its long narrow wings, bright red bill and legs, black skull cap, light grey body, and white tail.

SEWARD

Seward (pop. 1,843 in 1980) sits majestically at the head of Resurrection Bay, a deep fjord lined on both sides by icecapped peaks. You arrive in Seward up this magnificent channel by ferry or along a beautiful 200-km highway from Anchorage. The 1,865-sq-km Harding Icefield is just to the southwest. The town, built on an alluvial fan created by Lowell Creek, once suffered seasonal flooding. In 1940, a diversion tunnel was constructed under Bear Mountain and the creek waters now pour harmlessly into the bay, just beyond the new Seward Marine Center. Seward was founded in 1903 as the terminus of what became the Alaska Railroad and because it was also an ice-free port. The town has a pioneer air; many buildings from the early days have been preserved and are still in use. Seward is a pocket-sized place, just right for finding your way around; a visit is recommended.

SIGHTS OF SEWARD

The Resurrection Bay Historical Museum in the basement of the City Hall, 5th and Adams (open Mon. to Sat. 1100-1600, Sun. 1300-1600, 50 cents admission), has exhibits relating to the history of the town. There's also a slide show, shown upon request. The library just across the street presents slides and movies to the public Mon. to Sat. at 1400. More free movies, lectures, and slide shows are presented at the Seward Marine Center (open Mon. to Fri. 1300-1700, Tues and Thurs. 1900-2030 also). The Center is operated by the Institute of Marine Science of the University of Alaska, Fairbanks. The research laboratories are on the waterfront just across the street. For an enjoyable short walk on a winding trail through the forest, look for the Two Lakes Trail behind AVTEC First Lake Facility, 2nd and C. There's a picnic area at the trailhead.

Mt. Marathon: The high, bare slope which hangs over Seward to the W is Mt. Marathon. The steep climb up to Race Point (920 m) can be very tiring if you're not in shape. Every 4th of July there's a race up and down the mountain and many do it in under an hour, but if you've come to enjoy yourself, allow at least four. Follow Jefferson St. due W up Lowell Canyon and look for the trailhead to the R just

beyond a pair of large water tanks. Keep R through the forest on the way up to avoid exhaustion. You can run all the way back down the mountain on a steep gravel incline, if your legs and nerves are good. Beware of slipping on the solid rock face near the bottom. The trail does not actually reach the summit of Mt. Marathon (1,403 m), but rather the broad E shoulder, which offers a spectacular view of Seward and the entire surrounding area.

hiking: There are many hiking possibilities up Resurrection River Road, which begins 5 km N of Seward. Thirteen km up this dirt track is a 3-km trail to Exit Glacier. A trail is being built up the Resurrection River Valley which will eventually permit access to the Russian Lakes and Cooper Landing. Ask at the Forest Service office about progress on this route. For information on the Lost Lake Trail near Seward see under "Outdoor Experiences" above.

others: The coastline and interior icefields SW of Seward have been declared Kenai Fjords National Park. There is no way into the park

SEWARD

1. Seward Marine Center
2. ferry office
3. Jinny Coffee Shop
4. Yukon Bar
5. Quikwash Laundromat
6. Flamingo Lounge
7. Great North Sports
8. New Seward Hotel
9. Seward Bakery
10. public library
11. city hall/museum
12. Horizons Travel
13. First National Bank
14. Mini-Mall Fast Foods
15. Van Gilder Hotel/Liberty Theater
16. Forest Service
17. post office
18. tourist office
19. AVTEC Cafeteria
20. AVTEC First Lake Facility

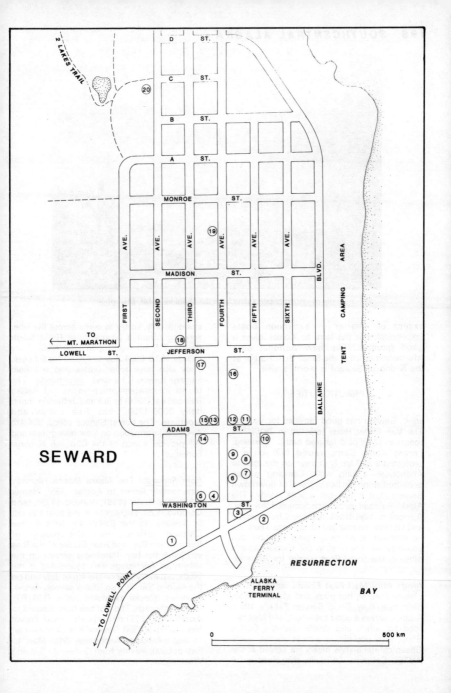

the all-encompassing view from the shoulder of Mt. Marathon

except on charter or excursion boats (expensive), but the ferry to Kodiak gives a good glimpse. The new national park information office in the Small Boat Harbor at the N end of Seward is worth a visit.

PRACTICALITIES

stay: Seward has good facilities for visitors. The Van Gilder Hotel (erected in 1916) has rooms at $24 s or d (shared bath). _camping:_ Forest Acres Campground ($3) is in a protected area 3 km N of town on the road to Anchorage—a long walk. Camping is also permitted along the beach just E of downtown Seward, but it can get a little windy. The Alaska Railroad yards once occupied this area. A modern toilet block has been built nearby and you may be charged $3 to camp. There are no showers at either camping location, but you may use the ones in the Harbormaster's office in the Small Boat Harbor for 75 cents.

food: Mini-Mall Fast Foods, across from Liberty Theater, has pizza and Mexican food, plus cheap beer. Good. Seward Bakery, 4th at Adams, serves a good breakfast, and Mexican food for lunch and dinner. Ginny's Coffee Shop, also popular, is almost always open. Cheap cafeteria-style meals are served at the AVTEC Cafeteria. Officially, this place is for students only, so try to come across like one. _services:_ Rent a bicycle from Great North Sports, 215 5th Ave. (open 1100-1900). They charge $6.50 for 4 hours, $10.50 for 8 hours. They also have roller skates and will hold luggage for you ($1 a day). _information:_ The tourist information office, in an old Alaska Railroad car (1916) at 3rd and Jefferson (open daily 0900-1700), has free coffee and brochures. The Forest Service office, 334 4th Ave., has information on local hiking trails and will provide a map of the Chugach National Forest.

from Seward: The Alaska Marine Highway runs weekly ferries to Kodiak ($35), Homer ($56), Seldovia ($56), Valdez ($35), and Cordova ($35). Highlights of the boat trip out of Seward are the Steller sea lions on the Chiswell Islands near the mouth of Resurrection Bay, and Bear Glacier to the R as you leave the bay. Passenger service on the railway to Anchorage was suspended in the 1950s, but every year on the 4th of July and on the second Sat. in Aug. (for a salmon derby), there are special excursion trains ($30 RT) from Anchorage. The TSI bus from Seward to Anchorage ($13) departs Horizons Travel Mon. to Fri. at 1330. Seward Bus Lines runs an 11-seat minibus to Anchorage ($15) Mon. to Sat. at 0900, leaving from Quikwash, 3rd and Washington.

WHITTIER

Whittier (pop. 198 in 1980) stretches along a narrow strip of land at the foot of the mountains on Passage Canal at the westernmost end of Prince William Sound. Whittier Glacier hangs directly above. Whittier is usually overlooked by tourists, who only use it as a transfer point to and from the ferry to Columbia Glacier and Valdez. Actually, this is one of the most scenic and appealing little towns in Alaska. It makes an excellent daytrip from Anchorage by train (100 km OW); stop over for a night instead of getting right on the ferry for Valdez.

SIGHTS OF WHITTIER

defense relics: Less well known than the Alaska Highway, the construction of the railway to Whittier was one of the great engineering feats of WW II. Two tunnels, one 1,497 m long, the the other 3,990 m long, were carved through the Chugach Mountains to link the military bases in Anchorage and Fairbanks to a secret saltwater port. Seward, the main ice-free port in Southcentral Alaska up to that time, was considered too exposed and vulnerable to Japanese attack, so from 1941 to 1943 the army blasted through the mountains

and laid the tracks which would insure the flow of supplies for the defense of Alaska. The Whittier route also shortened the distance to Anchorage and Fairbanks considerably. After the defeat of Japan, the military pulled out of Whittier, but a year later they were back as a new Cold War began with the Soviet Union. Whittier became a permanent base and large concrete buildings were built at that time; in them most of the local residents still live today. The 14-story Begich Towers (1948-1954), an unlikely skyscraper in this small village, is near another anomaly, the "City Under One Roof," which once housed 1,000 men and was the largest building in Alaska. The base was deactivated in 1960 and the buildings were damaged in the 1964 earthquake. The Begich Towers have been restored and are now converted into apartments. The military presence today is limited to an oil pipeline which supplies the military installations at Anchorage.

others: There is a small museum (open 1400-1700, closed Tues. and Thurs., donation) in room 107 at the Begich Towers, just down the hall from the post office. Every summer thousands of black-legged kittiwakes (the

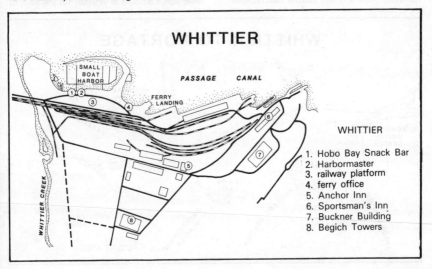

WHITTIER

PASSAGE CANAL

SMALL BOAT HARBOR

FERRY LANDING

WHITTIER CREEK

WHITTIER

1. Hobo Bay Snack Bar
2. Harbormaster
3. railway platform
4. ferry office
5. Anchor Inn
6. Sportsman's Inn
7. Buckner Building
8. Begich Towers

gulls with the black wing tips) migrate to a rookery on the cliffs directly opposite Whittier. The area is inaccessible on foot, but the state ferries pull up to it so visitors can have a look.

Portage Pass Trail: This highly recommended day hike from Whittier affords splendid views of Passage Canal, Portage Glacier, and the Chugach Mountains. On a clear day the views of the glacier from the Portage Pass area are far superior to those obtained from the Portage Visitor Center, which is accessible by road from Anchorage. From Whittier station, walk back 2 km along the road beside the railway line to the oil tanks and tunnel at the foot of Maynard Mountain. Cross the tracks on the dirt road to the L, but do not cross the river. Take the road to the R and climb SW along the flank of the mountain up a wide, easy track. If you walk briskly, you can be at Portage Pass (230 m) less than an hour after leaving the station. There are places to camp beside Divide Lake, but beware of strong winds at the pass. From the lake follow the stream down towards the glacier, then find a way via a tributary on the R up onto one of the bluffs for a view of Portage Lake. Deep crevasses in the blue glacial ice are clearly visible from here. During the gold rush, prospectors continued W over the glacier towards the mining areas N and S of Turnagain Arm. Portage Glacier has receded

far enough since those days that this route is now impossible and you must go back the way you came. This hike is highly recommended; allow a minimum of 3 hours for the round trip. Note that there is no clear trail beyond Divide Lake; you must find your own way. Do not attempt to walk on the glacier itself, as the crevasses can be fatal.

PRACTICALITIES

stay: There are 2 hotels in Whittier, both above large public bars and restaurants. The Sportsman's Inn has rooms with private bath at $27 s, $31 d, and is the better. The Anchor Inn is $30 s, $35 d. *camping:* The only designated camping area in Whittier is the gravel parking lot on the excursion boat wharf and a $5 fee must be paid at the Harbormaster's office. Camp free in the bush somewhere in town out of sight of the road or, best of all, up at Divide Lake beyond Portage Pass (see above).

from Whittier by train: There is no road or trail to Whittier, so everyone arrives by train or boat. The Alaska Railroad has daily service to and from Anchorage ($9 OW, $16 RT), which allows you to spend the day in Whittier and return to the city in the evening. If you're arriving on the ferry from Valdez, you must wait about 5 hours in Whittier for the train to

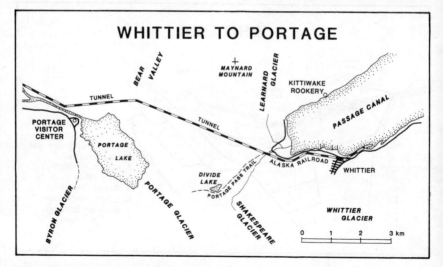

The view of Portage Glacier from Portage Pass is unsurpassed; Divide Lake in the foreground is a good place to camp.

Anchorage, a good opportunity to look around. There is a more frequent shuttle train between Whittier and Portage ($4 OW), a good place from which to hitch to Seward or Homer.

from Whittier by ferry: The Alaska Marine Highway has ferry service 5 times a week to Valdez ($34). A Whittier-Cordova ticket costs the same and allows a stop-off in Valdez for free. The tourist boat *Glacier Queen* sails daily from Whittier to Valdez ($67 including lunch and refreshments). *the route:* The boat ride

from Whittier to Valdez is unforgettable, with clear views of numerous glaciers all the way. Only the tourist boat sails right up to the face of Columbia Glacier; the state ferry stays 5 km out for political reasons (government competing with private business). Although the trip up to the face is certainly exciting, the view from farther out is in a way superior because you look across an iceberg-packed bay to a 4-km-wide tidewater glacier and follow its curving, icy course back up into the 3,650-m-high Chugach Mountains. On a good day, this trip is perhaps the finest boat ride in Alaska.

foster A Carr

harbor seals

VALDEZ

Valdez (pop. 3,079 in 1980), at the end of the Valdez Arm of Prince William Sound, is completely surrounded by magnificent snowcapped peaks. The Small Boat Harbor is extremely picturesque. Rafts of sea otters are often spotted in Valdez Bay. During the 20th C. Valdez has weathered some fairly earth-shaking events. A trail from Valdez to Eagle on the Yukon River opened in 1901 as a military route parallel to the existing telegraph and cable system to the goldfields. Stampeders poured through. In 1906, a branch route was developed from Gulkana to Fairbanks. This was upgraded to a wagon track by 1913. In 1964 the most violent earthquake ever recorded in North America shook Valdez and a tidal wave swept over the waterfront. The town was so badly damaged that it was relocated at a new site 6 km northwest. Nothing but an empty field remains of old Valdez. Today the $9 billion, 1,300-km-long pipeline brings oil from Prudhoe Bay on the Arctic Ocean S to Valdez, where it is pumped into tankers. Taxes paid by the

The 1280-km long Trans-Alaska Pipeline ends at the marine terminal opposite Valdez. The crude oil is stored in 18 tanks, each capable of holding over half a million barrels. Supertankers take on the oil year-round for shipment south.

pipeline company have made Valdez rich and the city is casting about furiously looking for ways to spend the money. Expensive new buildings around town are evidence of this, but there are also gimmicks like toilets that flush automatically when the weight is taken off the seat. A new $50-million container port and grain terminal have been built 4 km E of town to handle shipments to and from Interior Alaska.

SIGHTS OF VALDEZ

downtown: The City Museum/Valdez Heritage Center (open daily 1000-1900, admission free) has historic photographs, an old lighthouse lens, and a rare North Pacific fur fish (extinct since the 1964 earthquake). Archives Alive in the Royal Center on Egan Dr. shows free films on Alaska and the Arctic, nightly at 1900. The program ends with a gripping newsreel on the 1964 earthquake, which shattered much of Southcentral Alaska. Free tours of the Vessel Control Center at the Coast Guard headquarters begin at 0930 and 1330, and include a slide show. Point of View Park, beside the Coast Guard office overlooking the Sheffield Hotel, offers an historical display and lookout. There's an even better lookout above the flashy new Civic Auditorium (check inside for events). You can stare directly across at the oil terminal from here, the lifeline that makes Alaska and the oil companies so wealthy.

hiking: The best hiking is up Mineral Creek Road, a dirt road which runs from behind the city water tower up through an old mining area, past waterfalls and glaciers. A couple of km by trail beyond the end of the road is an old stamp mill. From mid-Aug. to early Sept. it's worth walking 1½ km up the Richardson Highway to the Crooked Creek Salmon Hatchery, where masses of fish can be seen spawning in the stream. *pipeline tours:* The Trans-Alaska Pipeline funnels 1,600,000 barrels of oil into Valdez daily. The marine terminal, where the oil is stored and loaded into tankers, is 19 km S of town on the far side of Valdez Bay. A 2-hour bus tour ($11), the only way to get inside the facility, leaves the 1900. A stop is made at an overlook above the complex for picture-taking.

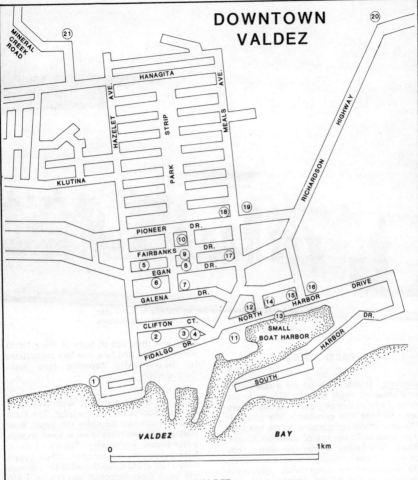

DOWNTOWN VALDEZ

VALDEZ

1. ferry terminal
2. Civic Auditorium
3. Coast Guard HQ
4. Point of View Park
5. National Bank of Alaska
6. Royal Center/Archives Alive
7. post office
8. City Museum
9. public library
10. City Hall
11. Sheffield Hotel
12. laundromat/showers
13. harbormaster
14. Pizza Palace Restaurant
15. tourist office
16. RV camping
17. First National Bank
18. Community College
19. Foodmart
20. Crooked Creek Salmon Hatchery
21. water tower

Passengers watch attentively for an iceberg to calve into Prince William Sound as the ferry *Tustumena* approaches Columbia Glacier.

PRACTICALITIES

camping: Hotels in Valdez are a ripoff—the very cheapest single goes for $55, so forget them. As far as camping goes, the city fathers seem to have their priorities a little jumbled. The only official campground for backpackers with tents is 10 km out of town on Airport Road. This facility is free (no water), but obviously barely accessible to people on foot. RV drivers, on the other hand, who could easily drive out to the campground, are allowed to park overnight free in a lot opposite the tourist office right in the center of town. Until the city manages to sort things out and provide realistic facilities, the best plan is to pitch your tent on the waterfront in the RV camp, among the bushes behind the tourist office, or along the road that runs around the S side of the Small Boat Harbor. In fact, people do this all the time. Public toilets are provided in the Harbormaster's office. Another place to look for a campsite is up Mineral Creek Road. Walk a little ways up the road, cross the first bridge, and head up the hill.

Keep your tent out of sight of the road to insure privacy, and take standard precautions for bear-country camping (see main "Introduction").

food: Of the several large supermarkets in Valdez, Foodmart is the cheapest. The Pizza Palace Restaurant opposite the Small Boat Harbor is the best place to eat in town, though a little pricey. *information:* There's a helpful, friendly tourist information office (open 0900-2100) at 245 E. North Harbor Dr. opposite the Small Boat Harbor. If you put up a $10 deposit, they'll loan you a bicycle to get around on free of charge!

from Valdez: The Alaska Marine Highway has ferry service to Whittier ($34) 5 times a week, to Cordova ($17) 3 times a week, and to Seward ($35) and Homer ($78 via Kodiak) weekly. A through ticket to Seldovia is also $78. Several of the ferries on the Valdez-Cordova run sail at night and spend the day in Cordova, which is convenient for sightseers. The ferries to Whittier and Seward give you a long-range view of Columbia

Glacier. The *Glacier Queen* of Columbia Glacier Tours, which approaches the face of the glacier, sails daily to Whittier ($65). *by bus:* Alaska Yukon Motorcoaches has a bus to Anchorage ($53) 3 times a week, to Fairbanks ($64) twice a week, leaving from the Sheffield Hotel. This company doesn't have an office in Valdez, so unless you've made a reservation elsewhere, you just have to front up and hope there's room. Valdez-Anchorage Bus Lines has a 10-seat van to Glennallen ($20) and Anchorage ($52), daily except Mon. at 1700 from the Royal Center.

PLACES NEAR VALDEZ

Columbia Glacier: This magnificent tidewater glacier just W of Valdez is one of the largest and most active in Alaska. It covers an area of 1,140 sq km and is 66 km long from the Chugach Mountains to Prince William Sound. Its terminus in Columbia Bay is 4 km wide, 80 m high above sea level, and an incredible 700 m deep below the water level. Columbia is the only glacier in Alaska which has not receded significantly in recorded history. Huge icebergs calve constantly into the sea as the glacier advances at a rate of almost 2 m a day. The excursion boats honk their horns near the face in the hope that the sound waves will give nature a hand for the benefit of the paying passengers. Although everyone hopes to visit during clear weather, a cloudy day has its own specialness; the glacial ice is more intensely blue. Hundreds of harbor seals may be seen lounging on the ice flows. Only the excursion boats sail right up to the face of the glacier where the cracking of the moving ice and the crash of the icebergs may be heard, but the longer view from the state ferry is also superb, as the eye follows a river of ice back into the mountains.

the Richardson Highway: A spectacular 190-km highway runs from Valdez to Glennallen. This highway, the Richardson, passes through Keystone Canyon with waterfalls cascading down sheer cliffs; over Thompson Pass, with its all-encompassing view of the Chugach Mountains; and past Worthington Glacier, which almost touches the pavement. More scenic wonders are jammed into the first 60 km of this highway than are seen on any other road in Alaska.

McCarthy: The abandoned Kennicott Copper Mine (1913-1938) near the village of McCarthy is accessible off the Richardson Highway along a 150-km dirt road through Chitina. Hitching requires time, but you're rewarded with the remote beauty of the area. From Chitina to Kennicott, the road follows the old route of the Copper River and Northwestern (CR & NW) Railroad, which once carried the ore to Cordova. Vehicular traffic ends at the Kennicott River, just before McCarthy. There are no stores in McCarthy, so bring food. The 10-km hike from McCarthy to Kennicott along the moraine of Kennicott Glacier is easy; continue on another 8 km to Bonanza Peak if you want a real workout. McCarthy is in the heart of Wrangell-St. Elias National Park, at the foot of the Wrangell Mountains. As yet, no park facilities (visitor centers, campgrounds, trails, etc.) have been established.

on the Copper River: If you have a canoe or inflatable rubber raft, you could float down the Copper River for 150 km, from Chitina to Million Dollar Bridge, past glaciers, wildlife, and the ruins of the railroad. As many as 20 million migratory birds pass through the Copper River Delta area below the bridge in early spring. From the bridge there's a 77-km road to Cordova.

CORDOVA

Cordova (pop. 1,879 in 1980), on Orca Inlet at the SE end of Prince William Sound, is surrounded by forests, small islands, and waterways which contrast beautifully with the bare snowcapped peaks of the Heney Range. Expect rain if you come here: Cordova gets 200 days of it a year. Prior to WW II, the town flourished as a terminus of the CR & NW Railroad from the rich Kennicott Copper Mine, 310 km NE, near McCarthy. The line was a major feat of engineering, pushed through by Michael J. Heney, the "Irish Prince," builder of the White Pass and Yukon Route from Skagway to Whitehorse. Construction began in 1907 and the railway operated until 1938, when a strike closed the copper mine and the operation folded for good. There is little trace of the railway in Cordova, but 77 km E is the famous Million Dollar Bridge which crosses the Copper River between Childs and Miles glaciers. One span of the bridge was destroyed by the 1964 earthquake, but the S end is accessible by road from Cordova. Today Cordova, with a large fishing fleet and many canneries, lives on commercial fishing.

SIGHTS OF CORDOVA

near town: The museum in the Centennial Building at 1st and Adams (open Mon. and Fri. 1300-1700, Tues. and Thurs. 1300-2100, Sat.

1300-1700/1900-2100) is surprisingly good. An excellent film about Cordova is shown while the state ferry is in. There's a good view of Cordova and the Heney Range from the city water reservoir, accessible up a rough gravel road near the small green shack with the white doors (where the aqueduct passes under Whitshed Road near town). This is an easy hike, ideal for anyone wishing to see something of the area and its vegetation without that much effort.

Crater Lake Trail: This excellent hike begins opposite Skaters Cabin on Eyak Lake, 3 km from town beyond the old cemetery, seaplane base, and municipal airstrip. The trail climbs 450 m in 3½ km through a beautiful forest, with panoramic views near the top of Eyak Lake and the Heney Range. The terrain around Crater Lake is fairly open and it would be easy to scale the surrounding summits, if you have the time and energy. Allow a minimum of 2 hours RT from the road to the lake. The trail is solid and very easy to follow; even if a wet wind is blowing, it will be relatively still in the forest, but be careful not to slip. Don't miss this one.

near the airport: Cabin Lake Road, directly opposite Cordova airport, leads 4 km to the head of Lake Elsner Loop Trail (10 km RT). The

The Crater Lake Trail near Cordova leads up through an enchanted forest.

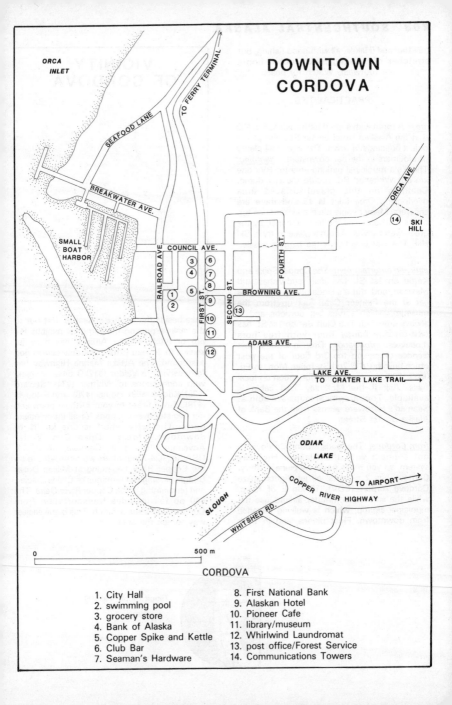

DOWNTOWN CORDOVA

ORCA
INLET

SEAFOOD LANE

TO FERRY TERMINAL

BREAKWATER AVE.

SMALL
BOAT
HARBOR

ORCA AVE.

SKI
HILL

14

COUNCIL AVE.

RAILROAD AVE.

FIRST ST.

SECOND ST.

FOURTH ST.

3   6
4   7
1   5   8
2
9
10
11
13
12

BROWNING AVE.

ADAMS AVE.

LAKE AVE.
TO CRATER LAKE TRAIL

ODIAK
LAKE

TO AIRPORT

COPPER RIVER HIGHWAY

SLOUGH

WHITSHED RD.

0 ————————— 500 m

CORDOVA

1. City Hall
2. swimming pool
3. grocery store
4. Bank of Alaska
5. Copper Spike and Kettle
6. Club Bar
7. Seaman's Hardware

8. First National Bank
9. Alaskan Hotel
10. Pioneer Cafe
11. library/museum
12. Whirlwind Laundromat
13. post office/Forest Service
14. Communications Towers

trail touched 6 lakes, all with good fishing, but stretches of muskeg make rubber boots appropriate footwear. Watch for bears.

PRACTICALITIES

stay: A room with shared bath costs $25 s, $30 d at the Alaskan Hotel on 1st St., one of the oldest buildings in town. There are still plenty of oldtimers in the bar downstairs. *camping:* There's a municipal parking area for RVs one km out Whitshed Rd. beside the city dump. Camping on this gravel-surfaced area overlooking Orca Inlet is $3 and there are showers. Many people pitch their tents on top of the bluff opposite the ferry terminal, by the green water tower. Another place to try is Ski Hill. The wet weather is the biggest hassle.

eats and entertainment: The Copper Spike and Kettle on 1st St. has deli sandwiches and Mexican food, but it's kinda pricey. The locals eat at the Pioneer Cafe, just up from the museum, which serves big portions and is always crowded. The Club Bar on 1st St. has two-for-one happy hour with free hors d'oeuvres. *information:* Drop in to the Forest Service office, on the 3rd floor of the post office building, 612 2nd St. (open Mon. to Fri. 0800-1700), for maps and information on local trails. Ask if the McKinley Trail cabin is available. Topographical maps are sold at Seaman's Hardware, across from the Bank of Alaska on 1st Street.

from Cordova: The roads around Cordova do not connect with the Alaskan Highway system, so you must travel by plane or ferry. Cordova has 2 airports: all jet flights utilize Cordova Airport (CDV), 18 km E of town, while the smaller, commuter airlines use the municipal airstrip, which is walking distance from downtown. Float planes land in Eyak

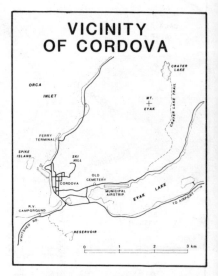

Lake beside the municipal airstrip. Get out to the main airport on the Airporter minibus ($7 pp) or hitch. Alaska Airlines has daily jet service to Juneau ($108), the only connection eastbound. The Alaska Marine Highway has ferry service to Valdez ($17) 3 times a week, with connections to Whittier ($34), Seward ($35), Kodiak ($59), Homer ($78), and Seldovia ($78). Buy a ticket to your furthest point and get free stopover coupons for all intermediate ports. The ferry wharf is one km N of downtown. *tours:* Open Door Water Adventures (Box 1185, Cordova, AK 99574, USA, tel. 424-7466) offers a 6-hour raft trip on the Copper River beginning at Million Dollar Bridge, passing the terminus of Childs Glacier, and terminating in the Copper River Delta. The $40 pp fee includes transportation from Cordova and a snack lunch. This is the easiest way to see the area.

Tlingit motif, Yakutat

SOUTHWEST ALASKA AND THE WEST ARCTIC COAST

INTRODUCTION

Southwest Alaska and the West Arctic Coast include the barren, windswept Aleutian Islands and the mainland's vast W coast, spotted with such small settlements as Dillingham, Bethel, Nome, Kotzebue, and Barrow. Both these sections of the state are extremely remote, making them difficult and expensive to reach, but also exotic and fascinating to visit. The flora and fauna are unusual and spectacular: fur seals, sea otters, and walrus abound. The Aleutians and more northern Pribilofs are a birdwatcher's paradise. Due to climatic conditions there are no forests beyond northern Kodiak Island and the adjacent mainland; the vegetation of most of the Alaska Peninsula and all the Aleutian Islands is open tundra. Several new national parks and preserves in the Brooks Range and around Kotzebue offer exciting possibilites for hikers and river runners in search of adventure. Any trip into these areas will involve spending a lot

of money, but you will be rewarded with a unique, unforgettable experience.

Southwest Alaska: From Denali National Park the Coast Mountains swing SW to become the Aleutian Range, Alaska Peninsula, and Aleutian Islands (a description of the Aleutians is found below). The Alaska Peninsula is an arm of extraordinary volcanoes, many very active. Great collapsed craters at Katmai and Aniakchak are now administered by the National Park Service. Kodiak Island (9,505 sq km) is the second largest island in the U.S. (at 10,458 sq km the Big Island of Hawaii is larger). This is the home of the Kodiak brown bear, largest meat-eating animal on earth; males can weigh up to 550 kilograms. Although there are over 2,000 of them on the island, it is unlikely any will be seen during a visit to the town of Kodiak and vicinity. With ferry service from Homer and Seward, Kodiak is the only easily accessible place in Southwest Alaska. Three times a year this ferry continues right down the Aleutian Chain to Unalaska, an opportunity that you won't want to miss if you're present at the time.

the West Arctic Coast: Bethel and vicinity, in Western Alaska, is a low lying, lake-filled delta area through which the Kuskokwim and Yukon rivers flow. Eskimo villages are scattered across the stark, treeless lowland. Further N is Nome, a gold rush town where dredging continues today. Continuing northward, across the rounded mountains of the Seward Peninsula, is the large Eskimo town of Kotzebue and, at the top of the continent on the Arctic Ocean, Barrow. Anyone considering a visit to these Eskimo settlements should be aware of racial tension. For the past 200 years, the Eskimos have watched the marine mammals and herds which once supported their society ruthlessly hunted by white men using more advanced technology. Whenever a valuable resource was discovered in their homeland, be it gold or oil, strangers arrived to grab it for themselves. The Eskimos' way of life has been seriously undermined by alcohol, American education, television, and the consumer society. The U.S. government is now attempting to solve the problem by throwing money at it. Large sums are being paid to the natives, and "experts" are helping them form American-style institutions. Where this will lead is still uncertain, but travelers among the Eskimos will sense the tension and even open hostility. This situation is compounded by white tourist promoters who send in profitable tour groups in increasing numbers to Kotzebue and Barrow. It is now practically impossible for a transient visitor to break through the wall of resentment; you have to be culturally self-sufficient in the Arctic.

"Wishing to get a walrus specimen for the Smithsonian Institution, I left the schooner in the dinghy with the Doctor and one man, pulled about half a mile and landed on the ice. Picking out the best specimen, a large male animal, I shot it, and started towing it off to the vessel. While doing so, we were attacked by a school of a hundred or more walruses. They would strike under the boat and rise all around trying to get their tusks over the gunwale. It became a fight for life. We stood up in the boat and fought them off with boat-hooks and oars. As is generally the case on such occasions when a rifle is most wanted, I could not get hold of mine as it was in the bottom of the boat, under other articles. The fight lasted only a few minutes, but it seemed like a lifetime, until the rifle could be gotten out. One shot frightened them all away, but they were not half so frightened as were those in the boat. To be in a small boat with the water alive with walruses, the blowing of the animals causing the water to foam, and to hear that terrible sound that only a mad walrus can make, is calculated to cause anyone's hair to stand on end." Lt. George M. Stoney of the U.S. naval exploration expedition on board the _Ounalaska_ (1884).

KODIAK

The town of Kodiak (pop. 4,756 in 1980), on the NE side of Kodiak Island, is at the same latitude as Stockholm, Sweden. The many small green islands in Chiniak Bay, just off the town, are freshly picturesque. First sighted by a Russian explorer in 1673, the first permanent Russian settlement in America was established on Kodiak Island in 1783. In 1792, the Russian governor, Alexander Baranof, shifted the town of Kodiak to its present site and made it capital of the colony, a position it retained until the definitive move to Sitka in 1804. Kodiak was the main U.S. naval base in Alaska during WW II. Today Alaska's biggest Coast Guard station occupies the site, 10 km SW of the town near the present airport. Kodiak, one of the 4 top U.S. ports in value of fish landed, boasts the largest fishing fleet in the state. Fifteen seafood processing plants operate year round, employing several thousand people. Kodiak is famous for its Alaska-sized king crabs.

SIGHTS OF KODIAK

in town: As you get off the ferry, a WW II liberty ship (the *Star of Kodiak*), converted to a cannery, is to the L, an old Russian stone wharf to the R, and Erskine House, which houses the Baranof Museum, is straight ahead. This is the oldest extant Russian building in North America, built in 1793 as a storehouse for sea otter pelts. The museum (open Mon. to Fri. 1000-1500, Sat. and Sun. 1200-1600, admission $1, students 50 cents) has a good representative collection from the Russian period. Just behind the museum, the Russian Orthodox church, rebuilt in 1946 after a fire, now shelters the remains of St. Herman of Alaska, the only Russian Orthodox saint in the Western Hemisphere. A group of less saintly believers is found interred in the Russian Orthodox cemetery at Erskine Ave. and Upper Mill Bay Rd., but the grounds and markers are in such a sad state of abandonment that all traces of these existences seem destined to fade before long. Kodiak's canneries, on the other hand, are thriving; take a stroll along Tagura Way or Shelikof St. to see them. The Small Boat Harbor is a great place to have your picture taken. The most unlikely cannery of them all is at Gibson Cove, 3 km W of town. Here lies the former Washington state ferry *Kalakala,* the

first streamlined, modernistic ferry in the world, converted to a cannery and finally closed. Veteran commuters from Bremerton will grow misty-eyed here from more than the weather.

wartime relics: Several coastal defense installations were set up to defend Kodiak from Japanese attack during WW II. One of these has now been converted into Fort Abercrombie State Historical Park, 8 km NE of town. The two 8-inch guns installed in 1943 were blown out of their housings when the facility was deactivated after the war; the broken barrels can be found among the brush just below the concrete turrets. The Park is worth a visit, not only for these crumbling remains, but also for the lovely sea views, spruce forest, birdlife, and hiking trails. Altogether, it is a beautiful, evocative place.

Horned puffins, symbol of the Alaska Center for the Environment.

hiking: The best hike near Kodiak takes you over Pillar Mountain (387 m) for a sweeping view of the town, the old naval airfield, and the entire NE corner of the island. Take note of the vegetation and wildflowers along the way. Begin by walking straight up Thorsheim St. as far as Maple St., where you turn L and go up Pillar Mountain Road. The route can be confusing as it passes through a subdivision, so ask directions if you get the chance. Follow

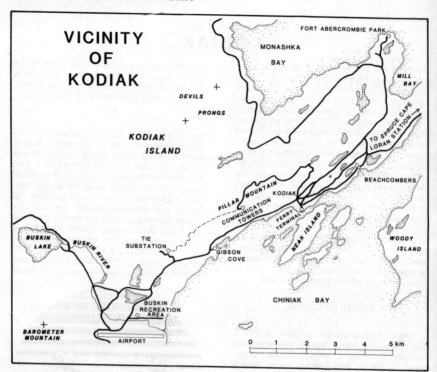

VICINITY OF KODIAK

the road to the communications towers on top of Pillar Mountain. The track down the SW side of the mountain is impossible for a car, but easy to follow on foot. If you want to begin from the Buskin River side, look for the gravel road running inland on the city side of the lakes, just a few hundred m before the point where the mountain begins to crowd the highway. The track turns uphill at the Tie Substation. A strong hiker could make it across Pillar in a couple of hours.

PRACTICALITIES

stay: All of the hotels in Kodiak are expensive. Weekly accommodations are sometimes available at the Gibson Cove Boarding House (tel. 486-6465) at $50 pp weekly (no daily rates) in a shared room (meals extra), but call before walking the 3 km from the ferry. _camping:_ The City of Kodiak provides no camping facilities. The only designated campgrounds in

the area are the state park facilities at Fort Abercrombie (8 km NE) and Buskin State Recreation Site (7 km SW). Tent camping at these is free, but limited to 7 days. If it gets crowded you may have to double up on campsites. The campground at Buskin River (which is near the airport), might be easier to hitch to, but Fort Abercrombie is more attractive. Camping elsewhere is illegal, so try to keep out of sight.

eats and entertainment: The cheapest place in town to eat is the Dairy Queen, which has a "whole meal deal" for $3. Somewhat more appetizing is Afternoon Delight, nearby in an old blue bus, with Mexican fast food and vegetarian sandwiches. El Chicano Restaurant, upstairs in the Center Street Plaza, is a little more expensive, but it's a good place to relax, and they serve large portions. Roaring rock 'n rollin' nightlife unfolds at Beachcombers on Mission Rd., 2 km NE of the ferry terminal. The old steamship _Queen of the_

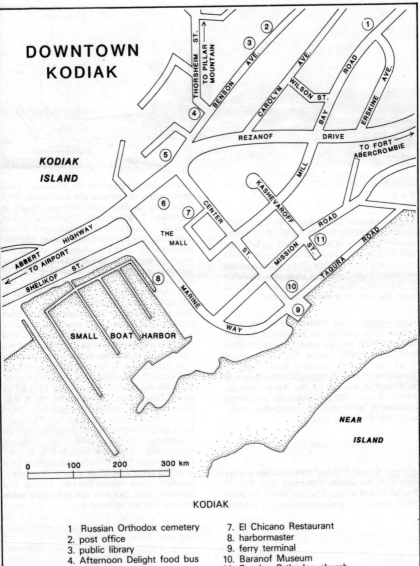

DOWNTOWN KODIAK

KODIAK ISLAND

NEAR ISLAND

0   100   200   300 km

KODIAK

1 Russian Orthodox cemetery
2 post office
3 public library
4 Afternoon Delight food bus
5 Dairy Queen
6 Krafts Supermarket
7 El Chicano Restaurant
8 harbormaster
9 ferry terminal
10 Baranof Museum
11 Russian Orthodox church

North from Victoria, B.C., rusts at rest next to the club.

tours: Alaskan Sea Adventures (Box 2225, Kodiak, AK 99615, tel. 486-4305) offers guided kayak trips on local waters at $15 pp half day, $35 pp full day, kayak rental included. With some advance notice they can arrange extended tours to remote areas where wildlife is abundant. This is good adventure if you have the time and money to spare.

from Kodiak: The Alaska Marine Highway offers ferry service to Homer ($27) and Seldovia ($27) twice a week, to Seward ($35) and Cordova ($59) weekly. The ferry terminal is at the end of Cannery Row, right in downtown Kodiak. A highlight of the ferry ride to Homer is the sail by the Barren Islands, home to over 100,000 seabirds and large colonies of seals. Puffins, cormorants, terns, and gulls circle the ship.

PLACES NEAR KODIAK

Katmai: Katmai National Park occupies a large chunk of the Alaska Peninsula, just NW of Kodiak Island across Shelikof Strait. In June 1912, one of the great cataclysms of modern history took place here as Mt. Novarupta blew its top, violently spewing ash and pumice for 3 days. One of the explosions was heard in Ketchikan, 1,440 km away. The fallout choked Kodiak, whose 500 inhabitants were evacuated in a daring marine rescue. Massive amounts of dust circulated in the upper atmosphere for 2 years, changing global weather patterns. Mt. Katmai collapsed simultaneously to form a crater lake. Hot ash and pumice piled up 200 m deep over a 104-sq-km area, forming the Valley of Ten Thousand Smokes. Steam once issued from thousands of fumaroles in the valley, but only a few remain today. Unfortunately, this fantastic wilderness is largely a preserve of the rich. It costs $220 RT to fly from Anchorage to King Salmon (AKN). It's only 65 km from King Salmon to Brooks River, but there is no road; Wein Air Alaska clips you another $110 RT to fly in. Direct flights from Kodiak to Brooks River are unavailable. The bus tour from Brooks River to the Valley of Ten Thousand Smokes (37 km OW) is $40. Wein also runs an expensive lodge ($80 pp double occupancy—no meals included) at Brooks River, where Park Service naturalists give evening talks and slide shows. You may, however, camp nearby for free. Katmai is a fantastic place, but you can get better value for your money elsewhere.

THE ALEUTIAN ISLANDS

From the tip of the Alaska Peninsula, an arc of 200 islands stretches 1,750 km SW to Attu I., separating the North Pacific Ocean from the Bering Sea. Here, the meeting of the mild Japanese currents with the icy Bering Sea causes fogs, rain, and snow. There is no permafrost, but the constant strong winds inhibit tree growth; only tundra and muskeg vegetation can be found. Frequent storms blow through (Unalaska experiences almost 250 rainy days a year), but due to the currents the sea never freezes. Just S of the chain is the very deep Aleutian Trench where vast tectonic plates meet: as the Aleutian Plate pushes under the Pacific Plate volcanos erupt and the earth quakes. The Aleutian Islands are part of the circumpacific 'ring of fire,' and 50 active volcanos dot the Alaska Peninsula and its submerged extension. High peaks drop abruptly to the sea. There are 14 large and 55 smaller islands (plus tiny islets), all dismal, windswept outposts in the northern Pacific Ocean. Surprisingly, prior to the arrival of the Russians, every island was inhabited by Aleut people, close relatives to the Eskimo. They were skillful hunters who lived in balance with the marine mammals and birds of their islands. The Russians enslaved and killed them, and their numbers plummeted from approximately 20,000 in 1741 to perhaps 2,000 a century later.

The Russians hunted the sea otters and fur seals of the islands to near extinction. Even today the U.S. Coast Guard must keep careful watch for plunderers, as Asian fishing boats steal in to the now uninhabited islands, under the most extreme weather conditions (when they know the patrol planes will be grounded) and sweep the sea clean of fish. Nothing is returned.

THE WAR IN THE ALEUTIANS

the Japanese challenge: During the spring of 1942, Japan was sweeping triumphantly across the Pacific to the gates of Australia and Hawaii. Singapore had fallen and China was in retreat. However, the strength of the U.S. aircraft carriers, none of which had been lost at Pearl Harbor, worried Fleet Admiral Isoroku Yamamoto, Commander-in-Chief of the Japanese Navy. He knew that time was on the side of the United States. To win, he would have to draw the American carriers into a great naval battle where his superior forces could crush them and end the war. His target was Midway, a tiny island at the end of the Hawaiian Chain, where the U.S. had recently built a base. To split the American forces, Yamamoto ordered a diversionary thrust at the

The smoking white cone of Shishaldin volcano (3,043 m) on Unimak Island is the highest peak in Southwest Alaska.

Priests of the Shinto, Buddhist, and Christian faiths returned to Attu in 1953 to lay the Japanese war dead finally to rest. The bodies were exhumed, collected, and cremated; the ashes were scattered to the wind.

Aleutians. On 3 June 1942 Japanese carrier-based planes struck at Dutch Harbor, a powerful new U.S. naval base in Unalaska Bay, but inflicted only slight damage. The next day they returned and did more damage, but the base continued to function. Unknown to the Japanese, secret air bases were then being built at nearby Umnak and Cold Bay, but weather conditions prevented a retaliatory strike by these facilities against the 2 Japanese carriers involved. Meanwhile, at Midway, the U.S. had broken the Japanese naval code, and Yamamoto's plans were falling apart. Their own strength divided, one Japanese carrier after another sank before the united American force. As a facesaving move, the retiring Japanese occupied undefended Attu and Kiska, at the W end of the Aleutian Chain, in the hope that bases on these islands would shield Northern Japan and drive a wedge between the U.S. and Russia.

the struggle for the islands: In Aug., 1942, the U.S. Navy occupied Adak Island and began building an airfield from which to attack Attu and Kiska. In Jan., 1943, the Navy leapfrogged to Amchitka Island, only 100 m E of Kiska, to provide an advanced U.S. base. Continuous bombing and a naval blockade weakened the Japanese ability to resist. On 11 May 1943 some 16,000 U.S.troops landed on Attu. Of these, 549 Americans were to die before the 2,650 Japanese troops entrenched in the mountains were overcome. On 29 May about 800 remaining Japanese staged a *banzai* charge. At first they overran the American

lines but were finally quelled by reserve forces. Only 28 Japanese prisoners were taken on Attu. With Attu in their hands, the Americans occupied nearby Shemya and began building a large airbase from which to bomb the Japanese Kurile Islands. The 6,000 Japanese on Kiska now faced the fate of their comrades on Attu. Late in July, however, Japanese

UNALASKA

destroyers managed to slip through the U.S. blockade in dense fog and evacuate their soldiers. Right on schedule, on 15 Aug. some 34,000 U.S. and Canadian troops landed, unopposed, on Kiska. Though there was no one to attack and rout, incredibly, they suffered a shocking 99 dead and 74 wounded through landing mishaps and other accidents. With their masterful evacuation, the Japanese had ended the Aleutian campaign.

the aftermath: Prior to WW II Alaska was a remote, neglected territory with a tiny population. The threat of invasion to North America prompted a massive overreaction on the part of the United States. A few thousand Japanese soldiers, occupying 2 small forlorn islands of little value, managed to tie up almost half a million men for several years and cause vast resources to be expended on projects such as the Alaska Highway, Canol Pipeline, Whittier railway, etc. The many large military bases, most of which are still with us, are reminders that the effects of the war in the Aleutians are still being felt today.

THE ISLANDS TODAY

Unalaska/Dutch Harbor: Unalaska Bay cuts into the N side of mountainous Unalaska Island, creating a great sheltered harbor. Dutch Harbor is on Amaknak, a small island in the bay opposite the village of Unalaska. The 2 are linked by a bridge. Area population was 1,322 in 1980. During Russian times, Unalaska was the main trading center in the Aleutians and a Russian Orthodox church remains to tell of their influence. Captain Cook spent 3 weeks at Unalaska in 1778, sharing experiences with Russian explorers. Today the many canneries at Dutch Harbor reflect the rich fisheries of nearby Bristol Bay. Crab canning is a specialty and a new freezer plant has been built. Akutan (pop. 55 in 1980), on a small island just NE of Dutch Harbor, is also an important fishing center.

getting there: Reeve Aleutian Airways charges $330 OW to fly from Anchorage to Dutch Harbor (DUT). The Alaska Marine Highway runs a ferry to Dutch Harbor 3 times a year, with stops at Chignik, Sand Point, King Cove, and Cold Bay. The fare is $136 OW from Homer and you can get a free stopover on Kodiak Island. Buy the return ticket Dutch

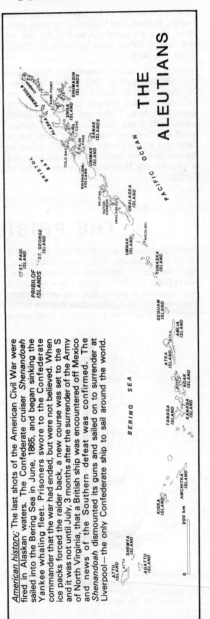

American history: The last shots of the American Civil War were fired in Alaskan waters. The Confederate cruiser *Shenandoah* sailed into the Bering Sea in June, 1865, and began sinking the Yankee whaling fleet. Prisoners swore to the Confederate commander that the war had ended, but were not believed. When ice packs forced the raider back, a new course was set to the S and it was not until July, 3 months after the surrender of the Army of North Virginia, that a British ship was encountered off Mexico and news of the Southern defeat was confirmed. The *Shenandoah* dismounted its guns and sailed on to surrender at Liverpool—the only Confederate ship to sail around the world.

Harbor-Cordova ($164 OW) and stop at Kodiak, Seward, and Valdez at no extra cost. These trips are usually in spring and fall, to pick up and deliver summer residents. Check ahead for dates.

others: The Aleut villagers on Attu were deported to Japan in 1942 by the Japanese. On their return to Alaska after the war, the U.S. government refused to allow them to resettle on Attu. Today the only inhabitants are the staff of the Coast Guard Loran station. Small Aleut villages exist at Atka (pop. 100 in 1980) and Nikolski (pop. 55 in 1980). Many of the islands in the Aleutian Chain are included in the Alaska Maritime National Wildlife Refuge.

military bases: The Air Force maintains a top secret base on Shemya and the Navy has a base on Adak, but security clearance is required to visit either. The town of Adak is a modern settlement with some 4,600 residents. There's everything from bowling alleys to gymnasiums, an indoor swimming pool, theater, library, bank, stores, and a television station. *Amchitka:* Despite its fragile geological situation, the U.S. used this remote volcanic island for underground nuclear testing until as late as 1971. In its first public action, the Vancouver environmental organization, Greenpeace, sent a protest vessel into the area and the resulting controversy led to the cancellation of the tests.

THE PRIBILOF ISLANDS

The Pribilof Islands lie in the Bering Sea, 1,450 km W of Anchorage. The 2 main islands, St. Paul (pop. 551 in 1980) and St. George (pop. 163 in 1980) are 65 km apart. There are also 3 tiny islets. All 5 experience the same damp, foggy weather as the Aleutians, 400 km to the south. Every summer a million fur seals arrive

Clothed in a waterproof cape of walrus intestines, wooden hunting hat on his head, this 18th C. Aleut is ready to embark in his *bidarka.*

in the Pribilofs from their winter range further S, to breed on the rocky, tundra-covered islands. Large bulls collect harems of up to 40 or more submissive females, which they guard jealously. Soon after Gerassim Pribilof discovered the islands in 1786, the Russians brought Aleut slaves to the uninhabited Pribilofs to slaughter the fur seals. So many were taken that by 1911 the seal population had dwindled to 150,000 and the animals were in danger of extinction. The U.S., Russia, Canada, and Japan then signed a treaty which banned ocean hunting and limited the number that could be taken on land. Today a U.S. government-sponsored "harvest" takes 45,000 non-breeding males each July. Besides the largest fur seal herd in the world, there are over 190 species of migratory seabirds to be seen in the Pribilofs. Literally millions of murres, kittiwakes, cormorants, fulmars, and puffins nest on the sheer cliffs above the seal rookeries. Nowhere else in North America is wildlife seen so easily and in such numbers.

getting there: The only way to the Pribilofs is by plane, for which Reeve Aleutian Airways charges $709 RT from Anchorage. Ironically, it's cheaper to buy a tour to St. Paul (SNP) from Alaska Exploration Holidays (838 W. 4th Ave., Anchorage, AK 99501, USA). This will run $656 for 2 nights, $716 for 3 nights, $826 for 5 nights, with airfare, bus tour, and hotel (pp double occupancy) included. Meals are extra. If you're set on doing something really wild during your trip N, this would be it.

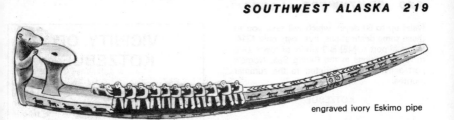

engraved ivory Eskimo pipe

THE WEST ARCTIC COAST

NOME

The town of Nome (pop. 2,301 in 1980) on the S side of the Seward Peninsula facing the Bering Sea, is 180 km N of the mouth of the Yukon River and 450 km E of Siberia. Eighty percent of the population is Eskimo. Nome attained fame in Sept., 1898, when gold was discovered at nearby Anvil Creek. A stampede began and by the turn of the century there were 30,000 people at Nome and tents lined the beach for 25 kilometers. Tension mounted as claim jumpers attempted to force the original prospectors off their claims. Then gold was found in the sands of Nome beach, which none could claim but all could work. Gold dredges still operate near town. During WW II Nome was a major transfer point for Lend Lease aircraft being sent to Russia. Almost 8,000 planes were turned over to Soviet airmen at Nome airfield.

sights: There's a museum (closed Sun. and Mon., admission free) in the library building on Front Street. Predictably, it specializes in Eskimo artifacts, and mementos of the gold rush. Every March the 1,688-km Iditarod Trail Sled Dog Race from Anchorage terminates in Nome and there is a winter carnival. _stay:_ The Community United Methodist Church Youth Hostel, 2nd Ave. and C St., charges $5.25 and is open year round. _getting there:_ There is no road from Nome to Fairbanks so, other than by dogsled in winter, the only way to reach Nome is to fly. Both Alaska Airlines and Wien Air Alaska offer Anchorage-Nome-Kotzebue-Anchorage for $419. Save money by asking for a one week advance purchase excursion ticket

Eskimo children with pet birds on the tundra near Hooper Bay.

(valid up to 60 days), which will take you to these same destinations, but costs only $314. Nome airport (OME) is 3 km W of town. Due to ice conditions in the Bering Sea, Nome's port activities are restricted to the summer months.

KOTZEBUE

Kotzebue (pop. 2,044 in 1980), on Kotzebue Sound near the mouths of the Noatak and Kobuk rivers, is 40 km N of the Arctic Circle. The sun rises on 3 June and doesn't set for 36 days. The Eskimos keep reindeer herds in the vicinity. To encourage tourism, the regional corporation has built a Museum of the Arctic, complete with Eskimo dancing and handicraft demonstrations. Adjoining the museum is a workshop where Kobuk jade is fashioned into jewelry. There is also a city museum, the Ootukahkuktukvik, in the middle of town. You must be able to pronounce the name correctly to enter. The airport (OTZ) is a 15-min. walk from the center of town.

BARROW

If you've got a lot of money to throw away, fly into Barrow (pop. 2,207 in 1980). The only reason to go to Barrow is vanity: to say you've been to the northernmost point in the U.S.

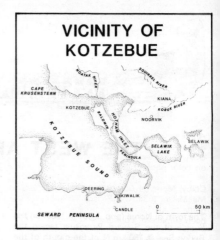

VICINITY OF KOTZEBUE

Barrow is the largest Eskimo village in the world; here "honkies" can have a taste of Alaska's racial tension. The Arctic ice pack is usually visible offshore. In spring the Eskimos still hunt whales, using traditional methods. The sun doesn't set from May to July and there are 51 days of darkness in winter. The airport (BRW) is walking distance from town, but there are no rooms at the Top of the World Hotel for under a hundred dollars.

boykinia

BOOKLIST

DESCRIPTION AND TRAVEL

Alaska Geographic. Alaska Geographic Society, Box 4-EEE, Anchorage, AK 99509, USA. A quarterly magazine with the emphasis on color photography.

Colby, Merle. *A Guide to Alaska.* New York, MacMillan, 1939. This Federal Writers' Project guide to Alaska half a century ago has never been surpassed. Look for it in a good library.

Exploring Alaska's Mount McKinley National Park. Anchorage, Alaska Travel Publications, 1976. This outstanding guidebook makes up for the lack of trails in the park by mapping and describing 25 recommended hikes off the road. Unfortunately, it is presently out of print.

Heller, Herbert L. *Sourdough Sagas.* Cleveland, World Publishing Co., 1967. Colorful tales of mishap and adventure about Alaska's prospecting pioneers.

Higgins, John. *The North Pacific Deckhand's and Alaska Cannery Worker's Handbook.* Albacore Press, Box 355, Eastsound, WA 98245, USA. Get this book for the evocative photographs, description of the fishing industry, and practical instructions on how to become a part of it all.

Marshall, Robert. *Alaska Wilderness.* Berkeley, University of California Press, 1970. A thrilling account of the author's exploration of the Central Brooks Range.

McGinniss, Joe. *Going to Extremes.* New York, New American Library, 1980. One man's journey to Alaska leads him to a series of characters as diverse as the state itself.

McPhee, John. *Coming into the Country.* New York, Bantam Books, 1979. Perhaps the best portrayal of Alaskan lifestyles ever written. Read it before your trip.

Moore, Terris. *Mt. McKinley, The Pioneer Climbs.* Seattle, The Mountaineers, 1981. An exciting history of man's challenge to North America's highest mountain.

Muir, John. *Travels in Alaska.* New York, Houghton Mifflin Co., 1915. Muir's classic narration of his experiences on the Stikine River and at Glacier Bay during 1879, 1880, and 1890.

Murie, Adolph. *A Naturalist in Alaska.* New York, Devin-Adair, 1961. Excellent insight into the fauna of Alaska.

Nienhueser, Helen, and Nancy Simmerman. *55 Ways to the Wilderness in Southcentral Alaska.* The Mountaineers, 715 Pike St., Seattle, WA 98101, USA. A compact trail guide, complete with maps, photos, and descriptions of the best the region has to offer.

Piggot, Margaret. *Discover Southeast Alaska with Pack and Paddle.* The Mountaineers, 715 Pike St., Seattle, WA 98101, USA. A superb guide to the trails and canoe routes of Southeast—full of photos, hiking maps, and useful tips. Highly recommended.

The Milepost. Alaska Northwest Publishing Co., Box 4-EEE, Anchorage, AK 99509, USA. For motorists, the best guidebook to Alaska and Western Canada. The highway maps and description make *The Milepost* a must if you're driving north. Although the information is accurate and comprehensive, specific listings of hotels, bars, and restaurants are limited to advertisers.

Wayburn, Peggy. *Adventuring in Alaska.* Sierra Club Books, 530 Bush St., San Francisco, CA 94108, USA. A guide to the remote wilderness regions of Alaska and how to get there. This book is recommended for anyone planning a major canoe, kayak, or rubber raft expedition in the state.

Westover, Beau. *A Season in Alaska.* Chico, Peregrine Communications, 1982. A guerilla guide to finding work in a cannery or on a fishing boat. This witty little resource book might help make you $20,000 in one summer.

Williams, Howel, ed. *Landscapes of Alaska.* Berkeley, University of California Press, 1958. A superb geography text.

HISTORY

Burton, Pierre. *Klondike.* Toronto, McClelland and Stewart, 1972. Brings alive the unforgettable characters who came out of the last great gold rush. A joy to read.

Chevigny, Hector. *Lord of Alaska.* Portland, Binfords & Mort, 1971. The biography of Alexander Baranof, manager of the Russian-American Company from 1791 to 1817.

Cohen, Stan. *The Forgotten War.* Pictorial Histories Publishing Co., 713 South 3rd West, Missoula, Montana 59801, USA. A pictorial history of WW II in Alaska and northwestern Canada.

Morgan, Murray. *One Man's Gold Rush, A Klondike Album.* Seattle, University of Washington Press, 1967. A feast of gold rush photography.

Okun, S.B. *The Russian-American Company.* Cambridge, Harvard University Press, 1951. This translation from the Russian gives a different view of the period up to 1867.

Sherwood, Morgan B. *Exploration of Alaska, 1865-1900.* New Haven, Yale University Press, 1965. The story of the opening of the interior.

Speck, Gordon. *Northwest Explorations.* Portland, Binford & Mort, 1954. Fascinating tales of the early explorers.

POLITICS AND GOVERNMENT

Alaska magazine. Alaska Northwest Publishing Co., Box 4-EEE, Anchorage, AK 99509, USA. A monthly magazine of life in the last frontier.

Dixon, Mim. *What Happened to Fairbanks?* Boulder, Westview Press, 1978. The social effects of the Trans-Alaska Oil Pipeline on Fairbanks, Alaska.

Hanrahan, John, and Peter Gruenstein. *Lost Frontier, The Marketing of Alaska.* New York, Norton & Co., 1977. A piercing analysis of what the multinationals have in store for Alaska.

Kresge, David T. *Issues in Alaska Development.* Seattle, University of Washington Press, 1977. A scholarly examination of the issues facing the state today.

Watkins, Mel, ed. *Dené Nation, The Colony Within.* Toronto, University of Toronto Press, 1977. The struggle of the Athapaskan Indians of Canada for a settlement similar to the one granted their brothers in Alaska.

ANTHROPOLOGY

Boas, Franz. *Race, Language, and Culture.* New York, MacMillan, 1940. Boas' anthropological work on the Northwest Coast Indians was definitive.

Bruemmer, Fred. *Seasons of the Eskimo, A Vanishing Way of Life.* Greenwich, New York Geographic Society, 1971. A photo essay on the Eskimos of Canada today.

Dekin, Jr., Albert A. *Arctic Archeology, A Bibliography and History.* New York, Garland Publishing, 1978.

Fejes, Claire. *Villagers.* New York, Random House, 1981. An account of contemporary Athapaskan Indian life along the Yukon River.

Swanton, John R. *The Indian Tribes of North America.* Washington, Smithsonian Institution, 1952. Specifically identifies all native groups.

ART AND LITERATURE

Bancroft-Hunt, Norman. *People of the Totem, The Indians of the Pacific Northwest.* New York, Putnam's Sons, 1979. A beautifully-illustrated history of the art of these people.

London, Jack. *The Call of the Wild.* This gripping tale of a sled-dog's experience along the gold rush trail was Jack London's most successful rendering of the spirit of the North.

Masterpieces of Indian and Eskimo Art from Canada. Paris, Musee de l'Homme, 1969.

Service, Robert. *Collected Poems.* New York, Dodd, Mead & Co., 1959. No one has ever better captured the flavor of northern life than the poet, Robert Service.

Stewart, Hilary. *Looking at Indian Art of the Northwest Coast.* Vancouver, Douglas & McIntyre, 1979. A concise analysis of the art forms of this powerful culture.

The Far North, 2000 Years of American Eskimo and Indian Art. Washington, National Gallery of Art, 1977. A catalog of an exhibition of native art.

ONWARD TRAVEL

A Moneywise Guide to North America. Travelaid, Box 28, Southwater Industrial Estate, Southwater, Sussex, England. Although short on maps and necessarily selective in what it covers, this book is an indispensible companion on any trip across or around the United States and Canada. Written for young people, it contains a wealth of the most interesting and unusual information, as well as specific instructions on how to survive on a tight budget. Concise and delightful.

Bisignani, J.D. *Japan Handbook.* Moon Publications, Box 1696, Chico, CA 95927, USA. A 520-page sensitive, in-depth travel guide to Japan on US$17 per day.

Brooks, John, ed. *The South American Handbook.* Trade and Travel Publications, The Mendip Press, Parsonage Lane, Bath BA1 1EN, England. By far the best guide to Central and South America, plus all the islands of the Caribbean. No traveler should visit Latin America without its 1,304 pages of fine print (US$30).

Buryn, Ed. *Vagabonding in the U.S.A.* And/Or Press, Box 2246, Berkeley, CA 94702, USA. A cornucopia of bizarre travel ideas, guaranteed to turn your wanderlust into a lifelong trip; a kaleidoscope of Americana.

Rand McNally Road Atlas [*United States, Canada, Mexico*]. Rand McNally & Co., 206 Sansome St., San Francisco, CA 94104, USA. The best collection of highway and city maps under one cover for the price.

Stanley, David. *South Pacific Handbook,* second edition. Moon Publications, Box 1696, Chico, CA 95927, USA. This 578-page guidebook by the author of *Alaska-Yukon Handbook* takes you to Hawaii and on to the most remote outer islands of the Pacific.

REFERENCE

Hulten, Eric. *Flora of Alaska and Neighboring Territories.* Stanford, Stanford University Press, 1968. A huge manual of the vascular plants—highly technical, but easy to consult.

Lada-Mocarski, Valerian. *Bibliography of Books on Alaska Published Before 1868.* New Haven, Yale University Press, 1969.

Murie, Olaus. *A Field Guide to Animal Tracks.* Boston, Houghton Mifflin, 1954. All North American mammals are included in this invaluable publication.

Orth, Donald J. *Dictionary of Alaska Place Names.* Washington, U.S. Government Printing Office, 1967.

Robbins, Chandler S., et al. *Birds of North America.* New York, Golden Press, 1966. A guide to field identification.

The Alaska Almanac. Alaska Northwest Publishing Co., Box 4-EEE, Anchorage, AK 99509, USA. A rich source of useful information about the state, all in one compact volume.

Tourville, Elsie A. *Alaska, A Bibliography, 1570-1970.* Boston, G.K. Hall & Co., 1974. Includes a simplified subject index.

Wickersham, James. *A Bibliography of Alaskan Literature, 1724-1924.* Fairbanks, Alaska Agricultural College, 1927.

GLOSSARY

Alcan—the Alaska Highway

alpine—elevated slopes above the treeline

argillite—a rock of compacted clay cemented by silica

aurora borealis—the northern lights; streams of light ascending in fan shape from the northern horizon

barbara—a large, semi-subterranean Aleut house

bidarka—a skin-covered Aleut kayak

billiken—a smiling comic mascot

boreal—subarctic

bore tide—a minor tidal wave caused by the shape or location of a bay

cache—a small, elevated chamber for food storage

calving—the breaking off of a piece of ice from a glacier

cheechako—a newcomer, tenderfoot, greenhorn

clutch—a group of eggs or chicks

Dene—the Athapaskan people

fish wheel—a device turned by the current of a river, scooping fish into a holding box

fjord—a narrow inlet flanked by steep cliffs

gandy dancer—a laborer on a railway line gang

husky—any sled dog

hypothermia—dangerous loss of heat energy due to exposure to wind, cold, rain

Inuit—Eskimo

lichen—alga and fungus growing in symbiotic association on rocks or bark

Lower 48—the 48 contiguous American states

monitor—a nozzle used to direct water into a hillside in hydraulic mining

moraine—a glacial deposit

mukluks—native boots made from animal skins

mush—to travel with a dog sled

muskeg—a grassy bog or swamp

northern lights—see *aurora borealis*

nunatak—a mountain peak poking up out of an icefield

oomiak—a walrus-skin Eskimo boat

orca—killer whale

Outside—an elitist term used by Alaskans to refer to anywhere out of state

parka—a hooded coat or jacket lined with fur

pemmican—dried or pounded buffalo meat or venison

permafrost—permanently frozen ground

petroglyphs—carvings on rocks

pingos—low, rounded mounds created by frost action, rising from the tundra

placer—a deposit of sand or gravel containing particles of gold

pleistocene—the glacial epoch in North America; the time of the great ice age

poke—a small bag of gold dust

portage—to carry a canoe around an obstruction or overland between waterways

potlatch—an elaborate ceremonial display of wealth at which valued gifts are given or destroyed to prove wealth or attain prestige

qiviut—wool of the musk ox

rack—moose or caribou antlers

raft—a group of floating sea otters

scrimshaw—the art of engraving on ivory

skiff—a rowboat

skookum—strong, active, a go-getter

slough—a backwater, side channel, or tidal flat

sluice—a long inclined trough with grooves or riffles on the botton where gold is caught as paydirt is washed through

sourdough—an oldtimer

symbiotic association—a mutually-supporting relationship between 2 dissimilar organisms

taiga—subarctic land of stunted coniferous trees

tsunami—a tidal wave caused by an earthquake or volcanic eruption

tundra—a treeless vegetation of mosses, lichens, herbs, and dwarf shrubs in arctic and alpine areas

tussock—a patch of solid ground in a bog, held together by dense grasses or roots

ulu—an Eskimo knife

Walrussia—Seward's Icebox; a deprecative term used by critics of the 1867 Alaska Purchase

williwaw—a sudden, violent rush of cold air over a mountain towards a low pressure zone

ABBREVIATIONS

AB—Alberta
AK—Alaska
APEX—advance purchase excursion
BC—British Columbia
C—Centigrade
C.—century
CA—California
CCC—Civilian Conservation Corps
CDN—Canadian
d—double
HI—Hawaii
L—left
MV—motor vessel
NWT—Northwest Territories
NY—New York
ON—Ontario
OR—Oregon
OW—one way
pp—per person
PQ—Quebec
R—right
RCMP—Royal Canadian Mounted Police
RT—round trip
RV—recreational vehicle
s—single
SS—steamship
t—triple
WA—Washington
YH—youth hostel
YMCA—Young Men's Christian Association
YT—Yukon Territory

INDEX

Answers to crossword puzzle
on page 232

It took 10 years of rambling and 3 trips around the world to convince Canadian travel writer, David Stanley, that some of the finest country this side of the Khyber Pass lay right in his own back yard. Now, all the traveling tricks learned during those years in Europe, South America, and Asia are applied to this exciting corner of North America. As he did with his *South Pacific Handbook,* Stanley researched the book exactly as it was written, right down to the last cold can of beans, soggy campsite, and long wait for a ride. He hit the road again soon after *Alaska-Yukon Handbook* was released, but promises to be back with a bigger and better second edition.

China On Your Own by Russell and Penny Jennings
This unique booklet is designed to supplement existing guidebooks, to assist the independent traveler in finding local transport and budget accommodations. Independent travel in China is a challenge. Its rewards include close contact with the local people as you travel with them, eat with them and sometimes share accommodations with them. You also enjoy lower travel costs compared to being on a guided tour. However, you have a language problem; making travel arrangements will be time-consuming and probably frustrating. This is where *China On Your Own* comes in.

LIMITED EDITION
1983

CHINA

On Your Own

A Do-It-Yourself Guide for the Budget Traveller

Russell and Penny Jennings

ALASKA ON A BUDGET

ACROSS

1 ____media
5 Origin of an idea
9 Better than none
13 Word with heart and head
14 Aluminum company
15 Budget accommodations in Anchorage
16 Tenderfoot
18 "____Richard's Almanac"
19 Aerosol: Shorthand
20 Officer-In-Charge: Initialism
21 Go-getter
23 Consumes hungrily
25 Untouched
27 Summon arboreal entities
29 Rarely bothers careful travelers
33 Teddy
36 Eye: Poetic
37 Govern by force
38 "____a hole to China..."
39 Japanese sword part
41 Word with horse and course
42 Symbols of clans
44 ____Abner
45 What glacial ice does slowly
46 Act out
47 Diamond Gertie's first bookkeeper
49 Had snakes for hair
51 Elevated food chamber
55 Meantime
58 "____, sis-boom-bah!"
60 Assn. of AK Naturalists: Acronym
61 World's greatest migrant
62 White Fang creator
65 Trojan masseur
66 ____a time
67 Eskimo home: Variation
68 Let it stand
69 Salmon catchers
70 Seeing Eye: Abbr.

DOWN

1 Tropical bird
2 Sneeze sound
3 Egg____
4 Lucky to, with Mt. McKinley
5 Mendenhall and Portage
6 Eccentric, for short
7 Where ptarmigan sleep
8 "____face for a potlatch"
9 Dangerous loss of heat energy
10 Frenzy
11 Launch Control Officers' Union: Initialism
12 Found in Matanuska Valley
14 Pacific tuna
17 Primary concern of budget travel
22 Prefix for eight
24 Alaska state flower
26 Misty patches of stars
28 What a carcass sometimes does
30 Dies____
31 Ecclesiastical: Abbr.
32 Best means of budget transportation
33 What a male mosquito won't do
34 Ancient Dead Sea kingdom
35 Rarely conducive to budget transportation
37 "____of the Wild"
40 Skin-covered Aleut kayaks
43 Sea: German
47 Compassionate treatment of animals
48 Reflection of sound waves
50 French mustard
52 Panhandle
53 Gringo, in Honolulu
54 Boredom
55 Suffix for inflammation
56 Where an eagle sleeps
57 Spruce or aspen
58 Altitude, for short
63 Whale: Prefix
64 City in Yugoslavia

South Pacific Handbook
by David Stanley

Here is paradise explored, photographed and mapped, the first comprehensive guide to the history, geography, climate, cultures and customs of this immense area. Backpack into the wilderness plateaus of Fiji, catch a ride on yachts, enjoy the cosmopolitan French life of New Caledonia, experience awesome Bora Bora by rented bicycle, live like a beachcomber in Tonga, dive on an eerie sunken Japanese war fleet in the Truk lagoon, witness the weaving of a 'fine mat' under a Samoan *fale,* travel in your own canoe or raft 100 km down the mighty Sepik River in New Guinea, go swimming with sea lions in the Galapagos. At 578 pages, no other travel book covers such a large expanse of the earth's surface. 162 illus., 160 black and white photos, 25 color plates, 127 island maps, 29 town plans, booklist, glossary, index. US$14.25.

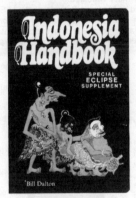

Indonesia Handbook
by Bill Dalton

Not only is *Indonesia Handbook* the most complete and contemporary travel guide to Indonesia yet prepared, it is a sensitive analysis and description of one of the world's most fascinating human and geographical environments. It is a travel encyclopedia which scans, island by island, Indonesia's history, ethnology, art forms, geography, flora and fauna—while making clear how the traveler can move around, eat, sleep and generally enjoy his unique travel experience in this loveliest of archipeligoes. 492 pages, 102 illus., 82 b/w photos. US$10.75.

Japan Handbook
by J. D. Bisignani

Packed with practical money-saving tips on travel, food and accommodation, this book dispels the myth that Japan is 'too expensive' for the budget-minded traveler. The theme throughout is 'do it like the Japanese,' to get the most for your time and money. From Okinawa through the entire island chain to Rishiri Island in the extreme north, this guide is a cultural and anthropological manual on every facet of Japanese life. 520 pages, 92 line illustrations, 29 charts, 112 maps and town plans, 200 photos, 35 color plates, an appendix on the Japanese language, booklist, glossary, index. US$14.25.

Practical Indonesian and Malay: A Communication Guide
by John Barker.
One of the most popular phrasebooks used by travelers and tourists to Indonesia, with grammar and pronunciation guide, special sections on doing business in Indonesia and on Indonesian body language. It also has outstanding tips on how to bargain, send goods, fill out forms, explore, shop. This small, easy-to-carry booklet has a tough cardboard cover, glossary, and even a supplemental appendix on differences in usage between Indonesian and the Malay language. 70 pages,

103 Hikes in Southwestern British Columbia, Second Edition by David and Mary Macaree.
From Vancouver Island to Manning Park, from the U.S. border to Lytton at the head of Fraser Canyon (including Garibaldi Park): complete trip descriptions, maps, photos. Extensive material on geology, natural history. 224 pages.

55 Ways to the Wilderness in Southcentral Alaska by Nancy Simmerman and Helen Nienheuser.
A year-round outdoor guide for residents and visitors in the Far North, with a wealth of hikes, snowshoe and ski tours, and canoe or kayak routes. Covering the area around Anchorage, the Kenai Peninsula, Talkeetna, Glenallen, Chitina and Valdez, the book's trips range from less than half a day to several days in length and from beach to mountaintop. Loaded with photos and maps. 168 pages.

Discover Southeast Alaska with Pack and Paddle by Margaret Piggott.
This delightfully written guide to the best outdoor experiences in Southeast Alaska—60 trips for all abilities, covering hiking, canoeing and kayaking in this magnificent wilderness area, from hikes of a few hours to week-long canoe traverses. Many can be done on foot from ferry or cruise ship dock. Loaded with information on flora, fauna, wilderness travel. 70 photos and 75 maps that really give the flavor of the area. 268 pages.

A Season in Alaska

A Guerrilla Guide to Lucrative Summer
Jobs and Short-term Employment

**If You Are Strong Enough, And Free, You Can
Earn $20,000.00 In The Next Three Months—
Maybe...**

A Season in Alaska by Beau Westover.
A Guerilla Guide to Lucrative Summer Jobs and
Short-term Employment. In Alaska, if he or she is
strong enough, it is still possible for a determined
individual to bust ass for a few months and then walk
away clean, holding an obscene roll of hundreds and a
ticket to anywhere in the world. 138 pages.

ORDER FORM

Quantity	Title	Bookrate to any-where in world	1st class USA, Canada, Mexico	Airmail to any-where in world
_____	SOUTH PACIFIC HANDBOOK, 2nd Ed.	$14.20	$16.00	$19.00
_____	JAPAN HANDBOOK	$14.20	$16.00	$18.00
_____	INDONESIA HANDBOOK	$10.75	$12.00	$17.50
_____	ALASKA-YUKON HANDBOOK	$ 2.00	$12.00	$17.50
_____	103 HIKES IN SOUTHWESTERN BRITISH COLUMBIA	$ 9.50	$10.50	$12.00
_____	55 WAYS TO THE WILDERNESS	$ 9.50	$10.50	$12.00
_____	DISCOVER SOUTHEAST ALASKA	$ 9.50	$10.50	$12.00
_____	A SEASON IN ALASKA	$ 6.95	$ 8.50	$ 9.75
_____	ALASKA KROSSWORDS	$ 3.50	$ 3.50	$ 4.25
_____	CHINA ON YOUR OWN	$ 5.25	$ 5.25	$ 6.25

sub-total _____

California
sales tax
(6 percent) _____

MOON catalog of
travel books $1.00

total _____

*All payments
in US dollars
please. Please
make all checks
out to Moon
Publications,
P.O. Box 1696
Chico, CA 95927
USA

Name_____

Street_____

City_____

State_____Zip_____

Country_____

READERS' QUESTIONNAIRE

(please return to Moon Publications, Box 1696, Chico, CA 95927, USA)

1) where do you live?_____

2) your age_____occupation_____

3) where did you purchase this book?_____

4) first place that you visited described in this book _____

5) your main means of transportation_____

6) type of accommodations used_____

7) was traveling cheaply important to you? yes ☐ no ☐

8) how many people went with you?_____ how long did you spend in the area?_____

9) which were your favorite places?_____
_____
_____

10) which places did you dislike?_____

11) did you work?_____where and what at?_____
_____
_____
_____

12) what was the best thing about this book?_____

13) did anything bother or annoy you?_____

14) would you like longer sections on history and economy?_____

15) what sort of things should we include next time?_____
_____
_____
_____

16) new destination areas you think should be covered_____
_____
_____

17) additional maps required _____
_____

18) if expanded, would you still buy a heavier, more expensive book?_____

19) should we cut back on the photos and illustrations?_____

20) should we lower the price by removing the color pages?_____

21) do you plan to return to Alaska or Yukon?_____

Please attach an additional sheet, if necessary. Thank you. MOON PUBLICATIONS